Business Information Management

Applying Business & Information Technology Skills for Workplace Readiness

The Development Team at B.E. Publishing

B.E. Publishing

www.bepublishing.com

Business Information Management

Applying Business & Information Technology Skills for Workplace Readiness

Business Information Management
ISBN: 978-1-626891-18-0
Copyright ©2017 by B.E. Publishing

Author
The Development Team at B.E. Publishing

Editors
Alissa Cafferky
Michael Gecawich
Kathleen Hicks
Elizabeth Kraushar
Diane Silvia
Joy Tavano

Graphic Design
Fernando Botelho
Mark Drake

Permissions
To use materials from this text, please contact us:

B.E. Publishing, Inc.
P.O. Box 8558
Warwick, RI 02888
U.S.A.

Tel: 888.781.6921
Fax: 401.781.7608
Email: permissions@bepublishing.com

All references made to specific software applications and/or companies used within this book are registered trademarks of their respective companies.

Printed in the U.S.A.

PUBLISHED BY

B.E. Publishing

Table of Contents

Introduction

Welcome to Business Information Management

Business Information Management is a comprehensive, skills-based textbook. In this textbook, you will use your computer applications skills as you produce professional documents. With a strong focus on workplace readiness and communication and writing skills, you will reinforce your touch typing skills, create word processing documents, develop spreadsheets, build databases, design desktop publishing documents, and make digital presentations using the appropriate software for the task at hand.

You will also explore the vital role technology has in the workplace, including the importance of managing information systems. This textbook culminates with students working in teams while collaborating on a final assessment.

Standards Alignment to TEKS (Texas Essential Knowledge and Skills)

This textbook has been designed exclusively for schools in the state of Texas. The contents, skills, projects, and lessons have been aligned with the TEKS (Texas Essential Knowledge and Skills) Standards published by the Texas Education Agency for Business Information Management courses. At the time this textbook went to press, the standards alignment document that was used to correlate this book with the TEKS was drawn from Proclamation 2017 from the document titled:

> Subject: Chapter 130. Career and Technical Education, Subchapter D. Business Management and Administration
>
> Course Title: §130.136. Business Information Management I (One Credit).

Each unit within this textbook includes a cover page that indicates the TEKS that are measured and met in that unit. For hands-on computer applications lessons, the TEKS measured and met are identified in the "New Skills/TEKS" section within each lesson. For easy reference, there is a TEKS correlations document available at **www.bepublishing.com**.

New Skills

The hands-on lessons in each unit are organized into a hierarchical skill-level format. With few exceptions, most of the lessons in this book build upon skills practiced in previous lessons.

Prerequisite Skills

This book is recommended for students in grades 9-12. It is expected that students have a basic working knowledge of using the following software applications (any version): word processing, spreadsheets, databases, presentations, and desktop publishing.

Materials Required

To use this textbook, students will need the following:

- Internet access
- Desktop or laptop computer
- Printer (optional)
- Word processing application
- Microsoft Access (for Unit 6: Databases)
- Spreadsheet application
- Presentation application
- Desktop publishing application

Software Note

The instructions for lessons requiring the use of software applications, such as word processing, spreadsheets, etc. are written in a generic format so they can be applied to various versions and utilize different applications. For example, the lessons in the word processing unit can be completed using any word processing application, such as Microsoft Word or Google Docs.

Note: There is one exception to the above. Unit 6: Databases requires students to use Microsoft Access (any version) to complete the lessons.

Using the Companion Website

This textbook is designed to be used in conjunction with the Companion Website (**www.MyCompanionSite.com**). Many of the lessons and projects require you to download worksheets, planning forms, or image files.

To download the necessary resources:

1. Go to **www.MyCompanionSite.com**.
2. Click on the **Business Information Management** thumbnail.
3. Select the appropriate folder for the unit and lesson you are working on.
4. Download and open the appropriate documents or logos.

Instructor Login & Resources

Instructors have access to a password-accessible instructor resource section via the Companion Website.

File Management

Since you will be completing a wide variety of lessons, most requiring you to save your work, it is imperative that you utilize proper file management organization. In Unit 4: File Management, you will create an organized file directory system for saving and storing files for units containing software application lessons as shown.

BIM

Unit 4 – File Management

Unit 5 – Word Processing

Unit 6 – Databases

Unit 7 – Spreadsheets

Unit 8 – Presentations

Unit 9 – Desktop Publishing

Pitch It!
INCORPORATED
"Making Your Idea The Next Big Thing"

Final Assessment – Pitch It!

The skills you practiced and learned in this textbook are integrated in a culminating final project (Unit 10) titled Pitch It! In this unit, you will work in teams to "pitch" a new product idea to Pitch It!, Inc., a product investment firm. Similar in format to the popular TV show "Shark Tank," you will combine your creativity, software application, and entrepreneurial skills in this exciting final assessment unit.

Understanding the Format of This Textbook

The lessons in this textbook have been organized into an easy-to-read, self-guided, visual format where you practice new skills and learn by doing. This textbook is divided into 10 units, each containing a set of individual lessons that focus on the following: technology and professionalism in the workplace, workplace readiness, technology resources, file management, word processing, databases, spreadsheets, presentations, and desktop publishing.

The final unit, "Pitch It!," is a culminating final assessment where you will utilize your information technology skills while working in teams to create a new product and introduce it to the market.

For easy reference, each lesson has been identified with a lesson name and number within each unit.

LESSON NUMBER

LESSON TITLE

OVERVIEW

PART OF UNIT

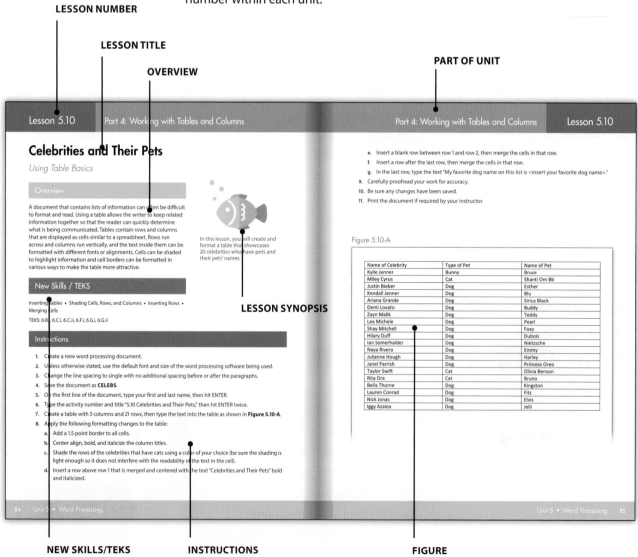

Lesson 5.10 — Part 4: Working with Tables and Columns

Celebrities and Their Pets

Using Table Basics

Overview

A document that contains lists of information can often be difficult to format and read. Using a table allows the writer to keep related information together so that the reader can quickly determine what is being communicated. Tables contain rows and columns that are displayed as cells similar to a spreadsheet. Rows run across and columns run vertically, and the text inside them can be formatted with different fonts or alignments. Cells can be shaded to highlight information and cell borders can be formatted in various ways to make the table more attractive.

In this lesson, you will create and format a table that showcases 20 celebrities who have pets and their pets' names.

New Skills / TEKS

Inserting Tables • Shading Cells, Rows, and Columns • Inserting Rows • Merging Cells

TEKS: 6.B.i, 6.C.i, 6.C.ii, 6.F.i, 6.G.i, 6.G.ii

Instructions

1. Create a new word processing document.
2. Unless otherwise stated, use the default font and size of the word processing software being used.
3. Change the line spacing to single with no additional spacing before or after the paragraphs.
4. Save the document as **CELEBS**.
5. On the first line of the document, type your first and last name, then hit ENTER.
6. Type the activity number and title "5.10 Celebrities and Their Pets," then hit ENTER twice.
7. Create a table with 3 columns and 21 rows, then type the text into the table as shown in **Figure 5.10-A**.
8. Apply the following formatting changes to the table:
   a. Add a 1.5 point border to all cells.
   b. Center align, bold, and italicize the column titles.
   c. Shade the rows of the celebrities that have cats using a color of your choice (be sure the shading is light enough so it does not interfere with the readability of the text in the cell).
   d. Insert a row above row 1 that is merged and centered with the text "Celebrities and Their Pets" bold and italicized.

Part 4: Working with Tables and Columns — Lesson 5.10

   e. Insert a blank row between row 1 and row 2, then merge the cells in that row.
   f. Insert a row after the last row, then merge the cells in that row.
   g. In the last row, type the text "My favorite dog name on this list is <insert your favorite dog name>."
9. Carefully proofread your work for accuracy.
10. Be sure any changes have been saved.
11. Print the document if required by your instructor.

Figure 5.10-A

Name of Celebrity	Type of Pet	Name of Pet
Kylie Jenner	Bunny	Bruce
Miley Cyrus	Cat	Shanti Om Bb
Justin Bieber	Dog	Esther
Kendall Jenner	Dog	Blu
Ariana Grande	Dog	Sirius Black
Demi Lovato	Dog	Buddy
Zayn Malik	Dog	Teddy
Lea Michele	Dog	Pearl
Shay Mitchell	Dog	Foxy
Hilary Duff	Dog	Dubois
Ian Somerhalder	Dog	Nietzsche
Naya Rivera	Dog	Emmy
Julianne Hough	Dog	Harley
Janel Parrish	Dog	Princess Oreo
Taylor Swift	Cat	Olivia Benson
Rita Ora	Cat	Bruno
Bella Thorne	Dog	Kingston
Lauren Conrad	Dog	Fitz
Nick Jonas	Dog	Elvis
Iggy Azalea	Dog	Jelli

LESSON SYNOPSIS

NEW SKILLS/TEKS

INSTRUCTIONS

FIGURE

Curriculum Guide

Curriculum Guide

Curriculum Guide

Curriculum Guide

LESSON			NEW SKILLS
Unit 6: Databases			
Part 1: Introduction to Databases			
Part 2: Creating Tables Using Datasheet View			
6.1	**Address Book**	*Creating Your First Database*	Creating a Blank Database • Naming and Saving a Database • Defining the Structure of a Database • Selecting Data Types • Naming and Creating Fields • Naming and Saving a Table • Adjusting Column Widths • Printing a Table • Closing a Database
6.2	**Address Book 2**	*Working with an Existing Database*	Opening an Existing Database • Adding New Fields • Using New Data Types • Formatting a Date/Time Field • Formatting a Yes/No Field
6.3	**Colleges**	*Working with Interactive Data Types*	Formatting Currency Fields • Using Hyperlinks • Formatting Number Fields
6.4	**Favorite U.S. Roller Coasters**	*Changing Data Types and Formatting Fields*	Deleting Fields
6.5	**Address Book 3**	*Working with Text and Formats*	Applying Bold and Italics • Changing Font and Font Size • Changing Alignment • Changing Font Color • Using Find and Replace • Sorting Ascending and Descending
Part 3: Creating Tables Using Design View			
6.6	**Sales at the School Store**	*Working in Design View*	Creating Tables Using Design View
6.7	**Income**	*Editing Field Properties*	Adding a Field Description • Setting a Field Size • Inserting/Deleting Fields • Moving Fields • Naming and Creating Fields in Design View • Exporting a Table from a Database
6.8	**Concerts**	*Applying Filters*	Changing Data Types • Applying a Selection Filter • Using Toggle Filter • Formatting Number View
6.9	**Multiple Oscar Winners**	*Editing Records*	Using Cut, Copy, and Paste
Part 4: Working with Queries			
6.10	**Winter Olympics and Paralympics**	*Working with Queries*	Using Multiple Tables • Using the Query Wizard • Running a Query • Sorting Query Results
6.11	**James Bond Movies**	*Specifying Criteria in Query Design*	Using Query Design View • Viewing Queries
Part 5: Creating Forms & Reports			
6.12	**Cars**	*Creating a Form*	Using Criteria to Filter Records • Using the Form Wizard
6.13	**Entertainment Data Warehouse**	*Creating a Report*	Using Find Duplicates Query • Using the Report Wizard • Using the External Data Wizard
6.14	**Graduation Announcements**	*Creating Mailing Labels*	Using the Label Wizard
6.15	**TechieTs.com**	*Determining the Database Requirements for a Business*	Designing and Creating a Database Based on a Business's Requirements
Unit 6 Review		Unit Review can be downloaded from the Companion Website: www.MyCompanionSite.com	

Curriculum Guide

Curriculum Guide

LESSON			NEW SKILLS
7.16	**Major Holidays**	*Sequencing Made Easy*	Using AutoFill to Complete a Sequence
7.17	**Presentation Rubric**	*Using Basic Calculations*	Using Basic Formulas: Addition • Copying and Pasting Formulas • Displaying Formulas • Using Cell References
7.18	**My Check Register**	*Adding Adjacent Cells*	Using AutoSum • Using SUM • Using Basic Formulas: Subtraction
7.19	**Town Camp Summer Payroll**	*Using Multi-Math Formulas*	Using Basic Formulas: Multiplication • Using Parentheses for Multi-Math Formulas
7.20	**Event Budget**	*Practicing Cell References*	There are no new skills being introduced in this reinforcement lesson.
7.21	**Basic Baseball Stats**	*Calculating Statistics*	Using Basic Formulas: Division
7.22	**Accounts Payable**	*Commonly Used Formulas*	Using Average, Maximum, and Minimum
7.23	**Skittles**	*Formatting Fractions*	Formatting Cells as Fractions
7.24	**Sales Projection**	*Working with Absolute Cell Reference*	Using Absolute Cell References
7.25	**Forever 21 Part 2**	*Determining the Number of Items*	Using the COUNTIF Function
7.26	**The Ultimate Pay Raise**	*Working with Conditions*	Using Conditions in Formulas
7.27	**Dream House Mortgage**	*Determining Loan Payments*	Using the Payment (PMT) Function
7.28	**College Savings**	*Determining the Future Value of Savings*	Using the Future Value (FV) Function
7.29	**Town Camp Summer Payroll 2**	*Calculating Payroll Deductions*	Using the ROUND Function • Rotating Cell Orientation

Part 5: Working with Shapes and Elements

7.30	**Dinner Menu**	*Working with Illustrations*	Inserting a Clip Art Image
7.31	**Paying the Bills**	*Annotating a Worksheet*	Inserting and Removing Comments or Notes for Cells
7.32	**Take a Ride**	*Adding Text Elements*	Inserting WordArt
7.33	**Binge Watch List**	*Adding Shapes*	Inserting Shapes
7.34	**Shoes, Shoes, Shoes!**	*Using Multiple Worksheets*	Referencing Cells from Other Worksheets • Printing Multiple Worksheets

Part 6: Working with Charts and Graphs

7.35	**Most Popular Features**	*Creating a Pie Chart*	Inserting a Pie Chart • Formatting a Pie Chart
7.36	**Sales History**	*Creating a Line Graph*	Creating a Line Graph • Formatting a Line Graph • Using the Fill Effects Feature in a Graph
7.37	**Sales Forecast**	*Creating a Column Chart*	Creating a Column Chart • Formatting a Column Chart • Aligning Text in a Chart
7.38	**Fast-Food Nutrition**	*Creating a Bar Chart*	Inserting a Bar Chart • Formatting a Bar Chart

Curriculum Guide

Curriculum Guide

Curriculum Guide

LESSON			NEW SKILLS
Part 3: Designing Professional Publications			
9.6	**Lunch Menu**	*Importing Text*	Importing Text
9.7	**Note Card**	*More Formatting with Text and Borders*	Changing Text Direction • Inserting and Formatting a Picture Border • Setting Margins
9.8	**Beginners Design Tips**	*Using Customary Standards and Styles*	There are no new skills being introduced in this reinforcement lesson.
9.9	**Doorknob Hanger**	*Formatting a Doorknob Hanger*	There are no new skills being introduced in this reinforcement lesson.
9.10	**Join the Club!**	*Formatting a Brochure*	There are no new skills being introduced in this reinforcement lesson.
9.11	**Fall Festival Flyer**	*Redesigning a Promotional Flyer*	There are no new skills being introduced in this reinforcement lesson.
Unit 9 Review		Unit Review can be downloaded from the Companion Website: www.MyCompanionSite.com	
Unit 10: Pitch It! Final Assessment			
10.1	**Overview and Project Setup**		
10.2	**What's the Big Idea?**	*Inventing Your New Product*	There are no new skills being introduced in this final assessment.
10.3	**Creating Your Product's Identity**	*Turning Your Product Into a Brand*	There are no new skills being introduced in this final assessment.
10.4	**Bringing Your Product to Life**	*Creating a Prototype of Your Product*	There are no new skills being introduced in this final assessment.
10.5	**Estimating Annual Gross Sales**	*Forecasting the Potential Sales of Your Product*	There are no new skills being introduced in this final assessment.
10.6	**Marketing Your Product**	*Designing a Magazine Print Ad*	There are no new skills being introduced in this final assessment.
10.7	**Advertising Vendor Database**	*Expanding the Advertising Potential*	There are no new skills being introduced in this final assessment.
10.8	**Putting It All Together**	*Creating the "Big Pitch" Presentation*	There are no new skills being introduced in this final assessment.
10.9	**The Big Pitch!**	*Delivering Your Presentation to Pitch It!, Inc.*	There are no new skills being introduced in this final assessment.
10.10	**Project Summary Report**	*Summarizing Your Pitch It! Project Experience*	There are no new skills being introduced in this final assessment.

Unit 1
Professionalism in the Workplace

Part 1   The Importance of Professionalism

Part 2   Soft Skills in the Workplace

Part 3   Rules and Regulations in the Workplace

TEKS

1.A.i, 1.A.ii, 1.B.i, 1.C.i, 1.C.ii, 1.D.i, 1.E.i, 1.E.ii, 1.E.iii, 1.F.i, 1.F.ii, 1.F.iii, 1.F.iv, 1.F.v

Part 1
The Importance of Professionalism

Even if you are not currently holding down a part-time job while attending school, at some point in the not too distant future, you will be working. You will be entering the exciting, and sometimes challenging, "real business world." Gone will be the days of your family buying your clothes, filling up your gas tank, making your dinner, and providing you with spending money. Once you enter the real world, you will be responsible for yourself.

While you may not know the answers to questions like "What career am I going to have?" and "How am I going to support myself?" you can at least begin to work on how you will succeed in whatever career you choose. There are a number of skills you can acquire today that will help you, regardless of what job you will hold in the future.

Although the remaining units in this book are dedicated to teaching you technology skills for the workplace, employers still rank the following as the top three skills they seek from employees:

1. Ability to work as a team
2. Ability to make decisions and solve problems
3. Ability to plan, organize, and prioritize work

This unit will introduce you to the importance of acting and conducting yourself as a professional in the workplace. **Professionalism** is defined as the competence or skill expected of a professional. In the workplace, how we look, dress, talk, write, and interact with others are continually being evaluated. Professionalism in the workplace is an expectation for everyone. Remember, *the single biggest thing you will ever sell is yourself*. Acquiring the skills and knowledge to be viewed as a true professional is one of the best things you can give yourself to jump-start your future career.

Characteristics of 'True Professionals'

Whether you become a chef, attorney, or athletic trainer, you will be expected to act as a professional. Some companies require uniforms, others a suit and tie, while others encourage casual dress. Regardless of the industry, profession, or job title, how you act and interact with co-workers and customers will be noticed, evaluated, and critiqued. True professionals possess a number of characteristics (see **Table 1.1**) that can apply to just about any industry, profession, and workplace environment.

Table 1.1

Characteristics of True Professionals	
Appearance	A neat appearance projects professionalism. At a minimum, try to meet or exceed the company's dress code. Proper hygiene and grooming are also essential.
Positive Attitude	Attitude is everything. Come across as confident, but don't overdo it or you will be seen as a "know-it-all."
Respect	Being professional means being respectful. Be courteous and considerate of others.
Communication	Develop good writing, speaking, and listening skills. When writing or speaking, always maintain a polite, courteous tone while still being able to get your point across.
Ethics	Some professions, such as doctors and lawyers, must follow a strict code of ethics. Even if your employer doesn't have a written code of ethics, you should display ethical behavior at all times.
Reliability	Actions, such as showing up on time, say "I'm reliable." Go the extra mile to get the job done.
Expertise	Professionals never stop learning. Always strive to become an expert in your chosen craft.
Organization	Keep your workplace neat and organized; you will be able to locate what is needed to get tasks done quickly.
Honesty	Tell the truth. If you make a mistake, own it.

Attitude Builds Character

Achieving the characteristics of a "true professional" requires the right mindset. You need to have an attitude that says, "I'm positive. I can get the job done no matter what."

When faced with adversity, do you see the glass as half empty or half full? Professionals see it as half full. You have to realize that some workdays will be good, and some may be bad. That's life. Regardless of the task (small, large, easy, or difficult), strive to be the employee that gets the job done.

We all have likes and dislikes. Think about the courses you are taking in school. For a number of reasons, you find some subjects more interesting than others. It could be the teacher, the subject material, or even the time of day the class meets. Chances are that the assignments you complete first are from the subjects you enjoy most. The workplace is no different. Sometimes you will be asked to work on projects that are exciting and engaging, while other times, the tasks might not be as enjoyable. In the workplace, it's important to maintain a strong work ethic and a positive attitude, regardless of the task you are assigned.

Do you see the glass as half empty or half full?

Part 2
Soft Skills in the Workplace

> Soft skills are all of the things that make a person a true professional.

Incredibly intelligent people are often measured by their IQ (Intelligence Quotient) scores, a number representing a person's reasoning ability. In the business world, however, people are measured by their EQ (Emotional Intelligence Quotient) or soft skills. **Soft skills** is a term often associated with a person's EQ, the cluster of personality traits, social attributes, communication, language, personal habits, interpersonal skills, management of people, leadership, and any other traits that characterize relationships with other people. Soft skills can be viewed as all of the things people do in the workplace that make them true professionals. **Table 1.2** highlights a list of the top 10 soft skills employers look for in employees.

Table 1.2

Soft Skills Employers Look For	
1. Communication	The ability to communicate with others
2. Teamwork and collaboration	The ability to work in teams and achieve the goals of the team
3. Time management skills	The ability to prioritize tasks and manage time so that deadlines are met
4. Flexibility and adaptability	Willingness to change and adapt to new procedures and new environments
5. Decision-making/Problem-solving	The ability to make decisions and solve problems
6. Leadership skills	The ability to lead by example and/or lead others
7. Creativity	The ability to apply both logic and creativity to solve problems
8. Responsibility	The ability to accept fault and not "pass the buck" onto someone else
9. Commitment	Dependability, reliability, enthusiasm, and willingness to work hard
10. Ability to work under pressure	The ability to work under stressful situations

Employment experts agree that your educational degree may get you an interview, but soft skills will get you the job—and help you keep it. The good news is that, like any skill, soft skills can be learned. Even if you think you already possess some or even all of the soft skills, practicing, perfecting, and mastering them will only help you down the road.

While there are many things that can be considered soft skills, let's focus on four of the most important areas: **communicating effectively**, **setting schedules and meeting deadlines**, **collaborating in teams**, and **time management**.

Communicating in the Workplace

How we communicate plays a vital role in the workplace. The words we choose, how we say or write them, our facial expressions, body language, and even our ability to listen all work together when communicating with people. In survey after survey, the ability to communicate with others is the number one skill employers look for when hiring. The growth in information communication technology tools have made communication skills more important than ever before. Organizations are communicating using online meeting programs, webcams, real-time customer service chats, blogs, and social media outlets, just to name a few. Whether your goal is to be a business owner or an employee of a business or organization, understanding the different types of communication skills is essential. Interacting with others is an everyday part of life in the workplace.

Three Types of Communication

There are three types of communication: **verbal**, **nonverbal**, and **written**.

1. Verbal Communication

How many times have you heard your parents or teachers say, "It's not what you said, it's how you said it?" How many times have you said something you didn't mean? In the workplace, employers may or may not have written policies on verbal communication guidelines. Whether they do or don't, it is expected that you communicate clearly, use appropriate language, and verbally communicate within the laws and regulations of the organization.

Verbal (or oral) communication is the sharing of information between individuals by using speech. Verbal communication consists of the words we speak, the way we form those words, and the tone in which we speak them.

In the workplace, saying the wrong thing can cost you your job and can even have legal ramifications. Sexual harassment, for example, is taken extremely seriously in the workplace. Even if you think you are joking, what you say can be offensive to others. Employment laws and regulations are covered in more detail later in this unit.

2. Nonverbal Communication

Nonverbal communication consists of body language and the cues that are given off while listening to someone else. Whether it's a conversation at a cubicle or during a formal meeting in a conference room, how we sit, stand, and use facial expressions all send nonverbal messages. When involved in a formal workplace conversation or meeting, follow these nonverbal communication tips:

- Nod your head to acknowledge you are listening.
- Make eye contact with whomever is speaking to you.
- Show an open body (keep shoulders back and arms uncrossed).

3. Written Communication

Written communication consists of anything that is written. The expansion of communication technology in our workplace has placed a strong emphasis on written communication skills. From Tweets and emails, to blogs and live chats, the writing skills of the "sender" are on center stage, being read and reviewed by readers.

According to an American Association of Colleges and Universities survey, employers reported that only 27% of recently hired college graduates have the written communication skills needed to succeed in the workplace. Due to the "accepted" abbreviations used in text messages (lol) and Tweets (#typo), written business correspondence is often riddled with typos, misused words, and grammatical inaccuracies. Nothing spoils a document faster than a typo or a grammatical error. Writing involves hard work, often taking several drafts to get it right. Follow the tips below for effective writing in the workplace.

When applying for a job, the first evaluation tool used to measure your qualifications is how well you write your resume and cover letter.

Tips for Writing Effectively in the Workplace

1. Know your audience.
Consider what your audience needs to learn from your document. The audience should be able to define the style, tone, and vocabulary of whatever you are writing. An email sent to a friend will have a different tone than one sent to your entire office.

2. Format business documents properly.
Learn the guidelines for formatting different documents, such as memos and reports. Use headlines, bullet points, numbering, and other features to make the document easy for the reader to understand.

3. Focus on content and style.
Use simple language that is as direct as possible. Make sure your communication serves a clear purpose and sticks to the subject.

4. Proofread thoroughly and revise accordingly.
Your first draft should never be your final product. Once you've finished writing, it's essential that you check for typos as well as grammatical errors. If needed, ask someone to read your work to ensure that it's not only free of errors, but will make sense to the intended audience.

5. Be concise.
Follow the "less is more" philosophy. Saying something in a few sentences is more effective than writing a long, complex paragraph to get the same point across. Respect your readers' time and write so that important information can be found quickly.

Goals, Deadlines, and Schedules

Renewing an expired driver's license, submitting a college application, taking the SAT, or completing a homework assignment—our lives consist of a series of deadlines, due dates, and to-do lists. Whether you're sending out birthday party invitations or getting to a meeting on time, without deadlines and due dates, people wouldn't know what tasks to complete first.

Without deadlines, creating organized schedules would be next to impossible. Following schedules keeps us organized and allows us to prioritize our lives. As your calendar fills up with meetings, deadlines, and a variety of activities, you can organize and prioritize the tasks and goals in your life accordingly.

Think about your daily schedule. You wake up at the same time each day, shower, get dressed, eat breakfast, and then head off to school before the homeroom bell rings. Then, it's off to your first period class. At the end of the school day, you might be involved in an after-school activity or a part-time job. When you return home, you have dinner, spend some leisure time, and then work on any assignments that are due. Then, you wake up the next day and follow the same schedule.

Like your school day, businesses operate in a similar fashion. Employees are asked to be at work by a certain time, get their to-do lists, and complete their assignments by their due dates. To accomplish goals by specified deadlines, organizations heavily rely on individuals, teams, and the ability for both to manage their time effectively.

Teamwork and Collaboration

Whether it's competing on an athletic field, participating in an academic decathlon, or helping a marketing department create a new advertising campaign, there's no 'I' in team ('I' meaning individual). **Teamwork** is defined as the cooperative or coordinated effort on the part of a group of persons acting together as a team or in the interests of a common cause. Teamwork is an essential skill in life and in the workplace.

As we've learned, the ability to work in teams is at the top of the list of skills employers look for in employees. Businesses rely on teams to work together to achieve a defined set of one or more goals within a certain timeline or deadline. To be on a team, you have to be a team player. A **team player** is a person who works well as a member of a team or group.

**Pitch It!**
In Unit 10, teamwork will be essential as you and a teammate will be "pitching" a new product idea to your instructor and classmates.

Characteristics of a Team Player

Team players possess qualities that allow them to be successful at what they do. For instance, strong team players must be active participants and put the team's objectives above their own. No matter how motivated you might be as an individual, you must also be motivated to work as a team. If you lack the initiative to be a team player, you risk missing the team's deadlines and possibly even lowering your teammates' morale. **Table 1.3** lists five qualities necessary to be an effective team player.

Table 1.3

Five Characteristics of a Team Player	
1. **Committed**	Team players give 110% to each project and must be willing to stick with the team for the duration of the project.
2. **Collaborative**	To achieve success, team players must be willing to collaborate and work well with all members of the team.
3. **Dependable and reliable**	Team players can be counted on to not only do their fair share, but be willing to do whatever it takes to see projects through until they are completed.
4. **Communicative**	Communication is key when working in a team environment.
5. **Enthusiastic**	Maintaining an energetic, positive attitude is essential for team players. When problems occur, team players help lift each other up so the project at hand can be completed.

Time Management

To meet life's deadlines, schedules, and to-do lists, you need time management skills. How many times have you waited until the night before a big test to start studying? Typically, the grade you receive is a direct correlation to the effort you put in. If you don't dedicate the time, you won't get the results you want. This is true in school as well as later in life. Failing to meet a deadline in the workplace may result in a negative reaction from your boss, or could even hurt your company as a whole. Cultivating time management skills early will help you succeed in your future career.

Whether you're working on a project alone or in a team, good time management habits will help you stay organized, prioritized, and productive. The time management tips on the following page are valuable in your personal life as well as in the workplace.

Time Management Tips

1. Define the goals of your project.
Ask yourself questions to help define your goals: What needs to be accomplished? What is the deadline for accomplishing these goals?

2. Create and organize your to-do lists.
List each task that needs to be accomplished. Once you've written down everything you can think of, organize the list in order of priority.

3. Prioritize your workday.
Start each day by figuring out what needs to be completed and in what order. What has to be taken care of right away, and what is lower priority? This way, you won't be scrambling to meet a deadline at the last minute.

4. Utilize technology, but don't let it become a time-wasting distraction.
It's easy to go on the Internet while conducting research for a paper and find yourself getting distracted. If necessary, turn off your phone and avoid social networking sites to increase your productivity.

5. Don't procrastinate.
Procrastinating can increase stress and make the end result of a project appear sloppy. On the other hand, if your task isn't a priority, it's acceptable to let it wait for a few days while you tackle more crucial deadlines.

6. Follow a schedule.
Try scheduling each task on a calendar, as well as the amount of time you are going to work on that task per day. If you follow a schedule, you will be amazed at how quickly you're able to finish your work.

7. Clear your clutter.
Sometimes staying focused is difficult when there are piles of paper and to-dos covering your desk. Put away everything that is unrelated to your current goal. That way, it's easier to focus on just one task at a time.

8. Consolidate tasks.
Multitasking has become routine in the workplace, but sometimes your brain struggles to switch between activities. Try to complete all of one type of to-do before switching to another. For instance, if you have to reply to several emails and you also have to write a report, finish the emails first rather than going back and forth.

Part 3
Rules and Regulations in the Workplace

Company policies and procedures outline the responsibilities of both employees and employers, and serve to protect workers' rights as well as employers' business interests. Rules, policies, common etiquette, and laws help workplace environments stay orderly, productive, and safe. These standards are established in three different ways:

1. Companies set their own policies and procedures for the workplace.

2. Employers and employees tend to follow unwritten rules of business etiquette.

3. Federal, state, and local governments make important workplace rules into laws and enforceable regulations.

Company Policies and Procedures

Policies and procedures set by companies are established to:

☑ Comply with all federal, state, and local regulations and laws.

☑ Keep employees safe.

☑ Reflect the company's mission statement and overall identity.

☑ Maintain the reputation and credibility of the company.

As long as they don't violate any civil rights and are in compliance with federal, state, and local laws and regulations, companies have the right to establish their own policies. Written policies and procedures of a business are typically found in the company's handbook. Upon being hired, employees are given a company handbook to read and review. The company handbook usually contains policies, rules, and procedures that help keep the workplace running smoothly.

The categories on the following page are commonly addressed in a company handbook, which all employees are expected to follow and comply with.

Typical Employee Handbook Categories

1. Dress code

Dress codes are used to ensure that workers are safe and dressed appropriately; they vary between workplaces. For example, some workers may wear a uniform to convey a corporate image, or factory workers may not be permitted to wear certain types of clothing that could catch on machinery.

2. Safety regulations

Safety regulations are in place to ensure that workers follow certain rules that will protect them from harm. The Occupational Safety and Health Administration (OSHA) is the main federal agency that protects workers' safety.

3. Smoking policies

Many state and local governments require workplaces to be smoke-free, which creates a safer, healthier work environment.

4. Drug and alcohol policies

Workplaces often have strict policies prohibiting drugs and alcohol in order to protect the well-being of their employees.

5. Computer usage policies

Companies may establish rules regarding personal use of the Internet, computer and network misuse, unauthorized access into company databases, software piracy, and so on. This is to improve employee productivity, as well as to protect the company.

6. Work hours, vacation, holiday, lunch and break policies, and time off policies and procedures

All employee handbooks should clearly state factors such as vacation days and the proper procedure for requesting time off. This offers employees a quick and easy way to reference the necessary information.

7. Federal, state, and local compliance rules and regulations

This section of the handbook may simply remind employees of the various laws pertaining to the company, as well as any related health and safety laws.

Unwritten Rules and Workplace Ethics

Many rules in the workplace are unwritten, but you are expected to follow them.

It is important to understand that some rules in the workplace may be unwritten. Though they are not typically included in an employee handbook, they are just as important.

Some of these rules may be simple matters of common sense and etiquette. For instance, there is probably not a rule in most employee handbooks that states you should knock on the door before entering someone's office. However, it is still an expectation that your colleagues will have.

Using common sense and treating others with respect will help you avoid breaking any unwritten rules of business etiquette. Some other common unwritten rules include:

- Respecting co-workers' workspace and privacy
- Not taking credit for others' ideas
- Being courteous
- Listening to others without interrupting
- Putting away cell phones during meetings

Business ethics apply to both the conduct of individuals as well as entire organizations. In other words, ethics in the business world govern everyday behavior in the workplace and in larger corporate practices. An example of unethical individual conduct in the workplace is lying, while an example of an unethical practice in business is discrimination. While laws are in place to prohibit businesses from this and other unethical behaviors, employees must be mindful of how they behave and ensure they are following a code of ethics in the workplace.

How Government Regulates the Workplace

Employment laws come from federal, state, and local sources. Employers are not allowed to choose which laws to follow even if there is an overlap; they must comply with all of the federal, state, and local laws that apply.

Regulatory Agencies

Federal, state, and local legislative bodies enact laws to protect both employers and employees. The government agencies that establish regulations to enforce those safeguards include:

Department of Labor

The Department of Labor is the primary federal agency that oversees employment law. To name a few, the Department of Labor oversees wages and hours, employer obligations, employee rights, and occupational safety.

Occupational Safety and Health Administration (OSHA)

OSHA is part of the Department of Labor and ensures safe, healthy working conditions for employees. OSHA not only enforces standards for workers, but also provides workplace safety training and education.

Equal Employment Opportunity Commission (EEOC)

The U.S. Equal Employment Opportunity Commission enforces federal laws prohibiting employment discrimination, including:

- Unfair treatment because of race, color, religion, sex (including pregnancy), national origin, age (40 or older), disability, or genetic information
- Harassment by managers, co-workers, or others in the workplace, because of race, color, religion, sex (including pregnancy), national origin, age (40 or older), disability, or genetic information
- Denial of reasonable workplace accommodations that the employee needs because of religious beliefs or disability
- Retaliation because an employee complained about job discrimination, or assisted with a job discrimination investigation or lawsuit

Labor Laws and Regulations

Several important laws and standards that impact the workforce include:

The Civil Rights Act

This landmark legislation outlawed discrimination based on race, color, religion, sex, or national origin. It also ended racial segregation in schools, in the workplace, and in public facilities. In addition, the Civil Rights Act granted workers the legal right to speak whatever language they prefer during break periods.

The Fair Labor Standards Act (FLSA)

The FLSA establishes minimum wage, overtime, recordkeeping, and child labor protections in the private sector of federal, state, and local governments.

State and Local Labor Laws

State laws include state minimum wage laws, child labor laws, minimum paid rest period requirements, and so on. State and local laws apply to everyone who lives or works in a particular state, commonwealth, territory, county, city, or town.

By visiting the Department of Labor's website, you can learn more about federal workplace laws and the various agencies that make up the Department of Labor. This website even includes informative blogs and news articles on employment-related topics.

Workers' Rights

Both state and federal laws protect employees from various types of discrimination. Discrimination in the workplace involves firing, hiring, demoting, or promoting someone based on prejudice. A few areas of possible discrimination are age, disability, race, and gender. If an employee feels they have been discriminated against, they may file a complaint with a state's employment agency or the Equal Employment Opportunity Commission (EEOC).

Regulations strive to protect workers' rights, but sometimes knowing what to do in a workplace situation can be more difficult than you might expect. Consider Joyce's dilemma in the following scenario:

Real-world Scenario

Joyce is the only woman working in a small office. Every morning, one of her co-workers, Bill, goes to a humor website and reads jokes out loud to the entire office. The jokes are always inappropriate and often discriminatory against women. While some people in the office laugh at Bill's jokes, Joyce feels uncomfortable. She has asked Bill to stop reading the jokes, but he refused and even accused her of not having a sense of humor. Joyce is considering telling their boss, but she is not sure if her complaints would fall under the category of sexual harassment. She is also afraid her boss or co-workers will be angry with her for speaking out. What should Joyce do?

As we've learned, there are many regulations in the workplace designed to protect workers. Something like sexual harassment is taken very seriously by companies, since it is a violation of the Civil Rights Act. What is considered sexual harassment varies depending on the situation, but can include unwelcomed advances, inappropriate requests, unwelcomed touching, and improper jokes. So, in this case, Joyce's problem is an example of sexual harassment.

An employee who feels they have been a victim of sexual harassment should keep track of any inappropriate practices directed at them and then report the issue. Joyce's best bet is to record each instance of the harassing behavior and then report the problem to her boss. Despite her fears of getting into trouble, the Civil Rights Act does not allow employers to retaliate against an employee who speaks out against harassment. Joyce should not be afraid to speak up.

 Recap

Professionalism is necessary for both an individual's and organization's success. As you enter the workforce, learning how to work in a team, how to make decisions and solve problems, and how to plan, organize, and prioritize will give you an advantage over many other employees. It is important to remember that true professionals have a positive attitude, are reliable, and have excellent communication skills; they also possess soft skills such as time management, leadership, and creativity.

Professionals are able to prioritize important tasks to meet goals and deadlines, and are able to create organized schedules to ensure all responsibilities are completed in a timely manner. Additionally, professionals adhere to any rules and regulations set by the company and by federal, state, and local laws. Knowing how to behave, communicate, and stay organized in the workplace are important aspects of professionalism that will help you thrive in any career path you choose.

Unit 1 Review

1. Visit **www.MyCompanionSite.com**.
2. Download and complete the **Unit 1 Review** worksheet.
3. Submit your completed worksheet to your instructor.

Unit 2
Information Systems

Part 1   Technology in the Workplace

Part 2   Information Systems & Communication Technology

Part 3   Technology Benefits and Drawbacks

Part 4   Integrating Information Systems into Business

TEKS

2.A.i, 2.A.ii, 2.B.i, 2.B.ii, 2.B.iii, 2.B.iv, 2.C.i

Part 1

Technology in the Workplace

Society has grown accustomed to swiping and tapping, sleek app designs, and devices that are capable of performing hundreds of functions and calculations, yet are smaller than the palm of your hand. In short, technology is cool!

Technology is Serious Fun

Whether it's surfing the net, using an app, or 'Googling,' technology is fun. Technology not only makes our lives easier, it also lets us travel the globe (virtually, of course), connect with friends and family from any place at any time, and find answers to questions in less than a second. Like its impact on our personal lives, technology plays a similar, but more serious, role in business.

The Business of Technology

Technology is a vital component in the modern workplace. Businesses use technology to accomplish tasks, keep things organized, communicate, and develop new methods for doing things more efficiently. Regardless of what career you choose to pursue, chances are you will be working with technology. You will be expected to know how to use technology applications and how those applications best serve the business and its customers.

All businesses, from multi-million dollar companies to mom and pop flower shops, depend on technology such as computers, printers, Internet routers, and fax machines. The key words here are "depend on technology." What would you do if your cell phone broke or stopped working properly? You would visit your local cell phone retail store to get it fixed or replaced.

Businesses face similar scenarios every day. The software won't load, the printer won't print, the Internet is down, or the keyboard is stuck. Like you with your broken cell phone, businesses need solutions to these and hundreds of other potential problems to properly manage and maintain their technology and the vast amount of information that technology produces.

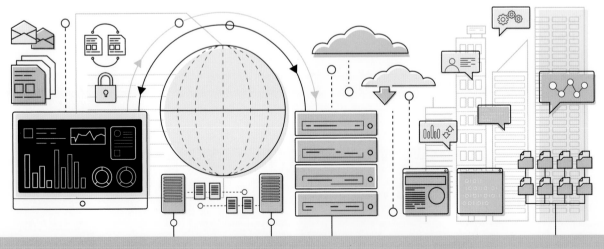

Information Systems & Communication Technology

Society is made up of many different systems. A **system** is an assembly of things, people, and processes that work together to form a unified whole. Examples of systems in society include:

- Transportation system
- Banking system
- Education system
- Judicial system
- Number system
- Language system

Systems give us structure. They let us organize our schedules, live within established rules and laws, and communicate in ways that we all understand. Imagine if we didn't have a language system—structured symbols and sounds that form words and represent ideas. Communication would be impossible. The mere fact that you are able to read this sentence proves this point.

Defining Information Systems

Like the systems required for society to function properly, the same is true for businesses and organizations: they need systems. For an organization to operate efficiently, everything within it, from the people to the technology, must communicate and coordinate with each other. The employees, computers, email, and phone system all need to work in synchronization so that information is distilled, organized, and communicated properly. These systems that businesses put in place are called information systems. **Information systems** are combinations of hardware, software, and technology networks that people build and use to gather, create, and distribute useful information.

Information systems are the "networks" of technology and people that organizations use to collect, filter, process, and communicate data, as illustrated below.

The Information System Process

| Technology Produces and Collects Information | Information Is Filtered Where It Needs to Go | Information Is Processed and Organized | Information Is Communicated to Proper Channels |

Information Communication Technology

The specific technology tools that organizations put in place to make business operations possible are referred to as **information communication technology** (ICT). Essentially, the communication technology contained within an information system must work effectively for organizations to operate successfully.

Information communication technology includes whatever technology is needed for a particular system to communicate and process information. Examples of information communication technology include:

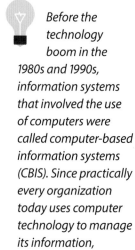

Before the technology boom in the 1980s and 1990s, information systems that involved the use of computers were called computer-based information systems (CBIS). Since practically every organization today uses computer technology to manage its information, the accepted term now is simply information systems.

- Email
- Video devices
- Online meeting software tools
- Online collaboration software tools
- Webcams

- Computer networks
- Software applications
- Printers
- Scanners

Components of Information Systems

Before the technology boom in the 1980s and 1990s, information systems were primarily manual processes where people did not rely on computers to work with information. For example, if a business needed to communicate with a customer, it had to either use a phone or send something in writing through postal mail. Today, email and text messages have become a primary business communication method.

Certain information systems support parts of organizations, others support entire organizations, and still others support groups of organizations. Each department or functional area within an organization can have its own collection of application programs, or information systems. Regardless of the type of information system, they all have common components. To build an information system, the following six components are required:

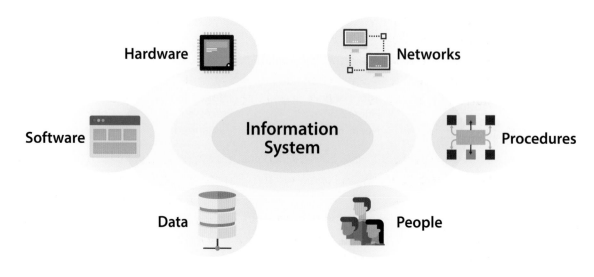

1. Hardware

Hardware is the machinery used to create content and manage and communicate information. This includes the physical parts of a computer system, such as the computer itself and the monitor, keyboard, scanner, and printer.

2. Software

Software programs are machine-readable instructions that direct the circuitry within a system's hardware to create, edit, organize, process, and analyze information. Examples include operating systems, spreadsheet and word processing software, and graphic design applications.

3. Data

Data is a collection of information that can be organized, analyzed, and utilized to better manage, understand, and communicate the information. Information is organized using databases, which are collections of related data so that groups of information, or records, can be stored and retrieved for a useful purpose. Typical examples of databases include employee records, product inventory, and product catalogs. In Unit 6, we will discuss databases in more detail.

4. People

People are the most important component in information systems. Without people, information systems cannot function. This includes anyone who uses or maintains the systems. Everyone who works in business, from someone who pays the bills to the person who hires and fires, uses information systems.

5. Procedures

For information systems to operate properly, people need to follow procedures. Procedures are the policies, rules, and guidelines that govern the operation of information systems. For example, procedures need to be established for an organization's accounting system, including who has authorization to access it and at what level. Organizations have to create manuals, file naming conventions, and a variety of other procedures so their information systems perform in the way they were intended. Requiring employees to log in and out of their computers at the start and end of each work day is an important security-related procedure.

6. Networks

While they may not always be required for every information system, networks are vital in today's virtually connected society. A network is how computers and other technologies within an information system communicate with one another. Organizations need networks to send emails, share files, stream videos, hold online meetings, and a multitude of other tasks. If you have access to the Internet in your home, you have a network.

The Role of Information Systems and Communication Technology

If you're involved with any of your school's athletic teams or clubs, what is your number one goal? To be the best, right? Companies and organizations are no different. They strive to be market leaders in their respective industry. Information systems and the technology used to support them help businesses achieve this objective. The strategic role of information systems is to support and enhance the goals and initiatives of organizations and to give them an advantage over their competition.

Information isn't worth much if it doesn't serve a purpose. That's what information systems and communication technology do for organizations: they make the information that the technology produces useful, accessible, and easy to communicate, which keeps the daily operations running smoothly.

To illustrate the important role that both information systems and communication technology play in an organization, let's see how they work for a school in the following scenario:

 Real-world Scenario

On any given day, there's a lot of news and information traveling around a school. From report card results, and plans about class dances, to agendas for staff meetings, schools generate and communicate important information every day. Think about all of the people who are in different departments and clusters within a school—teachers, guidance counselors, support staff, maintenance, student body, and many others. While each of these departments work separately, there are information systems and various communication technology tools in place that let them work together, such as:

- Email
- School website
- Public announcement system (PA)
- Student information system (SIS) where student data is kept

- Social media (such as Twitter and Facebook)
- Texting (for alerts and notifications)
- Phone system
- Large screen information displays

With different systems in place, organizations can perform all types of different tasks in separate parts. However, as long as the information system and the communication technology work together in a way that makes sense, the information and data can be shared and used across all of the moving parts.

Part 3

Technology Benefits and Drawbacks

We have discussed and explored the role and components of information systems and the communication technology used to support them. As technology rapidly evolves, grows, and offers new methods for doing things, organizations are constantly faced with the challenges of evaluating their current information systems, as well as implementing new systems and the technology required to support them.

To plan for changes and make informed strategic decisions, organizations continually weigh the pros and cons technology offers. Having this knowledge aids in the planning of integrating new information systems and supporting potential changes to existing ones. **Tables 2.1** and **2.2** compare some of the benefits and drawbacks that technology brings to businesses.

Table 2.1

Benefits That Technology Brings to Organizations

Stores and analyzes information
Data can be stored in a variety of formats, from spreadsheets to databases

Assists with making decisions
Technology performs calculations and other functions to help companies swiftly take action on decisions

Assists with business processes
Everyday operations occur more smoothly

Makes use of their data
Various technologies offer ways to help companies analyze and utilize data

Reduces workload
Using technology can increase collaboration and productivity, which lessens the workload

Improves workplace communication
Email, texting, and other technologies allow for rapid, convenient communication

Saves time and money
Money can be saved because it's much faster to move information around

Promotes learning anytime, anywhere
Online courses and remote learning resources are available to anyone with an Internet connection

Provides immediate connectivity
Voice, data, and visual technologies improve efficiency and accuracy

Saves on travel
Technology offers a substitute for physical travel, which is a more expensive means of communicating and conducting business

Expands purchasing power
Technology increases options in the marketplace, providing access to otherwise unavailable goods and services

Allows expansion to other markets or industries
The geographic scope of potential markets has increased through modern technology

Offers greater availability
For instance, clients can be given access to a company website or voicemail 24/7

Bridges the cultural gap
Different cultures can quickly communicate, thus increasing awareness and reducing prejudice

Creates new jobs
Many new and interesting jobs, such as database programmers, have been created

Table 2.2

 Drawbacks That Technology Brings to Organizations

Poses security issues
Information on the Internet or on computers is vulnerable to hackers, viruses, and other threats

Poses privacy issues
Sensitive information of individuals and companies could be illegally accessed by outside sources

Reduces employee retention
Technology can replace certain jobs

Increases reliance on technology
If a computer crashes or a machine breaks, individuals may not be able to finish their work until it is fixed

Involves malfunctions
Any issues can slow down a work day

Needs to be replaced
Technology needs maintenance and can be expensive to replace

Creates distractions
Time-saving benefits of technology can sometimes be outweighed by the distractions it creates

Needs to be learned
As new technologies evolve, employees must learn them, which may cause added stress

Causes confusion
People may miscommunicate, since emails and texts cannot convey tone or body language

While technology has some negative effects, it has an overwhelmingly positive impact on a business's overall success and its employees' opportunities.

Part 4

Integrating Information Systems into Business

The long-term success of a company depends upon the adequacy of its strategic plans. To properly manage existing and new information systems, businesses need to keep all aspects of the business in mind. For instance, most wireless devices that exist today require daily charging. If a business wanted to implement new wireless devices to support its information system, factors such as cost, staff training, and overhead expenses (additional electricity) would need to be evaluated before a decision is made. Information Systems Planning (ISP) is a vital part of an organization's success.

Information Systems Planning

To properly implement and develop new information systems, there are three key areas organizations need to evaluate and analyze:

1. The Organization's Plans and Goals

Identifying the long- and short-term plans and goals of an organization is essential to planning for new information systems, as well as evaluating existing ones. For example, if one of the goals of an organization is to increase the amount of advertising in the upcoming busy season, additional money, time, and labor will be required. Funds must be budgeted accordingly, which can affect other aspects of the organization, such as upgrading software or purchasing new printers.

2. The Current Information System in Place

Evaluating the current information system in place allows organizations to measure it against the plans and goals that have been identified. For example, does the organization have the necessary hardware to support new initiatives? If one of the goals of an organization is to reduce travel costs by utilizing online meetings, does the current information system possess the technology to support this? What are the cost savings involved in making this decision? Can those savings be utilized in other areas of the business?

3. The Rewards and Risks of an Information System's Technology

As we've learned, there are a variety of risks and rewards associated with technology. While many people get excited about using the latest and greatest tech widgets and gadgets, for businesses, impulse purchases can be a dangerous thing. However, at times it is necessary for a business to upgrade its technology in order to stay competitive in today's market.

Applying Information Systems Planning to Business Needs

As illustrated in the diagram to the right, each of the three information systems planning steps need to influence one another in order for the individual or business to make their final decision on whether to implement new systems.

Businesses must continually decide whether to update their equipment or maintain what they currently have. For example, consider the scenario below, which discusses whether or not a small business should modernize its information system.

Organization's Goals & Plans

Information Systems Planning

Information Systems Rewards & Risks

Current Information Systems

Real-world Scenario

The Kickstand is a small, independently owned bicycle shop. Mike, the owner, has been using the same point-of-purchase equipment (an older model cash register) for customer purchases since The Kickstand opened 10 years ago. Inventory is recorded and managed on a spreadsheet. Still, the shop is able to function smoothly, and bike sales have stayed steady for the past few years. Mike is thinking of upgrading to a digital system such as a computerized register and database. He needs to evaluate his options and determine whether the upgrade is worth the cost. He must also consider the dependability of a potential system and its security.

How can Mike make this business decision? From what you've learned in this unit, what are some questions he can ask himself? To determine what is best for his shop, Mike decides to evaluate his goals, his existing system, and the rewards and risks of upgrading.

Let's dive in a little further using the knowledge you've gained thus far.

In order to decide whether to upgrade his technology, Mike needs to first define the short- and long-term goals for his business.

Short-term Goals	Long-term Goals
As a short-term goal, he would like to hire two new employees to help him in the more hectic summer season.	For the long-term, he would like to increase his annual sales, which have been stable but have not improved for years.

Now that the short- and long-term goals are defined, Mike needs to evaluate the technology he already uses at The Kickstand.

Cash Register	Spreadsheet Software	Credit Card Reader
His cash register is 10 years out of date. When checking out a customer, he and his employees handwrite paper receipts, which slows down the line and sometimes irritates the customers.	He uses spreadsheet software on his laptop for bookkeeping tasks such as employee salaries, inventory, and so on. The spreadsheet software meets his needs, but at times the amount of information becomes overwhelming and he has been told that database software might be more efficient.	Recently, customers have also been complaining that his credit card reader is slow. A few people have suggested that he upgrade to a credit card payment system that uses an app on his smartphone and a small portable card reader.

With The Kickstand's technology needs identified, Mike needs to weigh the risks and rewards of upgrading.

Risks	Rewards
Running a bicycle shop can be expensive, especially since Mike plans to hire two new employees. Buying new equipment, such as a computer, a digital cash register, better bookkeeping software, and a more up-to-date credit card reader, will be costly. It might also be costly in terms of time, since he will have to train his workers how to use the new equipment.	However, if Mike upgrades his system, he could please his employees, who will be able to complete their work more quickly and efficiently, as well as his customers, who will receive better service when they purchase from The Kickstand. New software will help him easily maintain his records and keep them organized and accurate. The Kickstand's technology will also be more modern, which will give the business a competitive edge. An additional benefit is the fact that Mike will not have to upgrade his system again for some time.

After deciding to upgrade his technology, Mike is confident that he has made the right decision. Employees and customers alike have commented that since the upgrade, the store runs much more smoothly. Mike has learned that sometimes businesses have to spend money to make money, and that there can be long-term rewards for investing now to improve current technology systems.

Recap

Innovations in technology, like information communication technology, have helped businesses, organizations, and individuals do things more efficiently and successfully. While technology has reduced the need for certain types of jobs, it has undeniably given rise to new fields and careers.

In fact, the benefit of information systems to a business's operations, and therefore its bottom line, has created greater opportunities for information systems professionals. Well-trained information systems professionals are critical to making sure businesses can communicate any time, anywhere; reduce workload; increase productivity; and make better use of data for more profitable decisions. Even if you don't intend to become an information systems professional, understanding how these systems work together for an organization will benefit you in any career path you choose.

Unit 2 Review

1. Visit **www.MyCompanionSite.com**.

2. Download and complete the **Unit 2 Review** worksheet.

3. Submit your completed worksheet to your instructor.

Unit 3
Managing Information Systems

Part 1   Information Technology Requirements

Part 2   Planning and Setting Up Information Systems

Part 3   Managing Information Systems

TEKS

3.A.i, 3.A.ii, 3.B.i, 3.B.ii, 4.A.i, 4.A.ii

Part 1
Information Technology Requirements

While browsing your Instagram app on your iPhone, you notice that it continually crashes. You visit the App store to download an update that addresses a variety of bug fixes, including the crash issue. During the download, a dialog box pops up reading: "The version of your iPhone does not support the update available for this app." In this scenario, you have two options: 1. Purchase a new iPhone, or 2. Live with the current version of the Instagram app.

Organizations and businesses face similar scenarios, only on a much larger scale. To better understand the technology challenges organizations face, let's take a look at some real workplace scenarios. As you read each one, think about what you would do to address and solve each problem.

The Right Tools for the Job

If you were asked to create a list of all of the technology you need in your life, what would it look like? Your list would probably contain two columns. In column one, you would list all of the tasks and activities you do with your technology. The second column would include a list of corresponding technology devices and the hardware and software applications used to accomplish the items in the first column. Your list might look similar to **Table 3.1** below.

Table 3.1

Task/Activity	Technology Required
Schoolwork	Internet access, computer/laptop/tablet, printer, and application software (Microsoft Word, Google Docs, etc.)
Listening to music	Earbuds, iPod
Texting	Mobile phone
Watching TV and movies	iPad, Television, Wi-Fi access
Using social media	Mobile phone, apps like Twitter, Instagram, etc.
Phone calls	Mobile phone
Watching YouTube	Computer/laptop/tablet, Internet access

In essence, your list is the "information systems" that would help you accomplish your goals, or in some way enhance your life.

Businesses and other types of organizations perform a similar—but more involved—exercise when looking at their information system requirements. Identifying and understanding the needs of an organization helps determine how to plan, set up, and manage an information system.

From giant corporations like Google and Amazon, to the quick lube oil change center just up the street, organizations need information systems. Regardless of the size of an organization, designing and developing information systems is no small task. No matter their size or needs, in order to properly implement their information technology systems, organizations follow a series of common steps, which will be discussed in detail in this unit.

Part 2

Planning and Setting Up Information Systems

As we learned in Unit 2, an information system is made up of six components: hardware, software, data, people, procedures, and networks. To work successfully, all businesses need an effective mix of these components in their information systems. There are many issues to consider when analyzing available technologies and evaluating how to best make them work together.

What to Consider When Building an Information System

Building an information system that properly supports the operations of an organization involves a series of phases. In order to ensure that the software and hardware tools meet the needs of people and their tasks, the first step requires careful, detailed planning. In that sense, developing an information system is very similar to building a house. Learn about the similarities in the following scenario.

 Real-world Scenario

To build a house, a series of sequential steps are followed to ensure the end result (the house) meets the requirements of the homeowner.

First, the homeowner must determine what they need in the house, such as:

- How many bedrooms and bathrooms?
- What style of woodwork?
- How big will the kitchen be?
- What materials will be best suited for the environment the house will occupy?

Once the requirements have been identified, the blueprint of the house can begin. With the blueprint in place, materials and supplies can then be purchased and the building process can begin. Once the home is built, a series of tests are required, for example:

- Does the electrical and heating system work properly?

With the testing phase complete, homeowners must maintain the house. Filters need to be changed, the lawn needs to be mowed, carpets vacuumed, etc.

Similar to building a house, the approaches used in designing and developing information systems vary based on the size, type, and needs of an organization. Additionally, the phases often overlap based on a number of factors, such as delays in implementation, cost changes, and availability of workers. However, every method of developing an information system follows the same basic set of principles and phases:

Phase 1: Identify Organizational and Technological Requirements

Phase 2: Determine Equipment and Supplies

Phase 3: Create Testing and Maintenance Systems

Phase 4: Create Troubleshooting Systems

Phase 1:
Identify Organizational and Technological Requirements

Identifying an organization's operational and technical requirements is the all-important first phase in good information system planning. Therefore, it is critical to carefully consider several issues right from the start:

1. Identify the needs of the organization
2. Address the challenges
3. Revise the requirements
4. Determine the technological environment
5. Identify technology requirements

1. Identify the needs of the organization

In this step, the organization generates a list that identifies all of its goals and initiatives. For example, an organization might aim to enter a new market, implement a new phone system, or decide to let employees work from home. By identifying its needs, the organization can get a clearer picture of what technology will be required to support them. Consider the following scenario as it relates to an organization identifying its operational and technological needs.

Real-world Scenario

Best Buy® is one of the retail leaders in selling technology and entertainment products and services. Due to increased customer demand, Best Buy needs to hire new technical support employees. By identifying its need for new employees (an operational requirement), Best Buy has also identified the need for new technology to support the new employees (a technological requirement).

As operational needs are identified, other related requirements are often discovered. As more information is gathered, it becomes obvious that certain problems or challenges have to be addressed.

2. Address the challenges

Depending on the size and nature of the business, identifying the challenges faced by an organization can involve input from several sources. Merely listing problems isn't worth much if the aim isn't finding solutions. In fact, every challenge can be viewed as an opportunity, rather than a problem. Analyzing each issue to determine its root cause is the key to finding solutions. Once a challenge has been identified, how and when it is addressed needs to be prioritized in line with the organization's goals. To illustrate this concept, consider the Auntie Anne's scenario below.

 Real-world Scenario

Auntie Anne's® is a national franchise chain specializing in making and selling flavored pretzels. Among its extensive review of challenges to its operations, executives at Auntie Anne's have identified the following issues:

- Based on customer feedback, more flavors need to be added to the menu.
- The demand for their homemade pretzel baking kits has increased, requiring the need to purchase new manufacturing equipment to produce more kits.
- The company website has been performing very sluggishly, causing a decrease in online sales.
- Employees who work at the national headquarters have been complaining that their workstations are too small.

 Upon evaluating the identified challenges, executives at Auntie Anne's agree that solving every issue all at once is not feasible or immediately necessary. Auntie Anne's must prioritize the list and determine what to do next. For example: What is causing the website to slow down? Do they update their website first, or should they add new product items to their menu to increase sales? What technology is needed to address and solve the problem?

3. Revise the requirements

With the organization's needs and challenges identified, the next step is to revise the information system requirements as needed.

 For example, after reviewing and prioritizing their operations evaluation, the executives at Auntie Anne's determined that new employee workstations were not a high priority when compared to other issues identified. Consequently, new workstations can be removed from the list for the time being. When evaluating their website issue, a problem with the web server is discovered, creating a need to revise that item's technical requirements.

4. Determine the technological environment

For technology to work, it has to be used within the environment, or technological platform, it was built for. In other words, certain technology will not work with other technology platforms. For example, you cannot play an Xbox game on a PlayStation. However, some software applications—and most hardware—can be used in multiple environments. If you have ever opened a file on a Mac system that was first produced on a Windows system, you have worked with two different computer environments.

Before the selection of software and hardware can be identified, organizations need to know their existing technological environments, or identify potential new ones.

Since technological environments are major factors that impact business operations, certain questions have to be asked to help build an information system plan, including:

- Is the software and hardware primarily Windows-based, Mac-based, web-based, or a combination of each?
- Are the software applications web-based or installed on the users' computers?
- Do the computers utilize wireless technology?
- Is any of the hardware needed for a particular task built to function only with a particular environment?
- What type of Database Management System (DBMS) is used?
- Do employees work remotely from home?

Since changes in technology can affect how a company conducts business, defining the environment is critical. When technology changes, so might the technological platform. For example, businesses that deliver content—like magazine, newspaper, and book publishers—have had to figure out ways of delivering their content in digital formats, such as eBooks and ePubs. Before the digital revolution, most of their production tools were geared toward print production. Because of this change in technology, these types of businesses had to change their operating strategy.

5. Identify technology requirements

The final step in this phase is to determine what technology best fits the needs of the organization. It is important to note that in this phase, the actual selection of technology does not yet take place. Instead, the technology requirements are outlined at this high level. For example, if an organization knows it must update its online transaction system, identifying this "need" is what is noted, not the actual selection of the technology device or software that will be implemented to meet this requirement.

Phase 2:
Determine Equipment and Supplies

In the lessons ahead, you will become familiar with various software packages and how they are used by businesses to accomplish real-world tasks.

Just like a carpenter who is building a house needs certain tools and materials to do so, organizations need tools and resources for their information system. The next phase in developing an information system is to determine what equipment and supplies best meet the needs and requirements of the organization. The equipment and supplies that are implemented serve as the tools for getting the job done right within the information system. Selecting the right software, hardware, and other peripherals such as wiring, networking, and materials is all part of this phase.

Software

Software programs are the machine-readable instructions that direct the operations of a computer system. Programs are used to organize, process, and analyze data, as well as to control how the hardware parts of the system function. Examples of software include operating systems, programming languages, and applications such as spreadsheets, word processing, and graphic design programs. These various programs are divided into two categories:

System Software manages and operates the computer hardware to provide a platform for other software applications. System software is commonly referred to as the operating system. Examples are Windows and Mac OS. Operating systems make it possible for different computer or technology components to work together.

Application Software directly assists users in doing their work. Application software typically performs a primary task, or related tasks. Word processing software, for example, enables users to create, edit, and distribute various documents including memos, letters, and reports.

If you had to type a paper and prepare a presentation for school, what software applications would you use? To get the job done, you would use a word processing application (like Microsoft Word or Google Docs) and a presentation application (like Microsoft PowerPoint or Google Slides). Each application serves a different purpose to complete the task, and different versions offer different features.

There are literally tens of thousands of software applications in existence today. Different software applications do different things. From the mobile phone apps you use, to the accounting systems that large corporations work with, a clear understanding of the task at hand is needed in order to select the right software. Like you, organizations need to evaluate and analyze software applications to ensure they meet their operational requirements and the needs of people they employ.

To properly evaluate software so the right purchases are made, organizations ask three questions:

1. What tasks must be accomplished?
2. What software features are available to do what is needed?
3. What are the cost and feature benefits of one software application compared to another?

Computer Hardware

For software to do its job, it needs the right hardware. Hardware refers to the actual machines, electrical wiring, and other mechanical components of a computer or information system. In other words, hardware is the components of a computer system that you can physically see and touch. Examples include the computer and its monitor, mouse, speakers, and printer. These and other hardware can be categorized as shown in **Table 3.2**.

Table 3.2

Processing	Input	Output	Storage
The computer components that manipulate data and turn it into information are referred to as processing devices. Examples: CPU (Central Processing Unit), motherboard, and memory	All computer hardware components that are instrumental in feeding data to a computer system are categorized as input devices. Examples: keyboards, mouse, touchpad, microphone, webcam, and scanner	Hardware components that deliver and display both data and information are referred to as output. Examples: monitor, speaker, headphones, and printer	The parts of the computer that are used to store data in whatever form are classified as storage devices. Examples: RAM (Random Access Memory), hard drives, USB sticks, and cloud

Other hardware peripherals, supplies, and accessories

For software and hardware to interact and function as intended, several other components are necessary. Accessories, supplies, and other supporting hardware peripherals also need to be considered when determining equipment and supplies. Identifying everything from power cords, to custom digital file storage requirements, to the right ink cartridges for each printer is an important part of information system planning. Again, figuring out what and how much is needed depends on that first consideration of what an organization needs to accomplish. As an example, consider the scenario below.

Real-world Scenario

Jeanette and Ryan have decided to pool their talents in marketing and design to start their own multimedia studio. Their focus will be print work, presentations, and web design. With their freelance and ad agency experience, they have what it takes to make their new business successful. In addition to combining their talents, they will need to evaluate what software, hardware, and technology services to acquire and how to get the most from their investment.

Not only do Jeanette and Ryan need to agree on what software is needed; they must also determine what their software needs are regarding equipment and supplies to get the job done. **Table 3.3** below illustrates what they have to consider.

Table 3.3

Task/Business Need	Hardware/Service	Software/Service
Connectivity	Network Routers, Cable, Wireless	Internet Service Provider
Communications with Clients and Colleagues	Computers, Mobile Devices	Email Client Software
Online Portfolio	Website	Web Design
Proposals and Correspondence	Printers	Word Processing
Presentations	Displays	PowerPoint
File Backup	Cloud Service, Portable Drives	File Management
Client and Project Records	Computers	Access
Design Production	Workstation Computers, Scanners	Adobe Creative Cloud
Color and Black & White Printing	High Resolution Color Printer, High Volume Black & White Printer	Utilizes All Software

Phase 3:
Create Testing and Maintenance Systems

Before an information system is fully implemented, it will need to be tested. Therefore, a necessary part of ensuring information system functionality is testing and maintenance. Like a car, a house, and even the human body, an information system and its technology require ongoing maintenance. Both testing and maintenance require establishing and following a framework of step-by-step policies, processes, and procedures to make sure all system components operate optimally.

An important consideration in this regard is preventative maintenance. A plan for regularly scheduled maintenance of each system component will help avoid down time and control the need for unanticipated and costly repairs. A well-defined protocol for how technology and supplies will be maintained may include:

- When should supplies, such as printer ink or toner and paper, be ordered?
- When will software updates be implemented?
- What is the replacement life of each piece of equipment?
- When will the organization's needs change?
- When will certain technology become obsolete?
- When are files backed up offsite so as not to lose data in case something happens?
- When will security updates and enhancements be applied?

Phase 4:
Create Troubleshooting Systems

Every good information systems plan "plans on something happening." Troubleshooting is a critical, yet often overlooked, process in developing information systems. Solving a technical problem and determining how to avoid it in the future must be approached in a systematic way. Some common technical issues may include:

- Mechanical or electronic faults
- User error or lack of experience
- Incorrect or outdated software drivers for hardware
- Software and hardware incompatibility
- Malicious software or security breaches

Tracking and fixing issues to minimize system weakness is an important part of the ongoing information systems management. Part 3 in this unit expands upon the importance of building and managing information systems.

Part 3

Managing Information Systems

Basic Information Systems Management Elements

Each information system is unique and dynamic. How an information system is built and maintained depends on the organization, its size and mission, as well as its ever-changing needs. Even though every system is different, as the phases of information system development discussed earlier suggest, there are standard processes and procedures used to make sure that an information system will function as intended. There are three basic areas to consider:

Cyber Security

Due to the interconnected nature of so much of our computing, information is easily shared, but is also easily compromised. Efforts to protect privacy, including identity management and information security, are one of the most important tasks of information systems management. Online threats can be a moving target, and so system security must concern itself with questions such as:

- What information needs to be protected?
- Who needs access to what content and for how long?
- Where are the system's vulnerabilities?
- How could our systems likely be attacked?
- How effective is our current cyber security?

Managing Ongoing Operations

As discussed, preventative maintenance will ensure that an information system operates efficiently and as expected. Optimum efficiency is better achieved when the maintenance process is a framework of step-by-step policies and procedures that includes such things as:

- Regular application and system software updates
- Regular updates to cyber security software and policies
- Inventory tracking and use of quality equipment-appropriate supplies
- Regular file backup
- Ongoing review of organizational goals and technological needs

Technical Support

No matter how good the plan or how secure and efficient an information system is, every organization has to be ready to address technical issues. As noted, a "troubleshooting system" has to be in place before a system hits the ground running. Everything, from user error to unexpected glitches, needs to be addressed with critical thinking and persistence until resolved. Each situation is different; however, the following steps can be used as a standard for troubleshooting:

1. Confirm that a problem exists

See for yourself. Do not simply accept that something is not working.

2. Locate the cause of the problem by process of elimination

The more you understand how the whole system works—which software controls which function; which hardware device is hooked up to which network—the easier it will be for you to find the issue. As you investigate the issue, step through what works so as to eliminate each step until the problem is encountered.

3. Correct the problem

Knowing how the system works and which components are reliant on each other will help you correct the cause of the problem. Do not be satisfied with eliminating the "symptom" of the issue. Fix the root problem so that it does not happen again.

4. Confirm that the problem has been corrected

Once the issue has been resolved, try to replicate the original problem by doing what caused it in the first place. If the problem does not occur, the issue has been corrected.

5. Make system adjustments to prevent recurrence of the problem

If possible, update the system components—software or hardware devices—to prevent the same issue from happening again.

⭐ Recap

Businesses must consider many factors when analyzing available technologies and evaluating how best to make them work together. These include knowing and understanding the four phases of building an information system: identifying organizational and technological requirements, determining equipment and supplies, creating testing and maintenance systems, and creating troubleshooting systems. While each of these phases may be time-consuming, the end result is well worth the effort for a business.

After an information system is implemented, procedures need to be put in place regarding cyber security, preventative maintenance, and technical support. Information systems are constantly evolving, and as a result, it is important for businesses to plan appropriately for how they will maintain, protect, and replace their technologies. Understanding the processes necessary for a business to manage, maintain, and update their information systems is a critical skill as you prepare to enter the workforce.

Unit 3 Review

1. Visit **www.MyCompanionSite.com**.
2. Download and complete the **Unit 3 Review** worksheet.
3. Submit your completed worksheet to your instructor.

Unit 4
File Management

Part 1   The Computer File System

Part 2   The Importance of an Organized File System

Hands-on Lessons:

Part 3   File Management Lessons   Lessons 4.1 – 4.3

TEKS

5.A.i, 5.B.i, 5.C.i

Part 1

The Computer File System

Before computers, documents containing data were stored using a manual file system. Documents were placed inside of manila file folders, which were labeled and organized using file cabinets. Today, manual (paper) filing systems have been replaced by computer filing systems that organize and store files electronically using folders and directories.

A **computer file** is a resource for storing information, which is available on a computer program and is usually based on some kind of durable storage. Like a file cabinet, a computer **directory** is an organizational unit or container used to organize folders and files into a hierarchical structure. File directories typically contain file **folders** that hold one or more files. Folders provide a method for organizing files, similar to a manila file folder containing paper documents in a file cabinet. When multiple folders, subfolders, and files are stored in the directory, a directory tree is formed. A **directory tree** is a hierarchy of directories that consists of a single directory called the **parent directory**, or top level directory, and all levels of its subdirectories.

Operating Systems

Files are organized and controlled by a computer system's operating system. An **operating system** is the collection of software that directs a computer's operations, controls and schedules the execution of other programs, and manages storage, input/output, and communication resources. The operating system is the most important program on a computer. Every general purpose computer must have an operating system to run other programs and applications. In addition to organizing files and directories, operating systems perform basic tasks, such as recognizing input from the keyboard, sending output to the display screen, and controlling peripheral devices such as disk drives and printers. Two of the most popular operating systems are Microsoft Windows and Mac OS.

Part 2

The Importance of an Organized File System

Computer files contain important information, so it's vital for people and businesses alike to create a file system that is well-organized. Think of an organized file system, such as your notebooks and binders for school. If your notes and handouts aren't filed in an orderly manner, finding what to study or what assignment to complete becomes a major challenge. Computer files follow the same rules as paper files. Storing and saving your files and using the folders that make sense to you is all it takes.

Steps to Creating an Organized File System

To create an organized file system, there is a series of simple steps and rules to follow.

Step 1: Storing Files

Establish where the files will be stored. Files can be stored on hard drives, network drives, external drives (i.e. USB sticks), or in the cloud (i.e. Google Drive).

Step 2: Creating a Directory Tree

Create folders and subfolders (if necessary) in an organized manner for storing files. To demonstrate, let's say you are currently enrolled in six courses at your school. The directory tree structure might look similar to the one shown below:

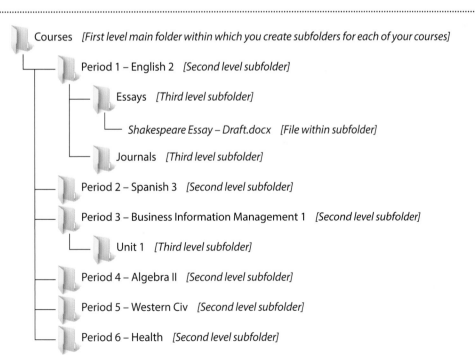

Courses   *[First level main folder within which you create subfolders for each of your courses]*

Period 1 – English 2   *[Second level subfolder]*

Essays   *[Third level subfolder]*

Shakespeare Essay – Draft.docx   *[File within subfolder]*

Journals   *[Third level subfolder]*

Period 2 – Spanish 3   *[Second level subfolder]*

Period 3 – Business Information Management 1   *[Second level subfolder]*

Unit 1   *[Third level subfolder]*

Period 4 – Algebra II   *[Second level subfolder]*

Period 5 – Western Civ   *[Second level subfolder]*

Period 6 – Health   *[Second level subfolder]*

Step 3: Saving and Naming Files

When it comes to naming files, there are two types: the files you create and those that you collect, such as a downloaded image. When naming files, use names that follow a logical pattern, are descriptive, and can be found easily by scanning with the eye or using a file search tool. Establish a good file naming convention. File naming conventions are rules that enable the titling of files and folders in a consistent and logical way.

For example, a good file name for a first draft of an English essay written on Shakespeare would be:

Shakespeare Essay – Draft.docx

All files contain a property known as a file extension. A **file extension** is a group of letters occurring after a period in a file name, indicating the format of the file. File extensions help to identify what software application was used to create the file, the software version (sometimes), and/or the format of the file. **Table 4.1** provides examples of various file extensions.

Table 4.1

Examples of File Extensions	
File Extension	**Software Application Used to Create the File or Its Format**
.pdf	Adobe Acrobat
.xlsx	Microsoft Excel
.docx	Microsoft Word
.jpg	An image file (photos, clip art, scanned documents, etc.)
.png	An image file that supports transparency

Most software application programs allow users to save files in different formats and versions. For example, you might be working with another classmate on a school project where sharing files is necessary. You might be using Microsoft Word 2016, whereas your partner has an older version of Word. So your partner can open and edit the Word file, you would need to save it as an older version of Word.

In addition to saving files as different versions, many software applications allow users to either save or export files in formats that can be read regardless of what application was used to create them. A good example is a PDF (Portable Document Format) file. The format of this file can be read using Adobe Acrobat, a free downloadable application that captures all of the elements of a printed document in electronic format.

Step 4: Knowing File Properties

In addition to the file name and extension, files contain a number of other properties (or attributes). File attributes you should be aware of are:

- File size
- The date the file was last saved or modified
- Security permissions (who has permission to access the file?)
- Author of the file (who created the file?)

Knowing the file properties can help you organize and find files using different sorting methods. For example, when viewing a folder that contains multiple files, you can sort the list by date, allowing you to quickly see what files were modified last.

Step 5: Copying, Moving, and Deleting Files

For a variety of reasons, copying, moving, and deleting files are a necessary part of keeping an organized file system. You may need to create a copy for backup purposes, or you may have saved a file to the wrong folder.

Copying, moving, and deleting files helps keep things organized. Think of this process as a messy, cluttered bedroom with clothes on the floor, cell phone and laptop chargers out of place, and papers spread out across the desk. To clean the room, you would have to move items to their proper place and throw out any garbage. It's important to use a similar mindset as you organize computer files.

CAUTION: Unless you are absolutely certain you no longer need the contents of a file, do not delete it. Once it's gone, it's gone for good. A good practice is to move files you don't "think" you need anymore to a folder called "Old Files," or something similar. This way, the file can be moved to keep your files and folders organized, but it's still available just in case.

Shortcut for Moving Files:

To copy a file, select (not open) the file. Simultaneously, hold down the **Ctrl** *key (Windows) or the* **Command** *(Mac) key and the letter* **C** *key.*

To paste the file, go to the desired location of the file, and hold down **Ctrl** *key (Windows) or* **Command** *key (Mac) and hit the letter* **V** *key.*

Step 6: Locating Files

All operating systems come equipped with file searching features. In the event you cannot locate a file, you can quickly search for all or part of a file name to locate it. Once located, you can determine if the file needs to be moved or copied to a different location.

 **Recap**

It is important to stay organized both personally and professionally, and understanding the value of file management is a good place to start. The steps to creating an organized digital file system are simple and can help you keep track of your digital photos, school assignments, and personal files. Your computer files will always be easily accessible when you build a logical directory tree, use consistent and meaningful file naming conventions, and recognize the various file types. Understanding how to store and save computer files efficiently is an important skill for life and will help you prepare to enter the business world.

Unit Directories

Setting Up a File Directory for this Book

Overview

The remaining units in this book contain a series of hands-on lessons that require you to produce a variety of documents using different software applications. Keeping your files organized will be essential to completing each unit. Using what you have learned thus far about file management, you will create a file directory system to help manage and keep the files you will be working with in an organized format.

In this lesson, you will create a file directory system that you will use to organize and save the files you will be creating in the remaining units in this book.

New Skills / TEKS

Creating a File Directory • Capturing a Screenshot

TEKS: 5.B.i

Instructions

1. Create a new folder on your storage drive (hard drive, network drive, web drive, etc.).

2. Name the folder **BIM**.

3. Create a file directory system identical to the one shown in **Figure 4.1-A**.

4. Take a screenshot of the file directory system you created. Be sure that the folders containing the files are open. To take a screenshot, follow the instructions below.

WINDOWS USERS:

    a. With the folder directory displaying on the screen, press the **PrtScn** (Print Screen) key.

    b. Using word processing software, create a new document. Use the key combination **(Ctrl+V)** to paste the screenshot into the document.

    c. Save the file as **BIM DIRECTORY** to the **Unit 4 – File Management** folder.

MAC USERS:

    a. With the folder directory displaying on the screen, use the **Command+Shift+4** key combination. This will automatically save the screenshot in .jpg format to your computer desktop. Typically, the file name for screenshots taken on a Mac are automatically assigned using the word "Screenshot" and date and time it was taken. For example: **Screenshot 2016-01-23 10:15 AM.jpg**

    b. Save the file as **BIM DIRECTORY** to the **Unit 4 – File Management** folder.

5. Print a copy of the screenshot if required by your instructor.

6. For the remainder of this book, save your files to their respective unit folders and subfolders.

Figure 4.1-A

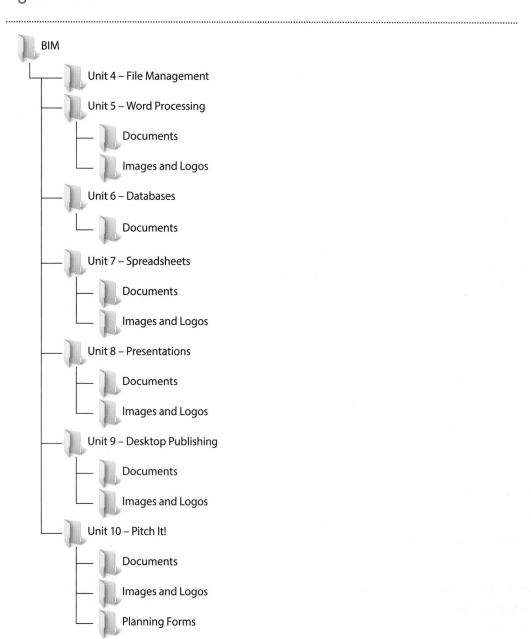

BIM
- Unit 4 – File Management
- Unit 5 – Word Processing
  - Documents
  - Images and Logos
- Unit 6 – Databases
  - Documents
- Unit 7 – Spreadsheets
  - Documents
  - Images and Logos
- Unit 8 – Presentations
  - Documents
  - Images and Logos
- Unit 9 – Desktop Publishing
  - Documents
  - Images and Logos
- Unit 10 – Pitch It!
  - Documents
  - Images and Logos
  - Planning Forms

File Formats

Saving Files in Different Formats

Overview

Assume the following scenario:

John Douglas is a self-employed graphic designer who works from his home. John works with a number of clients, and a necessary part of his job is sharing and exchanging files with them. John's customers use a variety of software applications, versions, and computer systems. Some have the latest and greatest software, while others use much older versions. Consequently, John needs to save his files in a variety of formats so they are readable by his clients. For example, John has the newest version of Microsoft Office, so any files he creates using these applications must be saved as older version file formats. John also uses Adobe InDesign, a popular page layout software, to produce finished documents. Most of his clients do not have this software, so John typically exports the files in PDF format, which allows his customers to quickly open and view the file.

In this lesson, you will create a file directory and then save a file in different formats to the directory.

New Skills / TEKS

Saving Files in Different Formats

TEKS: 5.B.i, 5.C.i

Instructions

1. Create a file directory system on your storage drive identical to the one shown in **Figure 4.2-A**.

2. Using word processing software, create a new document.

3. Save the document as **ORGANIZING FILES** to the **Lesson 4.2 > Documents** folder.

4. At the top of the document, type the following:

> **Organizing computer files involves being skilled in the following areas:**
> 1. **Storing files**
> 2. **Creating directories**
> 3. **Saving and naming files**
> 4. **Knowing the properties of files**
> 5. **Copying, moving, and deleting files**
> 6. **Locating files**

5. With the document still open and using the same file name, use the Save As or Export options to save or export the file in Rich Text Format (.rtf) to the **Lesson 4.2 > Documents > Different Formats** folder.

   NOTE: Rich Text Format is a cross-platform file format that is readable by many word processing applications.

6. Save or export the file in PDF (.pdf) format to the **Lesson 4.2 > Documents > Different Formats** folder.

   NOTE: If saving or exporting the file in PDF format is not an option, save or export the file in Plain Text (.txt) format.

7. Take a screenshot of the file directory system you created. Be sure that the folders containing the files are open. To take a screenshot, follow the instructions below.

WINDOWS USERS:

   a. With the folder directory displaying on the screen, press the **PrtScn** (Print Screen) key.

   b. Using word processing software, create a new document. Use the key combination **(Ctrl+V)** to paste the screenshot into the document.

   c. Save the file as **DIRECTORY SCREENSHOT** to the **Lesson 4.2 > Images** folder.

MAC USERS:

   a. With the folder directory displaying on the screen, use the **Command+Shift+4** key combination.

   b. Save the file as **DIRECTORY SCREENSHOT** to the **Lesson 4.2 > Images** folder.

8. Print a copy of the screenshot if required by your instructor.

Figure 4.2-A

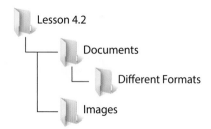

Lesson 4.2

    Documents

        Different Formats

    Images

Organizing Files

Copying and Moving Files

Overview

In this unit, you learned the value and importance of keeping an organized file system. For this lesson, assume the following scenario:

Your science teacher has given your class the following assignment:

Using word processing software, write a five page report about the solar system. To illustrate the content in the report, include images of several planets that make up the solar system.

In this lesson, you will work with copying, moving, and backing up files.

New Skills / TEKS

Copying and Moving Files

TEKS: 5.A.i, 5.B.i

Instructions

1. Create a file directory system on your storage drive identical to the one shown in **Figure 4.3-A**.

2. Using the Internet, search and find images of the following planets:

    Earth

    Mars

    Jupiter

    Saturn

3. Save each image to the **Solar System Paper > Documents** folder.

4. Rename each image file using its planet's name (Earth, Mars, etc.).

5. Move the files from the Documents folder to the Images folder.

6. Make a copy of all four image files.

7. Move the copied files to the **Solar System Paper > Images > Back Up Images** folder.

8. Take a screenshot of the file directory system you created. Be sure that the subfolders containing the files are open. To take a screenshot, follow the instructions on the following page.

WINDOWS USERS:

a. With the folder directory displaying on the screen, press the **PrtScn** (Print Screen) key.

b. Using word processing software, create a new document. Use the key combination **(Ctrl+V)** to paste the screenshot into the document.

c. Save the file as **SOLAR SYSTEM SCREENSHOT** to the **Solar System Paper** > **Images** folder.

MAC USERS:

a. With the folder directory displaying on the screen, use the **Command+Shift+4** key combination.

b. Save the file as **SOLAR SYSTEM SCREENSHOT** to the **Solar System Paper** > **Images** folder.

9. Print a copy of the screenshot if required by your instructor.

Figure 4.3-A

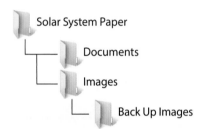

Unit 5
Word Processing

What is Word Processing Software?

Word processing software is used to create, edit, share, and print documents from a computer or similar device. Whether it's a resume, MLA style report, or business letter, word processing software has become a necessary document creation tool. Word processing software is used by businesses across all industries throughout the world. While there are many different word processing software applications available, they all give users the ability to perform the same basic tasks.

Word processing is essentially adding to and editing a document's content, with editing a document being the standard function word processing offers. Editing a word processing file simply means making changes to the text, graphics, or objects contained in the file. **Figure 5.0** lists some of the most common word processing editing tasks.

Figure 5.0

Basic Text Editing	Basic Graphic Editing	Basic Objects Editing
Inserting and deleting text	Drawing, resizing, and rotating shapes	Adding rows and columns to tables
Copying and pasting text	Adjusting alignment and position	Adjusting table column width and row height
Grouping, moving, and rotating text	Applying shadows and other effects	Inserting, formatting, and changing charts and graphs
Changing font style, color, and effects	Adding and changing fill and outline colors	Hyperlinking text to a website
Adjusting text size, paragraph, and character styles	Resizing and cropping pictures	

Why Learn Word Processing?

TEKS

6.A.i, 6.B.i, 6.B.ii, 6.C.i, 6.C.ii, 6.E.i, 6.E.ii, 6.E.iii, 6.E.iv, 6.F.i, 6.G.i, 6.G.ii

Word processing is the most commonly used computer application in business. It is a vital communication tool and is therefore one of the most critically important computer skills that you should learn. Word processing on a computer has become so popular because of the ease in which it enables composing and editing words, sentences, paragraphs, chapters, shapes, and objects.

Text color, size, and style can be changed with the click of a mouse. Images, objects, charts, and graphs can be easily inserted to enhance the appearance of the document, and page numbers can be generated automatically. Finally, the fact that word processing software can alert you of spelling errors and grammar mistakes can only help to ensure that the document you create is perfect!

Word processing software requires you to add text using an input device such as a keyboard. In this unit, you will be completing lessons that will not only improve your word processing skills, but by practicing proper touch typing techniques, you will improve your ability to create and type documents efficiently and accurately. Although the word processing lessons do not focus heavily on using the numeric keypad, you will gain significant numeric keypad practice in the spreadsheet unit and will ultimately improve your numeric keypad touch typing skills.

Types of Word Processing Software

For the most part, all word processing applications are inherently capable of doing the same thing—creating, editing, sharing, and printing documents. However, there are some considerations to make when choosing word processing software.

For instance, if you need to create complex documents such as reports that contain graphics and charts, Microsoft Word is a good choice.

For more basic word processing tasks, Google Docs may be a better fit since it is simple to use and offers document sharing and collaboration.

Larger businesses that distribute word processing software to thousands of employees typically have unique needs that dictate their word processing software application, such as cost, application training, document security, and document version control. In this case, a business-oriented version of Microsoft Word is a popular choice.

The Most Popular Word Processing Software

Microsoft Word is a widely used word processing software designed by Microsoft. Word is a component of the Microsoft Office Suite, but can be used as a stand-alone product. It was launched in 1983, and has since set the standard for other word processing software. Word works with Windows and Macintosh operating systems.

Pages is a word processing software that was developed by Apple, Inc. It is part of the iWork productivity suite, and runs on Apple's OS X and iOS operating systems. The first version of Pages was released in 2005, and the most recent version is offered for free to anyone with an iOS device.

Google Docs is a free web-based word processing application in which documents can be created, edited, and stored online. Files can be accessed from any computer with an Internet connection and a web browser. Google Docs was released to the public in 2007, and is integrated with Google Drive.

Identifying Different Types of Business Documents

Businesses use a variety of business documents to communicate and conduct business in a professional environment. From brief email messages and memos to complex legal documents and financial reports, it is essential that all business documents be well-written and free from typographical, grammatical, and factual errors.

You will find below a variety of business documents used in businesses today.

Memorandum

A memo is a form of written communication that moves within a company or organization and is written in a direct, professional tone. Typically, a memo calls attention to a specific topic or issue and addresses it.

Memos can be sent to an individual, a small group, or an entire business or organization. A printed memo provides an easy way to ensure that all recipients have received the same message.

Block Style Business Letter

A block style business letter is a format that is commonly used when writing a business letter. Recipients may include customers, colleagues in other businesses, service providers, and job applicants. Using a standard letter format, such as a block style, shows you understand what is commonly used in the business world.

It is important to become familiar with the various parts of a block style letter and their proper placement because as you enter the business world, you will find that concise, professional writing presented in a standard way is expected and appreciated.

MEMORANDUM

TO: All Staff

FROM: Joe Meridan, Owner *jm*

DATE: April 2, 20__

SUBJECT: New Flavor Kickoff Party

As you know, I have been working on a new flavor for Creamy Creations. I experimented with dozens of combinations and think I finally found the perfect new summertime recipe. It takes into consideration the fun of summer, the need to cool off, and the lazy attitude most people love to have in the months ahead.

The new flavor is called Melt-Away-Melon and includes the following ingredients:

- vanilla ice cream base
- swirls of cantaloupe puree
- crushed chocolate covered macadamia nuts

I have prepared the initial twenty gallons for taste testing. Please join me this Thursday, April 6, at 8:30 p.m., for a private staff party. In the meantime, as always, please keep this new flavor "under your hat" until it has passed the staff "taste test." Attached is the invitation. I look forward to seeing you all there.

jt

Attachment

---

68 Hillbrook Road
Columbus, OH 43215
January 10, 20__

Ms. Jennifer Crosswell
Greater Columbus Convention Center
400 North High Street
Columbus, OH 43215

Dear Ms. Crosswell:

Enclosed please find my volunteer application for your review. I am interested in working at the Jordan Perry event that will be held on February 14, 20__. I saw the advertised position in last Sunday's *Columbus Dispatch.*

As you can see, I have extensive experience in event marketing. I have volunteered at various church festivals, local carnivals, and walk-a-thons. At my last volunteer post, I assisted organizers of the Walk for Cancer by welcoming walkers at registration. My supervisor that day said I was one of the friendliest, most responsible volunteers she has ever had. Besides being a huge Jordan Perry fan, I believe my work experience and history as a hard working individual make me qualified for the job.

I look forward to speaking with you further about my qualifications. Please feel free to contact me at the above address or call me at 614-555-3219. Thank you for your consideration.

Sincerely,

Sara Birch

si

Enclosure

Resume

A resume is a professionally presented document that introduces you to a prospective employer.

A resume is often the first piece of communication an employer gets from you and is meant to encourage the opportunity for an interview that can lead to a job offer. It is important to convey how you can meet the needs of an organization by showcasing your abilities and skills.

Although there are many formats that you can use, a resume typically highlights your education and work experience, as well as any clubs, sports, or organizations you have participated in. Awards and accomplishments that are related to the job you are applying for may also be included.

Business Report

Business reports often include information in a format that is more formal, and usually longer, than a business letter.

Reports can cover a variety of topics. For example, a School Committee may prepare a detailed business report about the latest research study on ways of improving students' scores on standardized tests.

Although the format and contents of business reports differ depending on the report's purpose, they typically include an introduction, summary, methodology and discussion, conclusion, and recommendation.

MLA Style Report

An MLA (Modern Language Association) style report is an academic report widely accepted in schools and universities.

When using MLA style, the author's last name and page number are included in the header at the right margin. The heading typically includes the author's name, the instructor's name, course name, and date. The title of the report is center aligned in initial caps, and the body of the report includes an introduction, body, and conclusion.

The types of sources used in the research will determine the format that should be used. However, all cited sources are always included on the last page of the report, titled Works Cited.

Press Release/News Release

A news release is a written communication directed to members of the news media. For example, a news release can announce an upcoming scheduled event, or detail an employee receiving a special award or recognition. When the media receives a news release first, they are more likely to consider digging deeper into the story or conducting an interview for further information.

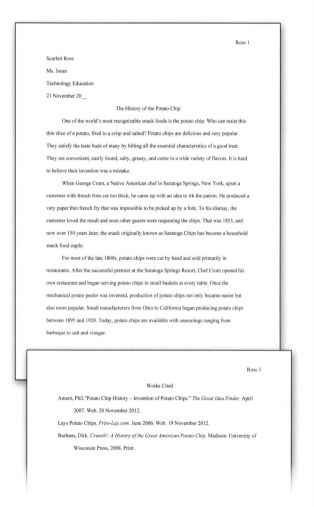

Newsletter

A newsletter is a regularly distributed business publication that is often used for building relationships and maintaining regular contact with customers and prospects.

A newsletter can serve many purposes, such as providing awareness about a business, demonstrating expertise in an area, and promoting products and services within a business. Although there is not a defined format that must be used, newsletters are typically formatted the same way from one issue to the next.

A great example of a newsletter that you may already receive is one that is published by your school. Whether it is delivered in print or electronic format (eNewsletter), this newsletter most likely serves as a communication tool for parents to learn about what is happening in the school and what events may be forthcoming.

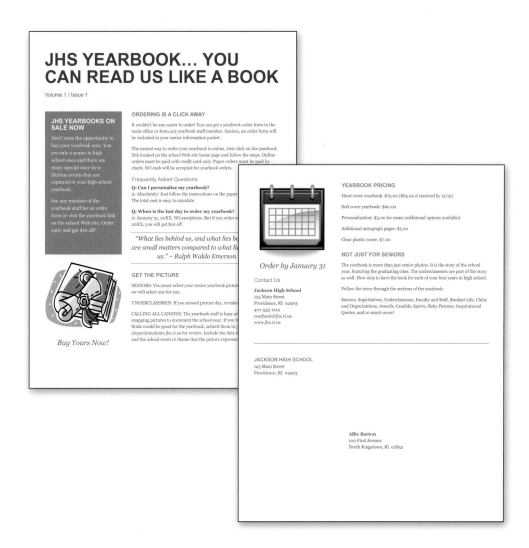

Hardware Requirements for Word Processing Applications

In this unit, you will create a series of documents that require the use of word processing software. As with all software applications, there are certain hardware requirements necessary to complete this task.

Hardware refers to the physical elements of a computer, so in this textbook's case, in order for you to use word processing software, you will need some type of computer to run the software, such as a desktop computer, tablet, or mobile phone. Some input devices that you will need include a mouse and a keyboard, or audio input if you are using voice recognition software. If you are going to print any of your word processing documents, you will need a printer. If the word processing software requires access to the Internet, such as Google Docs, then a router and Internet connection are required.

A LOOK AHEAD TO YOUR FINAL ASSESSMENT

Pitch It!™

As a final assessment (Unit 10), you will be divided into teams and "pitch" a new product idea to your instructor. This assessment will give you exciting, first-hand knowledge of how word processing can be used as a tool for creating and organizing information. Pay close attention to the skills you will be learning in this unit, as you will draw on them again in the "Pitch It!" final assessment.

My Favorite Things

Creating Your First Document

Overview

Word processing has become such a common tool that one might take its power for granted. Creating documents and making changes to existing documents is second nature to many people. Imagine having to recreate an entire document only to have a second version with slight changes. Luckily, computer applications, such as Microsoft Word and Google Docs, allow users to create new documents from existing ones without having to start from scratch.

In this lesson, you will see how a word processing document can be saved using one file name, revised, and saved with a new file name.

New Skills / TEKS

Creating, Naming, and Saving a Document • Revising, Renaming, and Saving an Existing Document • Changing Font and Font Size • Printing a Document • Closing a Document

TEKS: 6.B.i, 6.C.i, 6.C.ii, 6.D.i, 6.F.i

Instructions

1. Create a new word processing document.
2. Change the line spacing to single with no additional spacing before or after the paragraphs.
3. Save the document as **LIKES**.
4. Change the font to Georgia.
5. Change the font size to 14.
6. On the first line of the document, type your first and last name, then hit ENTER.
7. Type the activity number and title "5.1 My Favorite Things" in font size 18 point, then hit ENTER twice. (Do not type the quotation marks.)

    NOTE: The rest of the document should be 14 point.
8. Type the name of your favorite outdoor activity, then hit ENTER.
9. Type the name of your favorite superhero, then hit ENTER.
10. Type the name of your favorite social media website, then hit ENTER.
11. Type the name of your favorite video game, then hit ENTER.
12. Type the name of your favorite kind of breakfast cereal, then hit ENTER.
13. Carefully proofread your work accuracy.

14. Print the document if required by your instructor.

15. Be sure any changes have been saved, then close the document.

16. Open the document LIKES to be revised and renamed.

17. Save the document as **DISLIKES**.

18. Change the title to "5.1 My Least Favorite Things."

19. Change your favorite outdoor activity to your least favorite outdoor activity.

20. Change your favorite superhero to your least favorite superhero.

21. Change your favorite social media website to your least favorite social media website.

22. Change your favorite video game to your least favorite video game.

23. Change your favorite kind of breakfast cereal to your least favorite breakfast cereal.

24. Be sure any changes have been saved.

25. Print the document if required by your instructor.

Super Cuts

Formatting Text

Overview

The mark of a true touch typist is someone who seldom lets their fingers leave the keyboard. As computers and laptops become smaller, manufacturers often eliminate common function keys to save keyboard space. For instance, an 11" Chromebook does not have a delete key. Smart users will quickly learn the keyboard shortcut keys for their system—such as Alt+Backspace for delete—and can edit documents in a fast and efficient manner.

In this lesson, you will practice using common shortcut keys found in any popular word processing software, such as Microsoft Word or Google Docs, to edit a list of information about yourself.

New Skills / TEKS

Applying Bold, Italics, and Underline • Increasing and Decreasing Font Size • Aligning Text • Using Cut, Copy, and Paste • Creating a Numbered List

TEKS: 6.B.i, 6.C.i, 6.C.ii, 6.D.i, 6.F.i

Instructions

1. Review **Figure 5.2-A**, which contains common shortcut keys that can be used in word processing software.
2. Create a new word processing document.
3. Unless otherwise stated, use the default font and size of the word processing software being used.
4. Change the line spacing to single with no additional spacing before or after the paragraphs.
5. Save the document as **SUPERCUTS**.
6. On the first line of the document, type your first and last name, then hit ENTER.
7. Type the activity number and title "5.2 Super Cuts" center aligned, then hit ENTER twice.
8. Type the responses to the statements provided below left aligned. Type one answer per line, and do not type the statements or preceding letters.
   a. Your nickname.
   b. The name of your school.
   c. Your cell phone number.
   d. Your hair color.
   e. Your eye color.
   f. Your height.

   g. Your lucky number.

   h. The name of the street you live on.

   i. The number of years you have lived at your present address.

   j. Your current career goal.

9. Carefully proofread your work for accuracy.

10. Select the appropriate text and make the following changes using shortcut keys only:

   a. Italicize your nickname.

   b. Bold the name of your school.

   c. Underline your cell phone number.

   d. Italicize, bold, and underline your hair color.

   e. Increase the font size of your eye color by 2 points.

   f. Decrease the font size of your height by 2 points.

   g. Center align your lucky number.

   h. Right align the name of the street you live on.

   i. Copy the number of years you have lived at your present address and paste it under your nickname.

   j. Cut your current career goal and paste it on the line under the name of your school center aligned.

11. Number the list using the auto numbering feature.

12. Carefully proofread your work for accuracy.

13. Be sure any changes have been saved.

14. Print the document if required by your instructor.

Figure 5.2-A

Common shortcut keys

CTRL+ARROW KEYS	move cursor 1 word		**CTRL+C**	copy selected text
SHIFT+ARROW KEYS	select text		**CTRL+X**	cut selected text
CTRL+A	select all		**CTRL+V**	paste selected text
CTRL+B	bold selected text		**CTRL+Z**	undo last action
CTRL+I	italicize selected text		**CTRL+S**	save a file
CTRL+U	underline selected text		**CTRL+P**	print a document
CTRL+[	decrease font size of selected text*		**CTRL+R**	right align text*
CTRL+]	increase font size of selected text*		**CTRL+E**	center align text*

* **Note:** Depending on the software application being used, a different shortcut may be required. Refer to your operating system's or application's help screen to see a complete list of keyboard shortcut keys you can use.

State Symbols

Enhancing & Formatting Text

Overview

It does not matter what word processing software you are using when it comes to making changes to the look of your documents. Your document becomes a piece of visual communication when you enhance your text. Simply changing the case of text or inserting a symbol can give your document a more appealing and professional look.

In this lesson, you will find what your state recognizes as a symbol or icon for various categories and then format those answers accordingly. You will also be required to list the sources you used to find your answers.

New Skills / TEKS

Changing Font Color • Changing Text Case • Inserting a Symbol • Applying Strikethrough • Inserting a Standard and Customized Bullet • Applying a Border

TEKS: 6.B.i, 6.C.i, 6.C.ii, 6.F.i

Instructions

1. Create a new word processing document.

2. Unless otherwise stated, use the default font and size of the word processing software being used.

3. Change the line spacing to single with no additional spacing before or after the paragraphs.

4. Save the document as **STATES**.

5. On the first line of the document, type your first and last name, then hit ENTER.

6. Type the activity number and title "5.3 State Symbols," then hit ENTER twice.

7. Type the answers to the questions provided in the "20 State Symbols and Facts" column shown in **Figure 5.3-A**. Single space your answers, do not number them, and do not type the questions.

   NOTE: Use a website such as www.50states.com to help find your answers. Carefully keep track of the sources that you use, as you will be expected to list them later in this lesson. If your state does not have a symbol or fact for a category, type NONE and then recommend one.

8. Apply the corresponding changes to your answer provided in the "Formatting Changes to Apply" column shown in **Figure 5.3-A**.

9. Below the last typed line, type the list of sources you used to find your answers.

10. Carefully proofread your work for accuracy.

11. Be sure any changes have been saved.

12. Print the document if required by your instructor.

Figure 5.3-A

20 State Symbols and Facts	Formatting Changes to Apply
What is your state's official name?	Right align the text.
What is your state motto?	Change the text color to purple.
What is your state capital?	Underline the text.
What is the population of your state?	Insert a standard bullet before the text.
What are the colors of your state flag?	Change the font size to 20 point.
What is your state nickname?	Bold the text.
What is your state flower?	Center align the text.
What is your state bird?	Insert a black border around the text.
What is the area in square miles of your state?	Double underline the text.
What is the largest city in your state?	Change the font size to 8 point.
What is your state tree?	Change the font to a style of your choice and make it 14 point bold.
What is your state song?	Use numbering to insert the number 1. in front of the text.
What is pictured on your state quarter?	Strikethrough the text.
What is your state animal?	Italicize the text.
What is your state gem?	Change the text to all caps.
What is your state insect?	Copy the text and paste it under your answer on a separate line.
What is your state fish or aquatic life?	Bold and underline the text.
What is your state reptile?	Insert a customized bullet before the text.
What is your state food or drink?	Insert the copyright symbol after the text.
Why do you like living in your state?	Underline the text with a dashed line.

How to Build a Website

Working with Bookmarks

Overview

You can save time when moving around a multi-page document with hyperlinked text. Instead of scrolling through a document with your keyboard or mouse to a desired section of text, word processing software users can jump to different parts of the document with bookmarks. Once you have typed a document, text can be easily formatted as a bookmark and text located in another place in the document can be linked to that bookmark.

In this lesson, you will create bookmarks so that you can easily move from one place to another within your document.

New Skills / TEKS

Inserting a Page Break • Inserting a Bookmark • Hyperlinking Text to a Bookmark

TEKS: 6.B.i, 6.C.i, 6.C.ii, 6.F.i, 6.G.i

Instructions

1. Create a new word processing document.
2. Unless otherwise stated, use the default font and size of the word processing software being used.
3. Change the line spacing to single with no additional spacing before or after the paragraphs.
4. Save the document as **WEBSITE**.
5. On the first line of the document, type your first and last name, then hit ENTER.
6. Type the activity number and title "5.4 How to Build a Website," then hit ENTER twice.
7. Type the text as shown in **Figure 5.4-A**.
8. Insert a new page (page break) into the document by pressing CTRL + ENTER.
9. Starting on the first line of page two, type the text as shown in **Figure 5.4-B**.
10. Insert a new page (page break) into the document.
11. Starting on the first line of page three, type the text as shown in **Figure 5.4-C**.
12. Insert a new page (page break) into the document.
13. Starting on the first line of page four, type the text as shown in **Figure 5.4-D**.
14. Insert a new page (page break) into the document.
15. Starting on the first line of page five, type the text as shown in **Figure 5.4-E**.

16. Select all of the text on page two of the document and insert a bookmark. Name the bookmark "Step1." Do not use any spaces when naming the bookmark.

17. Go to page one and select the text "Step 1. Choose a Host." Hyperlink the selected text to the bookmark named "Step1."

18. Select all of the text on page three of the document and insert a bookmark. Name the bookmark "Step2." Do not use any spaces when naming the bookmark.

19. Go to page one and select the text "Step 2. Decide on a Domain Name." Hyperlink the selected text to the bookmark named "Step2."

20. Select all of the text on page four of the document and insert a bookmark. Name the bookmark "Step3." Do not use any spaces when naming the bookmark.

21. Go to page one and select the text "Step 3. Build Each Page." Hyperlink the selected text to the bookmark named "Step3."

22. Select all of the text on page five of the document and insert a bookmark. Name the bookmark "Step4." Do not use any spaces when naming the bookmark.

23. Go to page one and select the text "Step 4. Publish Your Pages." Hyperlink the selected text to the bookmark named "Step4."

24. Go to page one of your document. Click on each of the hyperlinks you created to be sure that they are all linked to the correct page within the document.

25. Carefully proofread your work for accuracy.

26. Be sure any changes have been saved.

27. Print the document if required by your instructor.

Figure 5.4-A

As technology improves, building a website has become a much easier task. Practically anyone can build a website to promote themselves, a company, or an organization.

Step 1. Choose a Host
Step 2. Decide on a Domain Name
Step 3. Build Each Page
Step 4. Publish Your Pages

Figure 5.4-B

Step 1. Choose a Host
A Host provides a virtual space for your website to live on the Internet, similar to renting a storefront for your business. There are three types of hosting options to choose from – free web hosts, virtual shared web hosts, and standard web hosts. Once you have determined which type of hosting fits your needs, you will need to choose a company such as GoDaddy, HostGator, or iPage. Registering with a hosting company will be done at the company's website where you will provide your billing information.

Figure 5.4-C

Step 2. Decide on a Domain Name
Your domain name is also referred to as the URL or web address. This is the name you will type into the URL bar of your Internet browser. The domain name must have an extension such as .com, .org, or .net. Businesses or personal websites use the extension .com or .net. Non-profit organizations use the extension .org. Your domain name should be one that is easy to remember.

Figure 5.4-D

Step 3. Build Each Page
Each page should include a navigation section that links to each page within your website. Pages should be built to include a header, body, and footer. The background color of each page should be a color that allows the text and images to be read with ease. Create a folder for images so they are accessed effortlessly when you are building your site.

Figure 5.4-E

Step 4. Publish Your Pages
Publishing your website to the Internet involves uploading each page of the site, as well as images to your hosting company's server. This is done through FTP transmission via the web host's server. Once your site is published, it will typically take up to 48 hours to propagate on the Internet and become live.

Fortune 500 Top 10 Companies

Working with Hyperlinks

Overview

Linking to websites within a document allows users to quickly access websites without having to type a website address (URL) into a webpage browser. You are able to format any text or image as a hyperlink directly in your word processing software. With more and more people finding information on the Internet, getting to a website from within documents gives users the ability to access information quickly.

In this lesson, you will hyperlink a list of the top 10 companies, ranked according to Fortune 500, to their corresponding websites.

New Skills / TEKS

Hyperlinking Text to a Website Address

TEKS: 6.B.i, 6.C.i, 6.C.ii, 6.F.i, 6.G.i

Instructions

1. Create a new word processing document.

2. Unless otherwise stated, use the default font and size of the word processing software being used.

3. Change the line spacing to single with no additional spacing before or after the paragraphs.

4. Save the document as **COMPANIES**.

5. On the first line of the document, type your first and last name, then hit ENTER.

6. Type the activity number and title "5.5 Fortune 500 Top 10 Companies," then hit ENTER twice.

7. Type the list of 10 companies provided in the "Company" column shown in **Figure 5.5-A**.

8. Hyperlink each company to its corresponding website address provided in the "Website Address" column shown in **Figure 5.5-A**.

9. Carefully proofread your work for accuracy.

10. If you have Internet access, check each hyperlink to verify that each link has been entered correctly.

11. Be sure any changes have been saved.

12. Print the document if required by your instructor.

Figure 5.5-A

Company	Website Address
Walmart	http://www.walmart.com
Exxon Mobil	http://www.exxonmobil.com
Chevron	http://www.chevron.com
Berkshire Hathaway	http://www.berkshirehathaway.com
Apple	http://www.apple.com
General Motors	http://www.gm.com
Phillips 66	http://www.phillips66.com
General Electric	http://www.ge.com
Ford Motor	http://www.ford.com
CVS Health	http://www.cvshealth.com

The Hunger Games

Using Find & Replace

Overview

There are many aspects that make word processing software so great, but nothing compares to the automated process of finding text in a document and replacing it with new text. A first draft often needs editing, and having to find recurring text throughout the document can become cumbersome. With find and replace, your computer does the searching and replacing for you, making the job easier and the results more accurate.

In this lesson, you will type a summary about one of today's hottest book and movie series, *The Hunger Games*, and replace text within the document.

New Skills / TEKS

Using Find and Replace

TEKS: 6.B.i, 6.C.i, 6.C.ii, 6.F.i

Instructions

1. Create a new word processing document.
2. Unless otherwise stated, use the default font and size of the word processing software being used.
3. Change the line spacing to single with no additional spacing before or after the paragraphs.
4. Save the document as **HUNGER**.
5. On the first line of the document, type your first and last name, then hit ENTER.
6. Type the activity number and title "5.6 The Hunger Games," then hit ENTER twice.
7. Type the article text exactly as shown in **Figure 5.6-A**.
8. Find and replace the words provided in the table below.

    NOTE: Be careful not to replace "Jennifer Lawrence" with "Ms. Lawrence."

Find	Replace
the hunger games	THE HUNGER GAMES
Lawrence	Ms. Lawrence
book	novel
movies	films
occupation	career

9. Carefully proofread your work for accuracy.

10. Be sure any changes have been saved.

11. Print the document if required by your instructor.

Figure 5.6-A

Book Trilogy Becomes a Phenomenon

The hunger games, by Suzanne Collins, is a series made up of three novels that have been developed into movies. Both the books and the movies have become a cultural phenomenon. They are among the top selling books and movies of all time. The popularity of the first novel inspired millions of fans to read the subsequent novels and run to theaters to watch the films. With its unique plot, strong main character, and highly praised lead actress, the hunger games have attracted a loyal fan base.

The series begins with the hunger games. Next is Catching Fire followed by Mockingjay. Author Suzanne Collins creates a unique universe where young characters are chosen to fight through a battle until only one opponent is left alive. The book's setting is unlike anything readers have seen before. A mix of science fiction and fantasy give readers a thrill. Katniss Everdeen, the story's main character, is chosen by lottery to participate in the hunger games, which is a televised fight between twelve boys and twelve girls, from the twelve different districts of the post-apocalyptic nation of Panem. Each participant is forced to eliminate the other competitors in any way they can.

As the story begins, Katniss is neither willing nor ready to fight to the death, but volunteers to take part in the battle in place of her younger sister. She knows she must survive the ordeal in order to get back home to care for her younger sister. Katniss lives in a coal mining town in District 12. This poor district affords little to its citizens, so Katniss learns to hunt for food for her family after her father dies in a mining accident. Katniss is strong-willed, determined, resourceful, responsible, and sometimes, sarcastic. The death of her father leaves her mother in a great depression, and in response, Katniss steps up to take care of both her mother and younger sister. She provides them with food, finding ways to forage, hunt, and trade. She is an especially skilled archer, and her name is derived from the official name for the Katniss plant, Sagittaria. Sagittaria comes from Sagittarius the Archer, and the Latin meaning is he who throws arrows.

Although Jennifer Lawrence did not begin her occupation when she was cast in the first of the hunger games movies, playing the part of Katniss Everdeen certainly launched her into worldwide stardom. Lawrence is an American actress who received an Academy Award for Best Actress nomination in 2010 for the independent drama Winter's Bone. Starring in the hunger games film series has established her as the highest grossing female action star. Between filming the subsequent films for the hunger games series, Lawrence went on to star in a romantic comedy alongside Bradley Cooper. In 2012, she won the Best Actress Oscar for her role in that film. Besides acting, Lawrence has become a style icon and was named the face of Dior Addict's beauty campaign.

The hunger games trilogy has had such success that many aspiring authors look to it for inspiration and motivation to keep writing. Suzanne Collins was able to create a story that had wide appeal and international attention. Young girls all over the globe look up to Katniss Everdeen and Lawrence as role models.

The Voice

Proofing Your Document

Overview

Creating work that is both interesting to read and without spelling or grammatical errors is essential in today's world. Although it is important to always proofread your work for errors, you can give yourself a head start with your word processing software's spelling and grammar check feature. It will find unintentional mistakes in your document and offer suggestions for how the error can be rectified. A built-in thesaurus can propose words to better describe what you are writing.

In this lesson, you will use spell check to find misspelled words and the thesaurus tool to find alternative words in a properly formatted news release. Remember to proofread your work carefully; the spell check does not always pick up everything.

New Skills / TEKS

Using Spelling and Grammar Check • Using the Thesaurus Tool

TEKS: 6.B.i, 6.C.i, 6.C.ii, 6.F.i

Instructions

1. Create a new word processing document.

2. Unless otherwise stated, use the default font and size of the word processing software being used.

3. Change the line spacing to single with no additional spacing before or after the paragraphs.

4. Save the document as **VOICE**.

5. On the first line of the document, type your first and last name, then hit ENTER.

6. Type the activity number and title "5.7 The Voice," then hit ENTER twice.

7. Type the press release exactly as shown in **Figure 5.7-A**; however, do not bold the words appearing in bold.

8. Run the spell check to replace the misspelled words.

   HINT: There are five misspelled words.

9. Use the thesaurus tool to find alternative words for the 10 words in bold.

   NOTE: Be sure the words you select make sense in the context of the sentence.

10. Underline each of the new replaced words.

11. Carefully proofread your work for accuracy.

12. Be sure any changes have been saved.

13. Print the document if required by your instructor.

Figure 5.7-A

FOR IMMEDIATE RELEASE

CONTACT:
Vera Vocals
Vocals Talent Agency
Phone: 555-456-7890
Email: sing@vocalstalent.com
Website: www.vocalstalent.com

THE VOICE ANNOUNCES AN OPEN AUDITION IN THE SUNSHINE STATE

Orlando, FL, <current date>—Imagine becoming the next **winner** of The Voice. Maybe u have what it takes to get the coaches to turn their chairs around. Find out by taking part in our **upcoming** audition. The producers of The Voice are in the process of selecting the most **talented** singers in America to compete on the **show**. The show features a **unique** format that is made up of five stages of competition. A grand prize winner is chosen in the finall stage of the competition and receives a recording contract.

Take a chance! You've got nothing to lose and **lots** to gain iff you are able to make it on The Voice! Auditions will be held next Saturday and Sonday at the Orlando Mall from 8 am to 5 pm. Warm up those vocal cords and get ready to **shine**!

Make your plans **soon** as spots will be filling up **very** fast. Arrive at the check-in booth and receive a wristband and an audition number. It is very **important** not to misplace your ticket number since this is the only way we know who you are. We expect there to be lots of singers on both Saturday and Sunday.

Email Vocals Talent Agency tooday to reserve your spot in the audition.

Movie Summary

Changing Paragraph Line Spacing

Overview

After researching your favorite movie on the Internet, you will write a plot summary of the movie that details the main point of the storyline. Your summary must include an introduction, body text that discusses the main plot points and mentions the lead actors in the movie, and a conclusion that explains how the movie ends. When you are finished, the plot summary should be between 175 and 300 words, and a list of sources must be included at the end of the document.

In this lesson, you will write a plot summary of your favorite movie, format the summary using double space, and list your sources.

New Skills / TEKS

Changing Paragraph Line Spacing • Writing a Summary • Using Word Count

TEKS: 6.B.i, 6.C.i, 6.C.ii, 6.D.i, 6.D.ii, 6.F.i

Instructions

1. Choose your favorite movie and research it using the Internet. Next, write a summary on paper that includes an introduction, body text discussing the main plot points and lead actors, and a conclusion explaining how the movie ends. The summary should be no less than 175 words and no more than 300.
2. Create a new word processing document.
3. Unless otherwise stated, use the default font and size of the word processing software being used.
4. Change the line spacing to single with no additional spacing before or after the paragraphs.
5. Save the document as **MOVIE**.
6. On the first line of the document, type your first and last name, then hit ENTER.
7. Type the activity number and title "5.8 Movie Summary," then hit ENTER.
8. Type, bold, and center align the title of the movie your summary is about.
9. Starting one line below the title, type the movie summary.
10. Change the line spacing of the entire document to double space.
11. Use word count to verify your document meets the minimum/maximum criteria.
12. At the bottom of your document, list the sources you used to research your movie.
13. Carefully proofread your work for accuracy.
14. Be sure any changes have been saved.
15. Print the document if required by your instructor.

Taking a Vacation

Creating a Bulleted List

Overview

Word processing software really helps with the appearance of a document. Lists are simpler to read when they are numbered and bulleted since they tell the reader the sequence, order, or grouping of a block of text. A customized bullet, such as an open box or a non-traditional numbering pattern, like letters, can enhance the look of any list in a document. Additions or deletions to the list are automatically renumbered.

In this lesson, you will insert bullets or numbers into four separate lists of top vacation spots.

New Skills / TEKS

Formatting Numbered Lists • Using Bullets • Formatting Customized Bullets

TEKS: 6.B.i, 6.C.i, 6.C.ii, 6.F.i

Instructions

1. Create a new word processing document.

2. Unless otherwise stated, use the default font and size of the word processing software being used.

3. Change the line spacing to single with no additional spacing before or after the paragraphs.

4. Save the document as **VACATION**.

5. On the first line of the document, type your first and last name, then hit ENTER.

6. Type the activity number and title "5.9 Taking a Vacation," then hit ENTER twice.

7. Type the four lists exactly as shown in **Figure 5.9-A**. Leave one blank line between each list.

8. Center align the title of the first list, "Top 5 Beaches," and change it to Arial, 16 point, and bold.

9. Center align the title of the second list, "Top 5 Cities," and change it to Comic Sans, 18 point, and bold.

10. Center align the title of the third list, "Top 5 Places to Vacation," and change it to Georgia, 14 point, and bold.

11. Center align the title of the fourth list, "Top 5 Ski Resorts," and change it to Verdana, 20 point, and bold.

12. Select only the list portion of the "Top 5 Beaches" and format it as a bulleted list using a standard bullet.

13. Select only the list portion of the "Top 5 Cities" and format it as a bulleted list using an open box bullet.

14. Select only the list portion of the "Top 5 Places to Vacation" and format it as a numbered list using traditional numbers (1, 2, 3, 4, 5).

15. Select only the list portion of the "Top 5 Ski Resorts" and format it as a numbered list using capital letters (A., B., C., D.).

16. Add the text "Maui" between Barcelona and Paris in your numbered list "Top 5 Places to Vacation."

17. Edit the title of "Top 5 Places to Vacation" to "Top 6 Places to Vacation."

18. Carefully proofread your work for accuracy.

19. Be sure any changes have been saved.

20. Print the document if required by your instructor.

Figure 5.9-A

Top 5 Beaches
Baio Do Sancho, Brazil
Grace Bay, Turks And Caicos
Rabbit Beach, Sicily
Playa Paraiso, Cuba
Playa De Ses Illetes, Balearic Islands

Top 5 Cities
Kyoto, Japan
Charleston, South Carolina
Siem Reap, Cambodia
Florence, Italy
Rome, Italy

Top 5 Places To Vacation
London
Bora Bora
Barcelona
Paris
Sydney

Top 5 Ski Resorts
Revelstoke, Canada
Meribel, France
Riksgransen, Sweden
Alyeska, Alaska
Zermatt, Switzerland

Celebrities and Their Pets

Using Table Basics

Overview

A document that contains lists of information can often be difficult to format and read. Using a table allows the writer to keep related information together so that the reader can quickly determine what is being communicated. Tables contain rows and columns that are displayed as cells similar to a spreadsheet. Rows run across and columns run vertically, and the text inside them can be formatted with different fonts or alignments. Cells can be shaded to highlight information and cell borders can be formatted in various ways to make the table more attractive.

In this lesson, you will create and format a table that showcases 20 celebrities who have pets and their pets' names.

New Skills / TEKS

Inserting Tables • Shading Cells, Rows, and Columns • Inserting Rows • Merging Cells

TEKS: 6.B.i, 6.C.i, 6.C.ii, 6.F.i, 6.G.i, 6.G.ii

Instructions

1. Create a new word processing document.
2. Unless otherwise stated, use the default font and size of the word processing software being used.
3. Change the line spacing to single with no additional spacing before or after the paragraphs.
4. Save the document as **CELEBS**.
5. On the first line of the document, type your first and last name, then hit ENTER.
6. Type the activity number and title "5.10 Celebrities and Their Pets," then hit ENTER twice.
7. Create a table with 3 columns and 21 rows, then type the text into the table as shown in **Figure 5.10-A**.
8. Apply the following formatting changes to the table:
    a. Add a 1.5 point border to all cells.
    b. Center align, bold, and italicize the column titles.
    c. Shade the rows of the celebrities that have cats using a color of your choice (be sure the shading is light enough so it does not interfere with the readability of the text in the cell).
    d. Insert a row above row 1 that is merged and centered with the text "Celebrities and Their Pets" bold and italicized.

   e.   Insert a blank row between row 1 and row 2, then merge the cells in that row.

   f.   Insert a row after the last row, then merge the cells in that row.

   g.   In the last row, type the text "My favorite dog name on this list is <insert your favorite dog name>."

9.   Carefully proofread your work for accuracy.

10. Be sure any changes have been saved.

11. Print the document if required by your instructor.

Figure 5.10-A

Name of Celebrity	Type of Pet	Name of Pet
Kylie Jenner	Bunny	Bruce
Miley Cyrus	Cat	Shanti Om Bb
Justin Bieber	Dog	Esther
Kendall Jenner	Dog	Blu
Ariana Grande	Dog	Sirius Black
Demi Lovato	Dog	Buddy
Zayn Malik	Dog	Teddy
Lea Michele	Dog	Pearl
Shay Mitchell	Dog	Foxy
Hilary Duff	Dog	Dubois
Ian Somerhalder	Dog	Nietzsche
Naya Rivera	Dog	Emmy
Julianne Hough	Dog	Harley
Janel Parrish	Dog	Princess Oreo
Taylor Swift	Cat	Olivia Benson
Rita Ora	Cat	Bruno
Bella Thorne	Dog	Kingston
Lauren Conrad	Dog	Fitz
Nick Jonas	Dog	Elvis
Iggy Azalea	Dog	Jelli

Homework Planner

Formatting Tables

Overview

Although word processing software automatically fits text into table cells with word wrap, it is often necessary to resize rows and columns to better accommodate the text inside them. A table can take on the look of a more graphic object on your page when you change cell alignment and text direction within cells. In addition, clip art can be inserted and resized to become part of the design of your table.

In this lesson, you will gain more practice working with tables to create a page from a homework planner.

New Skills / TEKS

Changing Column Width • Changing Cell Alignment • Changing Row Height • Changing Text Direction • Inserting an Image in a Table • Centering a Table Horizontally

TEKS: 6.B.i, 6.C.i, 6.C.ii, 6.F.i, 6.G.i, 6.G.ii

Instructions

1. Create a new word processing document.

2. Unless otherwise stated, use the default font and size of the word processing software being used.

3. Change the line spacing to single with no additional spacing before or after the paragraphs.

4. Save the document as **PLANNER**.

5. On the first line of the document, type your first and last name, then hit ENTER.

6. Type the activity number and title "5.11 Homework Planner," then hit ENTER twice.

7. Create a table with 4 columns and 11 rows, then type the text into the table as shown in **Figure 5.11-A**.

8. Apply the following formatting changes to the table:

   a. Resize each column as indicated below:

Subject:	1.5"
Assignment:	4"
Due	0.75"
Done	0.75"

   b. Center the table horizontally on the page.

   c. Merge and center row 1.

   d. Adjust the height of row 1 to 0.5".

e. Change the text in row 1 to 18 point, and center it horizontally and vertically.

f. Shade row 1 to light gray.

g. Bold the column titles.

h. Adjust the height of row 2 to 0.5".

i. Center the text in row 2 horizontally and vertically.

j. Adjust the height of the last row to 1.5".

k. Merge the cells in the last row.

l. Change the text direction in the "Notes" row so that the text "Notes" is rotated 90 degrees to the right.

m. Change the text "Notes" to 18 point.

n. Insert an image of a school in the bottom right corner of the last row.

HINT: Use text wrap if necessary.

o. Resize the image so that it is no more than 0.5" high and 0.5" wide.

9. Carefully proofread your work for accuracy.

10. Be sure any changes have been saved.

11. Print the document if required by your instructor.

Figure 5.11-A

Daily Planner for November 16			
Subject	Assignment	Due	Done ☑
Biology	Ecosystems Project	11/30	
U.S. History	Colonial Development Article Response	11/17	☑
Spanish	Study for tomorrow's vocabulary quiz	11/17	☑
Geometry	Problems 11-25; Complete Online Assessment	11/18	
English	Read pages 35-75	11/17	☑
Art	Sketch object from nature	11/20	
Chorus	Watch last year's performance video	11/18	☑
Personal Finance	Update daily spending plan	11/19	
Notes:			

So You Think You Can Dance

Formatting Text into Columns

Overview

Text in newspapers or magazines is often formatted in columns. Columns make text easier to read because they reduce the number of words per line a reader has to read. Text continues from the bottom of one column to the top of the next. Fully justified text gives the document a tidy and professional appearance.

In this lesson, you will type an article about *So You Think You Can Dance*, a televised dance competition, and format the article into two columns.

New Skills / TEKS

Creating Two Columns • Justifying Text

TEKS: 6.B.i, 6.C.i, 6.C.ii, 6.F.i

Instructions

1. Create a new word processing document.

2. Unless otherwise stated, use the default font and size of the word processing software being used.

3. Change the line spacing to single with no additional spacing before or after the paragraphs.

4. Save the document as **DANCE**.

5. On the first line of the document, type your first and last name, then hit ENTER.

6. Type the activity number and title "5.12 So You Think You Can Dance," then hit ENTER twice.

7. Type the text exactly as shown in **Figure 5.12-A**.

8. Change the title of the article to 24 point, bold, and center aligned.

9. Justify only the body text of the article.

10. Format the body of the article into columns, adhering to the following guidelines:

    a. Number of columns: 2

    b. Width of columns: 3"

    c. Space between columns: 0.5"

    d. Equal column width

    e. No line in between columns

    NOTE: The column option may not be available in all word processing applications being used.

11. Carefully proofread your work for accuracy.

12. Be sure any changes have been saved.

13. Print the document if required by your instructor.

Figure 5.12-A

So You Think You Can Dance

So You Think You Can Dance is a televised American dance competition in which contestants compete to win the title of America's best dancer. The show is taped over several months but is edited to air for eight to nine weeks. Auditions are held in various cities in America and the best dancers are chosen to be part of the top twenty. These dancers perform live on television and viewers are able to vote for their favorite dancers each week. The two dancers with the lowest votes each week are eliminated from the competition until only one dancer remains.

So You Think You Can Dance airs on the Fox television network. It has reached over ten million viewers since it began in 2005. It was the number one summer show when it premiered and continues to compete with that spot against America's Got Talent. The series was meant to rejuvenate the visibility and appreciation of dance as an art form in the United States and to give exposure to struggling dancers. It has certainly done just that. With thousands of young aspiring dancers watching the show, So You Think You Can Dance is not only a form of entertainment, but an inspiration for many to continue their training. Many of the show's contestants have grown up watching the show and maintained dreams of one day competing themselves.

The show is hosted by Cat Deeley and has had a variety of judges since its start. A season typically has anywhere from two to three judges, but at times there have been nine judges at the table. Since its start, executive producer Nigel Lythgoe has been a permanent judge. His background in dance, choreography, and television production make him a certified expert to be in the position of choosing who makes it into the top twenty. Throughout the season, judges critique each performance; however, at some point in the season, the viewers control who leaves and who moves on in the competition. Other judges have included Mary Murphy, Adam Shankman, Paula Adbul, and Jason Derulo.

Each week dancers are randomly given a style of dance to perform in duets or small groups. Dance styles have included jazz, hip hop, contemporary, ballroom, Latin, Bollywood, and classical ballet to name a few. Besides showcasing the dancers, the talents of the choreographer are praised and applauded. The show gives a face to the most talented and hardworking choreographers in the industry. Filming is done during rehearsals and clips of it are shown prior to each performance. This look behind the scenes is just as much a treat for the viewer as the actual performance. Often dancers and choreographers are shown struggling with perfecting the performance and acting goofy. Explanations about the meaning behind the dance are given, offering a better understanding of what the viewer is about to see. This gives the audience a deeper appreciation of each performance. Many of the choreographers on the show have gone on to be nominated and win Emmy awards.

Winning So You Think You Can Dance is a terrific honor. The winner clearly has a passion for dance and shows the unbelievable commitment to the art throughout the season. Winners as well as other contestants have gone on to star on Broadway, tour with top selling music soloists and groups, as well as appear in other television shows or commercials. Past winners have also continued on with the show as all-star performers or choreographers. Long time viewers of So You Think You Can Dance appreciate seeing their favorite past dancers.

Video Game Ratings

Setting Custom Tabs

Overview

Tab stops can be formatted to have alignment built in. When using a tab stop with center alignment, the center of the text will be at the tab stop position. When using a tab stop with right alignment, the text will be right aligned at the tab stop position. It is difficult, not to mention time consuming, to align text by using the space bar. Jumping quickly to a formatted position in the document with the tab key can save time and ensure precision in your document.

In this lesson, you will create a three-column list about video game ratings by setting tabs formatted with left, right, and center alignment.

New Skills / TEKS

Setting Left, Right, and Center Tabs

TEKS: 6.B.i, 6.C.i, 6.C.ii, 6.F.i

Instructions

1. Create a new word processing document.
2. Change the line spacing to single with no additional spacing before or after the paragraphs.
3. Save the document as **RATINGS**.
4. Change the font to Georgia, 11 point.
5. On the first line of the document, type your first and last name, then hit ENTER.
6. Type the activity number and title "5.13 Video Game Ratings," then hit ENTER twice.
7. Type the heading exactly as shown in **Figure 5.13-A**, then hit ENTER twice.
8. Set the following tabs:
   a. Left aligned tab at 0.75"
   b. Center aligned tab at 3.25"
   c. Right aligned tab at 6"
9. Type the text exactly as shown in **Figure 5.13-A**. **HINT:** Use the tab key to align text into columns.
10. Change the font of the text "Video Game Ratings by the Entertainment Software Rating Board" to 14 point, bold, and center aligned.
11. Change the line spacing of the entire document to double space.
12. Carefully proofread your work for accuracy.
13. Be sure any changes have been saved.
14. Print the document if required by your instructor.

Figure 5.13-A

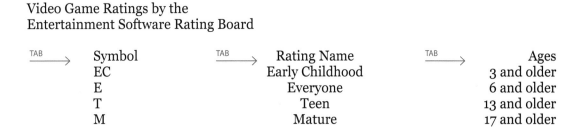

Video Game Ratings by the
Entertainment Software Rating Board

Symbol	Rating Name	Ages
EC	Early Childhood	3 and older
E	Everyone	6 and older
T	Teen	13 and older
M	Mature	17 and older
RP	Rating Pending	Not yet assigned

Social Media for Teens

Applying Tab Leaders

Overview

Aligning text within your document is easy with setting custom tabs. Using dot leaders in front of custom tabs helps with the readability of the document. Often seen in a book's table of contents, dot leaders draw the reader's eye across the page so that they can easily determine which chapter corresponds to which page. Other common documents that utilize dot leaders include restaurant menus, store hours signs, and party invitations.

In this lesson, you will format a custom tab stop that contains dot leaders in a document about social media use.

New Skills / TEKS

Using Dot Leaders

TEKS: 6.B.i, 6.C.i, 6.C.ii, 6.F.i

Instructions

1. Create a new word processing document.
2. Change the line spacing to single with no additional spacing before or after the paragraphs.
3. Save the document as **SOCIAL**.
4. Change the font to Comic Sans, 11 point.
5. On the first line of the document, type your first and last name, then hit ENTER.
6. Type the activity number and title "5.14 Social Media for Teens," then hit ENTER.
7. Type the heading exactly as shown in **Figure 5.14-A**, then hit ENTER.
8. Set the following tabs:
   a. Left aligned tab at 1.5"
   b. Right aligned tab at 5" with dot leaders
9. Type the text exactly as shown in **Figure 5.14-A**.
10. Change the heading text to 14 point, bold, and center aligned.
11. Change the line spacing of the entire document to double space.
12. Carefully proofread your work for accuracy.
13. Be sure any changes have been saved.
14. Print the document if required by your instructor.

Figure 5.14-A

Percent of Teens Using Social Media Platforms

Facebook 71%
Instagram 52%
Snapchat 41%
Twitter 33%
Google+ 33%
Vine 24%
Tumblr 14%

From the Top to the Bottom

Using Headers and Footers

Overview

It is often necessary to format documents with the same information on the top or bottom of every page. Word processing software is also able to automatically output document information, such as the page number and total number of pages in the file. Headers and footers only need to be formatted once, and they will show on the top and bottom of every page of your document, making them very useful for long papers.

In this lesson, you will create a header and footer in a two-page document.

New Skills / TEKS

Inserting a Header • Inserting a Footer • Inserting Page Numbers • Inserting the Date

TEKS: 6.B'i, 6.C.i, 6.C.ii, 6.G.i

Instructions

1. Create a new word processing document.

2. Unless otherwise stated, use the default font and size of the word processing software being used.

3. Save the document as **TOP**.

4. Create a header that contains the following information as shown in **Figure 5.15-A**.

   a. Type your name in all caps, then hit the Tab key.

   b. Type the activity number and title "5.15 From the Top to the Bottom," then hit the Tab key.

   c. Insert the current date.

5. Create a footer that contains the following information as shown in **Figure 5.15-B**.

   a. Type the word PAGE in all caps center aligned.

   b. Insert the page number.

6. At the top of the page, type the text "This is my first page and it contains a header." as shown in **Figure 5.15-C**.

7. Insert a page break so that your document has a second page.

8. At the top of page two, type the text "This is my second page and it contains a header, too." as shown in **Figure 5.15-C**.

9. Carefully proofread your work for accuracy.

10. Be sure any changes have been saved.

11. Print the document if required by your instructor.

Figure 5.15-A

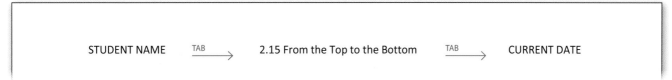

STUDENT NAME   TAB →   2.15 From the Top to the Bottom   TAB →   CURRENT DATE

Figure 5.15-B

PAGE #

Figure 5.15-C

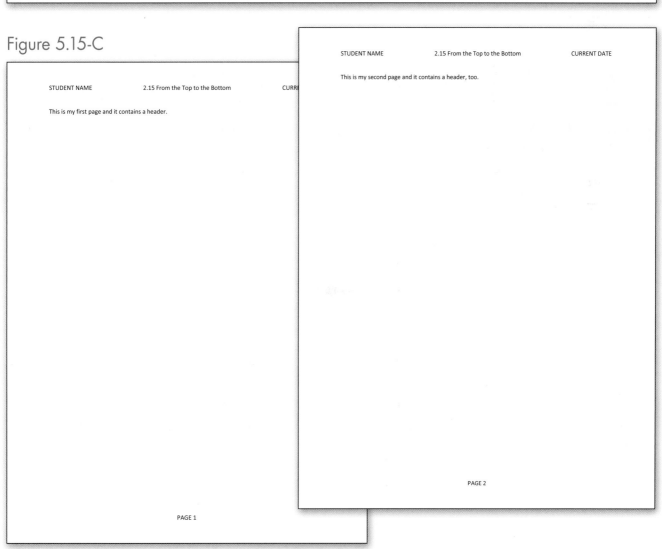

STUDENT NAME   2.15 From the Top to the Bottom   CURR...

This is my first page and it contains a header.

PAGE 1

STUDENT NAME   2.15 From the Top to the Bottom   CURRENT DATE

This is my second page and it contains a header, too.

PAGE 2

School Lunch Menu

Vertically Centering Text

Overview

Not every document should be created in a portrait orientation. Holding a standard 8 ½ x 11" paper vertically may constrain your design or restrict the layout options for text and graphics. Your page can easily be converted to landscape orientation so that the page is wider. Text and graphics may be more appealing to the eye if your page is printed with a customized margin.

In this lesson, you will create a lunch menu that is vertically and horizontally centered on a landscape document.

New Skills / TEKS

Formatting Page Orientation • Setting Custom Margins • Adding a Page Border • Centering Text Vertically

TEKS: 6.B.i, 6.C.i, 6.C.ii, 6.F.i

Instructions

1. Create a new word processing document.

2. Unless otherwise stated, use the default font and size of the word processing software being used.

3. Change the line spacing to single with no additional spacing before or after the paragraphs.

4. Save the document as **LUNCH**.

5. Change the page orientation to landscape.

6. On the first line of the document, type your first and last name, then hit ENTER.

7. Type the activity number and title "5.16 School Lunch Menu," then hit ENTER twice.

8. Type the name of your lunch menu. For example, "Lunch Menu for Tuesday."

9. Hit ENTER twice and type "Starter."

10. Hit ENTER and type the name of a type of soup.

11. Hit ENTER twice and type "Option 1."

12. Hit ENTER and type the name of an entrée.

13. Hit ENTER twice and type "Option 2."

14. Hit ENTER and type the name of an alternative entrée.

15. Hit ENTER twice and type "Sweet."

16. Hit ENTER and type the name of a dessert.

17. Change the name of your lunch menu to 16 point, bold, and all caps.

18. Italicize all of the text on the menu, then center the text vertically and horizontally.

19. Set the top, right, and left margins of the page to 3". Set the bottom margin to 1".

20. Add a page border to your document.

21. Carefully proofread your work for accuracy.

22. Be sure any changes have been saved.

23. Print the document if required by your instructor.

Spring Scene

Using Shapes

Overview

Using shapes in a document is a great way to practice formatting objects in any applications. Shapes can be drawn and formatted in different sizes with different fill colors and outline thicknesses. Shapes can be rotated and placed on top of other shapes, and multiple shapes can be grouped together to make working with them easier. Drawing tools can enhance the overall message of a flyer or newsletter and add interest to a presentation or webpage.

In this lesson, you will practice using a variety of drawing tools to create a spring scene.

New Skills / TEKS

Using Shapes • Using Shape Effects • Changing Shape Fill • Changing Shape Outline • Resizing Shapes • Grouping Shapes

TEKS: 6.B.i, 6.C.i, 6.C.ii, 6.G.i, 6.G.ii

Instructions

1. Create a new word processing document.

2. Save the document as **SPRING**.

3. Insert a header that has your name left aligned, and hit ENTER.

4. Type the activity number and title "5.17 Spring Scene" and close the header.

5. Change the page orientation to landscape.

6. Using Shapes, create a spring scene. Use **Figure 5.17-A** as a guide.

   a. Tree—Using the cube shape, draw a cube for the trunk that measures 4" high and 1" wide with brown fill and no outline. See icon **Ⓐ**.

   b. Tree—Using the cloud shape, draw a cloud for the leaves that measures 3" high and 4" wide with green fill and no outline. See icon **Ⓑ**.

   c. Tree—Group the tree trunk and leaves together.

   d. Tree—Duplicate the tree one more time so that there are two trees in the scene. Change the color of the leaves in the new tree to a different shade of green (if desired). See icon **Ⓒ**.

   e. Butterfly—Using the heart shape, draw a heart with black fill and no outline to begin making the wings. The size does not matter right now.

f. Butterfly—Using the circle and triangle tools, draw three circles and one triangle. Fill the shapes with a color of your choice (not black) and no outline, and place them symmetrically on the heart wing. Be sure they appear in front of the heart. See icon **D**.

g. Butterfly—Group the heart wing with the circles and triangle and duplicate it once.

h. Butterfly—Using the oval tool, draw an oval for the butterfly's body and a circle for the butterfly's head. Size them in proportion to your heart with black fill and no outline. See icon **D**.

i. Butterfly—Stack the oval body and circle head, then using the scribble tool, draw two black antennae on top of the head. See icon **D**.

j. Butterfly—Rotate and position the two heart wings onto one side of the body and group the two wings. Next, duplicate the two wings and flip them horizontally, then position them on the other side of the butterfly. See icon **D**.

k. Butterfly—Group all elements of your butterfly (head, body, antennae, wings) and resize it to measure 2.5" high and 2.5" wide. See icon **D**.

l. Butterfly—Rotate the butterfly at a slight angle. See icon **D**.

m. Sun—Using the sun tool, draw a sun that measures 2" high and 2" wide with yellow fill and no outline. See icon **E**.

n. Sun—Using the smiley face tool, draw a smiley face that measures 1" high and 1" wide with yellow fill and a 3 point black outline. Place the smiley face on top of the center of the sun. See icon **E**.

o. Grass—Using the Explosion tool, draw a shape that measures 2" high and 3.5" wide with green fill and no outline. See icon **F**.

p. Grass—Duplicate the Explosion shape multiple times to fill the bottom of the page and place each explosion to cover any empty space at the bottom of the page. See icon **F**.

q. Background—Format the page color to blue.

r. Rainbow—Using the rectangle tool, draw a rectangle that measures 0.5" high and 11" wide with red fill and no outline. See icon **G**.

s. Rainbow—Duplicate the rectangle five more times and fill each one with a different rainbow color—orange, yellow, green, blue, and violet. See icon **G**.

t. Rainbow—Position the rectangles so that the colors are arranged with violet on top of blue, blue on top of green, green on top of yellow, yellow on top of orange, and red beneath them all, but each color still shows slightly. See icon **G**.

u. Rainbow—Group all rectangles, rotate on a diagonal, and resize it to stretch across the page. See icon **G**.

v. Rainbow—Order the entire rainbow to appear behind all other page elements (except the background). See icon **G**.

7. Be sure any changes have been saved. Your document should look similar to **Figure 5.17-A**.

8. Print the document if required by your instructor.

Figure 5.17-A

Dynamic Desktop

Inserting and Formatting Pictures

Overview

Clip art was once only available to graphic designers, but has become a common tool for all computer users. Clip art is any non-photographic image and was at one time only available in print. As technology improves and desktop publishing becomes more popular, a person no longer needs to physically clip the image from a book and copy it. Clip art can be found directly in your word processing application or searched for on the Internet. Pictures can also be inserted into a document and resized, rotated, and arranged.

In this lesson, you will practice finding, resizing, rotating, and placing clip art or pictures on a page.

New Skills / TEKS

Inserting a Picture • Resizing a Picture • Rotating a Picture • Using Layout Options • Applying a Border to a Picture

TEKS: 6.C.i, 6.C.ii, 6.G.i, 6.G.ii

Instructions

1. Create a new word processing document.

2. Save the document as **DESKTOP**.

3. Insert a header that has your name left aligned and the activity number and title "5.18 Dynamic Desktop" right aligned.

4. Change the page orientation to landscape.

5. Insert a cube shape to represent a desk that is 3.5" high and 9" wide with a fill color of your choice and a 1 point black outline. Place the cube in the lower half of your page.

6. Using the pictures or clip art provided with your word processing application or the Internet, find one image for the following four items typically found on someone's desk. Use **Figure 5.18-A** as a guide.

    • Laptop

    • Eye glasses

    • Pencil holder

    • Coffee mug

    HINT: Select images with a transparent background.

7. Resize the images as needed so that they are in correct proportion with the desk.

8. Move and rotate the images as necessary so that they appear to be sitting on the desk.

   HINT: Use the wrap text feature as needed to adjust the placement of your images.

9. Find a photograph of a person or pet and insert it on your page.

10. Resize the photograph to be approximately 1" high and 1" wide and apply a border (frame) around the photograph. Move the photograph so that it appears to be sitting on the desk.

11. Be sure any changes have been saved.

12. Print the document if required by your instructor.

Figure 5.18-A

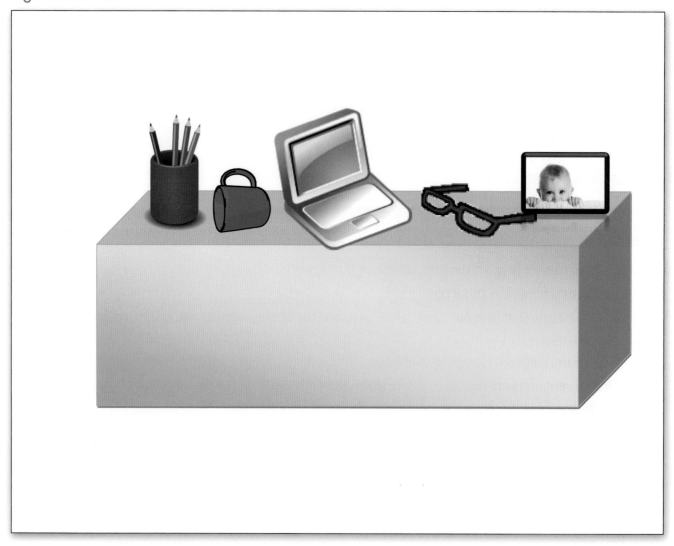

Right Here, Right Now

Working with Text Boxes

Overview

One of the features of placing an object such as clip art, WordArt, or a picture in your document is that it can be moved easily with your mouse. On the other hand, text that is typed on a line cannot be freely placed in different spots on the page. However, when a text box is used, text is contained in a box that can be positioned anywhere on the page. Text boxes can be resized and have optional borders. Using a text box eliminates the frustration of having text interfere with other elements on the page since it can be placed exactly where you want it.

In this lesson, you will use text boxes and graphics to create a collage of current news headlines.

New Skills / TEKS

Inserting a Text Box • Resizing Text Boxes • Wrapping Text Within a Text Box • Grouping a Text Box with Other Objects

TEKS: 6.B.i, 6.C.i, 6.C.ii, 6.D.i, 6.D.iii, 6.F.i, 6.G.i, 6.G.ii

Instructions

1. Create a new word processing document.

2. Unless otherwise stated, use the default font and size of the word processing software being used.

3. Save the document as **NOW**.

4. Insert a header that has your name left aligned and the activity number and title "5.19 Right Here, Right Now" right aligned.

5. Find current news articles about the following topics:

   • Today's weather forecast

   • A local news story

   • A national news story

   • A sports story

   • Your horoscope

6. Type headlines for the articles in five separate text boxes with no borders.

7. Resize the text boxes so that they each measure 1" high and 1.75" wide.

8. Wrap the headline text within each text box (if necessary).

9. Insert an image relating to the corresponding headline above each text box.

10. Group the text box and the image so that they become one object.

11. Arrange the objects so they are visually appealing and that all objects fit on one page.

12. Carefully proofread your work for accuracy.

13. Be sure any changes have been saved.

14. Print the document if required by your instructor.

Days of the Week

Working with Design Elements

Overview

Word processing software is clearly a tool for written communication, but by using graphic enhancements in your text, you can transform a written piece into a visual communication. Starting a sentence or paragraph with a larger-sized initial letter, also known as a drop cap, can add visual appeal to a document. Drop caps are commonly used in story books and magazines, and can help the reader distinguish where one paragraph ends and another begins. This interesting design element can direct a reader's attention to specific parts of the document.

In this lesson, you will format letters as drop caps, change text case, and format WordArt to enhance a document and make it more visually appealing.

New Skills / TEKS

Using WordArt • Formatting a Drop Cap

TEKS: 6.B.i, 6.C.i, 6.C.ii, 6.F.i

Instructions

1. Create a new word processing document.

2. Save the document as **DAYS**.

3. Insert a header that has your name left aligned and the activity number and title "5.20 Days of the Week" right aligned.

4. Change the line spacing to single with no additional spacing before or after the paragraphs.

5. On the first line of the document, type the text exactly as shown in **Figure 5.20-A**.

6. Apply the following formatting changes to the document:

   a. Change the font to Georgia, 11 point.

   b. Change the title "Days of the Week Origins" to bold, center aligned, and all caps.

   c. Change the first letter of each day at the beginning of each paragraph to a drop cap, dropped two lines within the paragraph.

   d. Bold each day's name throughout the document.

   HINT: Do not bold "Monday's Child."

   e. Change the title "Days of the Week Origins" to WordArt with the color and size of your choice.

   HINT: You may need to add spacing at the top of your document to fit the WordArt.

7. Carefully proofread your work for accuracy.

8. Be sure any changes have been saved.

9. Print the document if required by your instructor.

Figure 5.20-A

Days of the Week Origins

Sunday was named for the sun. People get their light and warmth from the sun. In the poem "Monday's Child," a child born on Sunday is fair, wise and good in every way.

Monday was named for the moon. The moon is very important to our life on earth. For many people, Monday is the start of the workweek. In the poem "Monday's Child," a child born on Monday is fair of face and is associated with beauty.

Tuesday was named after the Norse god, Tiw. This god was known for his sense of justice. In the poem "Monday's Child," a child born on Tuesday is thought to be graceful and with good manners.

Wednesday was named for the most powerful Norse god, Woden, also known as Odin. In the poem "Monday's Child," a child born on Wednesday is full of woe. This is the only negative characteristic of the week.

Thursday was named for the Norse god Thor. Thor is best known for wielding a giant hammer that only he and Odin can lift. In the poem "Monday's Child," a child born on Thursday has far to go and their talents will take them far in life.

Friday was named for another powerful Norse god named Frigg. He was the god of peace and fertility. In the poem "Monday's Child," a child born on Friday is big-hearted and generous.

Saturday was named for the Roman titan Saturn. Saturn was the father of six of the Roman gods, including Jupiter. In the poem "Monday's Child," a child born on Saturday is hardworking, responsible, and dedicated.

Logo Links

Applying Hyperlinks to Images

Overview

Hyperlinks can give a computer user a quick way to get to a website. Similar to hyperlinking text, hyperlinking graphics works the same way. Once the hyperlink is attached to a picture in your document, anyone with access to the file and the Internet can click the picture and be brought to the webpage.

In this lesson, you will expand on a skill you practiced in a previous lesson by hyperlinking a set of images to website addresses within a document.

New Skills / TEKS

Hyperlinking Images to Websites

TEKS: 6.C.i, 6.C.ii, 6.G.i

Instructions

1. Create a new word processing document.

2. Save the document as **LOGOS**.

3. Insert a header that has your name left aligned and the activity number and title "5.21 Logo Links" right aligned.

4. Starting on the first line of the document, insert an image for each of the 10 companies shown below. Use the Internet to find a logo image with a transparent background for each company and then resize the images to approximately 1" high and 1" wide.

    a. Apple Computers
    b. Google
    c. Amazon
    d. Starbucks
    e. Walt Disney
    f. Southwest Airlines
    g. American Express
    h. General Electric
    i. Coca-Cola
    j. FedEx

5. Add a page border to your document in the size and color of your choice.

6. Position each logo so that the spacing is distributed evenly.

    HINT: Use the wrap text feature as needed to adjust the placement of your images.

7. Hyperlink each logo to its corresponding company website.

8. If you have Internet access, test each hyperlink to ensure it is linked properly.

9. Carefully proofread your work for accuracy.

10. Be sure any changes have been saved.

11. Print the document if required by your instructor.

SWOT Analysis Diagram

Working with a Template

Overview

An effective way to identify **S**trengths, **W**eaknesses, **O**pportunities, and **T**hreats (SWOT) related to a business is by conducting a SWOT analysis through using a simple diagram. After you create the diagram, you can save it as a template that can be used as often as you need it. Read through all of the instructions and glance at the model before proceeding with creating the diagram.

In this lesson, you will create a SWOT analysis diagram that you can use whenever you need to analyze a business idea—your own, or someone else's.

New Skills / TEKS

Creating and Saving a Template • Aligning Objects

TEKS: 6.C.i, 6.C.ii, 6.F.i

Instructions

1. Create a new word processing document.

2. Save the document as **SWOT ANALYSIS**.

3. Insert a header that has your name left aligned and the activity number and title "5.22 SWOT Analysis Diagram" right aligned.

4. Create a text box that is 3" high and 3" wide.

5. Select a fill color for the text box. Depending on the fill color you choose, use black or white as the font color (whichever gives you the most contrast with the background).

6. Change the line spacing to single with no additional spacing before or after the paragraphs.

    NOTE: Repeat this step before typing in all text boxes in this lesson.

7. Using Arial, 18 point for the title, with the bulleted items 14 point, bold, and left aligned, type the text as shown in **Figure 5.22-A**. See icon **Ⓐ**.

8. Copy and paste a new text box to the right of the original text box. Align the new text box with the original text box, as shown in **Figure 5.22-A**.

9. Change the fill color for the second text box and type the text using Arial, 18 point for the title, with the bulleted items 14 point, bold, and left aligned as shown in **Figure 5.22-A** (note that the title in this text box is right aligned). See icon **Ⓑ**.

10. Paste two additional text boxes and align them side by side below the first two text boxes as shown in **Figure 5.22-A**. See icons **Ⓒ** and **Ⓓ**.

11. Change the fill color for each of these text boxes and type the text using Arial, 18 point for the title, with the bulleted items 14 point, bold, and left aligned as shown in **Figure 5.22-A** (note the placement of the text box titles). See icons **C** and **D**.

12. Carefully proofread your work for accuracy.

13. Save the file as a template.

14. Print the document if required by your instructor.

Figure 5.22-A

Professional Business Documents

Identifying Various Business Documents

Overview

Businesses use a variety of business documents to communicate and conduct business in a professional environment. From brief email messages and memos, to complex legal documents and financial reports, it is essential that all business documents be well-written and free from typographical, grammatical, and factual errors.

In this lesson, you will use the Internet to find examples of several types of business documents and place them in a table.

New Skills / TEKS

Identifying Business Documents

TEKS: 6.A.i, 6.B.i, 6.C.i, 6.C.ii, 6.F.i

Instructions

1. Create a new word processing document.

2. Save the document as **BUSINESS DOCUMENTS**.

3. Unless otherwise stated, use the default font and size of the word processing software being used.

4. Change the line spacing to single with no additional spacing before or after the paragraphs.

5. Insert a header that has your name left aligned and the activity number and title "5.23 Professional Business Documents" right aligned.

6. On the first line of the document, type the heading text "Types of Business Documents," then hit ENTER.

7. Insert a table with 3 columns and 4 rows, then type the text into the table as shown in **Figure 5.23-A**.

8. Bold and center align the text in the table.

9. Change the height of rows 1 and 3 to 3.75".

10. Using the Internet, find an image for each of the corresponding business documents and insert into the appropriate cell in the table.

    HINT: Use the wrap text feature as needed to adjust the placement of your images.

11. Change the font size of the heading text "Types of Business Documents" to 24 point, bold, and center aligned.

12. Resize each image so that it fits appropriately in the cell.

13. Carefully proofread your work for accuracy.

14. Be sure any changes have been saved.

15. Print the document if required by your instructor.

Figure 5.23-A

Block Style Business Letter	News Release	Resume
MLA Style Report	Newsletter	Memorandum

Recommendation Letter

Writing a Letter of Request

Overview

A letter of request is an effective way to ask someone for a recommendation, goods, services, and more. You could write to a company to request a sample product, or you could write to a prospective employer asking if they have internship opportunities available to students. Many students request recommendation letters from teachers as part of their college application packet. Asking for a recommendation can happen in casual conversation, but formatting and sending a letter that asks for a recommendation shows your professionalism.

Using the mail merge function in your word processing software makes the job of creating multiple copies of the same letter easier, and also allows for personalization. The multi-step process will save you time since you only have to type and edit the letter once, and once the mail merge has been set up, the three letters you are required to send can be produced and distributed to the intended recipients very quickly.

In this lesson, you will first carefully review the parts of a business letter and how to properly format it in block style format. You will then compose a letter of request using the mail merge feature in your word processing software.

New Skills / TEKS

Writing an Effective Letter of Request • Formatting a Block Style Letter • Creating a Mail Merge for Letters

TEKS: 6.A.i, 6.B.i, 6.C.i, 6.C.ii, 6.D.iii, 6.E.i, 6.F.i, 6.H.i, 6.H.ii

Instructions

1. Create a new word processing document.
2. Change the line spacing to single with no additional spacing before or after the paragraphs.
3. Save the document as **REQUEST**.
4. Set the margins as follows: Top to 2", Left, Right, and Bottom to 1".
5. Change the font to Times New Roman, 12 point.
6. Begin the mail merge process by setting up your address book. Connect to an existing list or create a new list. In either case, the list should contain the following information for three teachers that you know:

Title	Address Line 1
First Name	City
Last Name	State
School/Organization	ZIP Code

7. Carefully review **Figure 5.24-A** to learn the proper format and parts of a block style letter.

8. Type the unformatted letter of request provided in **Figure 5.24-B** and follow the steps below:

   a. Use block style format as shown in **Figure 5.24-A**.

   b. Type your home address as the return address.

   c. Use the current date for the date.

   d. Insert merge fields (or address block) for the inside address and salutation as shown in **Figure 5.24-B**.

   e. Compose an original paragraph for paragraph two. Include information about your school accomplishments up to this point in your life. Consider telling about your extracurricular activities, any part-time jobs you have held, your hobbies, any awards or recognitions you have received, and/or any special skills you have.

   f. Use your full name as the sender's name.

9. Be sure any changes have been saved to **REQUEST**.

10. Complete the mail merge.

11. Carefully proofread your work for accuracy.

12. Save the merged document as **MERGED**.

13. Print the documents if required by your instructor.

14. Using a blue or black pen, sign your name in the signature block of each letter and distribute to the intended recipients if required.

Figure 5.24-A

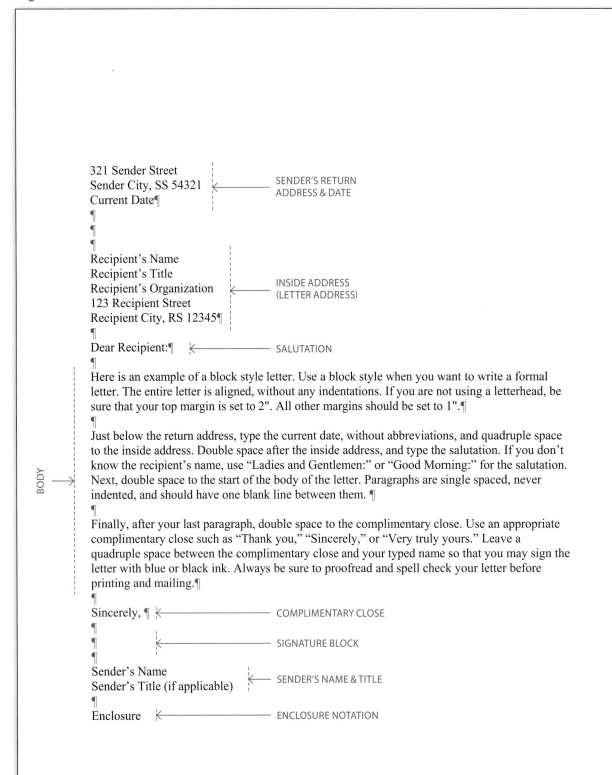

321 Sender Street
Sender City, SS 54321 ← SENDER'S RETURN
Current Date¶   ADDRESS & DATE

¶

¶

¶

Recipient's Name
Recipient's Title
Recipient's Organization ← INSIDE ADDRESS
123 Recipient Street   (LETTER ADDRESS)
Recipient City, RS 12345¶

¶

Dear Recipient:¶ ← SALUTATION

¶

Here is an example of a block style letter. Use a block style when you want to write a formal letter. The entire letter is aligned, without any indentations. If you are not using a letterhead, be sure that your top margin is set to 2". All other margins should be set to 1".¶

¶

Just below the return address, type the current date, without abbreviations, and quadruple space to the inside address. Double space after the inside address, and type the salutation. If you don't know the recipient's name, use "Ladies and Gentlemen:" or "Good Morning:" for the salutation. Next, double space to the start of the body of the letter. Paragraphs are single spaced, never indented, and should have one blank line between them. ¶

¶

Finally, after your last paragraph, double space to the complimentary close. Use an appropriate complimentary close such as "Thank you," "Sincerely," or "Very truly yours." Leave a quadruple space between the complimentary close and your typed name so that you may sign the letter with blue or black ink. Always be sure to proofread and spell check your letter before printing and mailing.¶

¶

Sincerely, ¶ ← COMPLIMENTARY CLOSE

¶

¶ ← SIGNATURE BLOCK

¶

Sender's Name
Sender's Title (if applicable) ← SENDER'S NAME & TITLE

¶

Enclosure ← ENCLOSURE NOTATION

BODY →

Figure 5.24-B

Return Address and Date: Your street, Your city, State ZIP Code, Current Date

Inside Address: «Title» «First_Name» «Last_Name» «SchoolOrganization» «Address_Line_1» «City», «State» «ZIP_Code»

Dear «Title» «Last_Name»:¶ I am in the process of compiling the things I need for my college application packet. My guidance counselor suggested that I include a few letters of recommendation from my teachers. I am hoping that you would be willing to write such a letter on my behalf.¶ USE THIS PARAGRAPH TO DETAIL THE ACCOMPLISHMENTS YOU HAVE HAD IN SCHOOL SO FAR. INCLUDE DETAILS ABOUT ANY EXTRACURRICULAR ACTIVITIES YOU HAVE BEEN INVOLVED IN, ANY PART-TIME JOBS YOU HAVE HELD, YOUR HOBBIES, ANY AWARDS OR RECOGNITIONS YOU HAVE RECEIVED, AND/OR ANY SPECIAL SKILLS YOU HAVE.¶ I have always appreciated your judgment and know your recommendation will be honest and sincere. My hope is to have my college application packet complete in the next month. I can make myself available to pick up a signed copy of your letter at your convenience.¶ Sincerely, Your Full Name

New Menu Announcement

Creating a Press Release

Overview

A press release is a written statement directed to the media. It can be used to announce a wide variety of newsworthy items. Farm to Tables, a small local restaurant, is about to kick off three new menu items that have been submitted by teen residents of the local community. The new menu items were the result of a recipe contest sponsored by the restaurant. Farm to Tables is excited about the new menu items and has decided to spread the word using a press release. The local newspaper limits the number of characters that can be submitted to their paper to 2,500.

In this lesson, you will prepare a press release for the local media to advertise the new additions to the menu of a local restaurant. The restaurant has provided copy for you, but you must properly format the press release as well as check that the maximum character count is not exceeded.

New Skills / TEKS

Formatting a Press Release

TEKS: 6.A.i, 6.B.i, 6.C.i, 6.C.ii, 6.F.i

Instructions

1. Create a new word processing document.

2. Save the document as **PRESS RELEASE**.

3. Insert a header that has your name left aligned and hit ENTER.

4. Below your name in the header, type the activity number and title "5.25 New Menu Announcement" left aligned. Close the header.

5. Change the line spacing to single with no additional spacing before or after the paragraphs.

6. Change the font to Times New Roman, 12 point.

7. On the first line of your document, type the heading in bold and all caps as shown in **Figure 5.25-A**. See icon **Ⓐ**.

8. Hit ENTER twice and type the contact information in bold as shown in **Figure 5.25-A**. See icon **Ⓑ**.

9. Hit ENTER three times and type the introduction in bold, all caps, and center aligned as shown in **Figure 5.25-A**. See icon **Ⓒ**.

10. Hit ENTER twice and change the line spacing to double space.

11. Type the body of the press release as shown in **Figure 5.25-A** with a 0.5" tab indent at the beginning of each new paragraph (but do not indent the first paragraph beginning with the date). See icon **D**.

12. Change <city, state> to your city and state and <current date> to today's date.

13. Use the thesaurus tool to find alternative words for the following two underlined words:

    stage

    enormous

    NOTE: Replace with the alternative word, then bold and underline.

14. At the end of the document, hit ENTER and insert the symbols to indicate the end of the press release as shown in **Figure 5.25-A**. See icon **E**.

15. Download and save the Farm to Tables logo from the Logos folder on the BIM Companion Website: **www.MyCompanionSite.com**.

16. In the upper right-hand corner, insert the Farm to Tables logo. Resize the logo so it is in proportion with the rest of your document as shown in **Figure 5.25-A**. See icon **F**.

    HINT: Use the wrap text feature as needed to adjust the placement of the logo.

17. Use the word count feature to calculate the number of characters with spaces.

18. On the bottom line of your document, type the number of characters followed by the words "characters in the press release" as shown in **Figure 5.25-A**. See icon **G**.

19. Carefully proofread your work for accuracy. Be sure to check the final character count (with spaces) and verify that your press release is under 2,500 characters.

20. Be sure any changes have been saved.

21. Print the document if required by your instructor.

Figure 5.25-A

A **FOR IMMEDIATE RELEASE**

B
Farm to Tables
Ophelia McDonald, Owner
2314 Commercial Drive
Lamont, CA 93241
Phone: 1-661-555-0313
ophelia@farmtotables.com
www.farmtotables.com

F

C   **FARM TO TABLES ANNOUNCES THE ADDITION OF THREE NEW MENU ITEMS CREATED AS A RESULT OF A RECIPE CONTEST**

D <city, state,> <current date>–Ophelia McDonald's Farm to Tables Restaurant has added three new items to its menu, ranging from dinner to dessert.

Farm to Tables is eager to share the reason why the three new items are being offered. During this past year, Ophelia McDonald has been getting lots of menu requests and suggestions from local teens about adding more vegetarian choices to its menu. Last September, a group of teens met with McDonald about an idea they had that could help identify what would be the most requested vegetarian dishes—a recipe contest.

McDonald was open to the idea and agreed to add the winning recipes to the menu starting in January for the New Year. Well, the idea was so appealing to teens in the community, that a group from the high school got local businesses to contribute prizes for the first-, second-, and third-place winners.

The contest was off and running starting October 15th and was open until October 30th. One hundred and seventy recipes were submitted. With a group of teen representatives as judges, that number was narrowed to fifty. These fifty contestants were asked to prepare the dish, submit a picture, and include a description of how it tastes. A booth was set up at the middle and

Figure 5.25-A (Continued)

high schools where teens were encouraged to come by to vote on the dish they found most appealing and most likely to purchase.

Nine lucky contestants moved on to the final **stage** of the competition—the taste test. It was decided that the teen leaders throughout the community would be the taste testers. There were three favorites among that group that received **enormous** raves and they are the following: Steamed Veggie Platter, Granny's Sweet Potato Pie, and the Fresh Kale and Apple Salad.

These amazing-tasting dishes have proudly been added to the Farm to Tables menu and dedicated to the teen winners who worked so hard at making sure their local eatery had something on the menu that represented their requests. These dishes will remain a tribute to the teens for years to come. Come one, come all, and taste for yourself!

 ###

 ____ characters in the press release

Spirit Week Memo

Creating a Memo

Overview

There are several ways to communicate to others within an organization. For issues that require an immediate response, phone calls and emails are best, but when something only needs to be announced, interoffice memorandums work well. A memo is a short, one page document that provides information to a group of people. It may include a request for action and should be clear in its message. The format of a memo is similar to an email since it includes who the memo is to and from, as well as the subject and the date it is written.

In this lesson, you will first carefully review the proper format of a memo. You will then recreate a memo written by the school principal and addressed to the faculty about an upcoming event.

New Skills / TEKS

Formatting a Memo

TEKS: 6.A.i, 6.B.i, 6.C.i, 6.C.ii, 6.F.i

Instructions

1. Create a new word processing document.

2. Change the line spacing to single with no additional spacing before or after the paragraphs.

3. Save the document as **SPIRIT**.

4. Set the margins as follows: Top to 2", Left, Right, and Bottom to 1".

5. Change the font to Arial, 12 point.

6. Starting on the first line of the document, type the title "MEMORANDUM" bold, center aligned, and in all caps.

7. Type the remaining text in the memo as shown in **Figure 5.26-A**. Blank lines are shown by the ¶ symbol. Use the Tab key to align the text separating the "TO," "FROM," "DATE," and "SUBJECT." Use your first and last name as the sender and the current date for the date.

8. Carefully proofread your work for accuracy.

9. Be sure any changes have been saved.

10. Print the document if required by your instructor.

11. Using a blue or black pen, initial the printed copy next to your name to show that you have reviewed the memo.

Figure 5.26-A

MEMORANDUM

¶
TO: All Faculty
¶
FROM: Your Full Name, Principal
¶
DATE: <Insert Current Date>
¶
SUBJECT: Spirit Week
¶
¶
It is so hard to believe it is nearing our school's annual homecoming! Thank you in advance to everyone who has already assisted to make this year's Spirit Week a memorable one. There are lots of things going on at the school during Spirit Week and we will need all hands on deck.
¶
The students and faculty have all voted for the Spirit Week daily themes. We had an overwhelming response for Pajama Day! The days and their themes are as follows:
- Monday – PJ Day
- Tuesday – Formal Day
- Wednesday – Geeks vs. Jocks
- Thursday – Twin Day
- Friday – School Colors Day
¶
I will need your help managing students during the Pep Rally. We will need to assign people ahead of time to dedicated areas of the gymnasium. Ideally, everyone will be sitting with their homeroom, but I do need some people posted outside of the gym. I am asking for a handful of faculty members to be on the lookout for roaming students. If you see anyone leave the Pep Rally, please intervene and get those students back to the gym or send them to the office.
¶
I know this will be one of the best Spirit Weeks we have ever had. Show the students what it means to have school spirit by participating in the daily themes and showing your enthusiasm at the Pep Rally.

School Newsletter

Recreating a Newsletter

Overview

A newsletter is a regularly distributed publication that addresses one main topic of interest to its subscribers. Newsletters are typically formatted the same way from one issue to the next and include stories written by third-party observers. Newsletter marketing is one way that businesses maintain communication with existing customers.

Here are some basic design guidelines for newsletters:

- Keep the layout simple and easy to read.
- Design the heading as the most prominent element on the page.
- Use a maximum of two to three fonts in the newsletter.
- Article headings should be no more than 14-point font and text no more than 11-point font.
- Place the most important information at the top of the newsletter.

In this lesson, you will recreate and design a newsletter for a high school. The students have already written the articles for you to format accordingly.

New Skills / TEKS

Formatting a Newsletter

TEKS: 6.A.i, 6.B.i, 6.C.i, 6.C.ii, 6.E.iv, 6.F.i

Instructions

1. Create a new word processing document.
2. Save the document as **NEWSLETTER**.
3. Change the line spacing of all paragraphs and text boxes to single with no additional spacing before or after the paragraphs.
4. Set page margins to 0.5" on all sides.
5. Use **Figure 5.27-A** as a guide as you recreate the newsletter.
6. On the first line of your document, type the title of the newsletter in Arial, 36 point, bold, center aligned, and in all caps as shown in **Figure 5.27-A**. See icon **Ⓐ**.

7. Type the subtitle using Arial, 10 point, italic, center aligned, and bullet symbols inserted where indicated as shown in **Figure 5.27-A**. See icon **Ⓑ**.

    NOTE: Replace Student Name with your name.

8. Insert a 1 point black line that measures 6" wide and position as shown in **Figure 5.27-A**. See icon **Ⓑ**.

9. Insert a section or continuous break.

10. Format the rest of the page as two 3.5" columns. Allow 0.5" between the two columns with a line inserted between them.

11. Type the remainder of the text in the newsletter as follows:

    a. Format each newsletter article heading using Arial, 14 point, bold, and center aligned as shown in **Figure 5.27-A**. See icon **Ⓒ**.

    b. Insert an image similar to the one shown. Resize the image to approximately 1" high by 2" wide and add a border as shown in **Figure 5.27-A**. See icon **Ⓓ**.

        HINT: Use the wrap text feature as needed to adjust the placement of the image.

    c. Format the body text of the newsletter using Arial, 11 point, and justified as shown in **Figure 5.27-A**. See icon **Ⓔ**.

    d. Format the "Reported by" line using Arial, 11 point, italic, and center aligned as shown in **Figure 5.27-A**. See icon **Ⓕ**.

    e. Using a text box with a 1 point border, type the text using Arial, 14 point, bold, and center aligned as shown in **Figure 5.27-A**. See icon **Ⓖ**.

12. Carefully proofread your work for accuracy. Your newsletter should look **similar** to **Figure 5.27-A**.

13. Be sure any changes have been saved.

14. Print the document if required by your instructor.

Figure 5.27-A

Ⓐ RAIDERS MONTHLY GAZETTE

Ⓑ *Westminster High School Newsletter • Issue 9 Volume 2 • by Student Name*

Ⓒ Are We Ready?

The day we all work for is almost here—GRADUATION! We're about to leave behind one chapter in our lives and begin another. We're all moving in many directions; some of us will be going on to college, others are joining the workforce, and yet others will be going into the military. Let's take the time we have left as high school seniors to thank the people (faculty, staff, and friends) who helped get us to our ultimate goal—GRADUATION!

Ⓕ Raiders Season Wrap-Up
Reported by Michael Murphy, Senior

All of the Westminster Raiders varsity teams finished their seasons with outstanding stats. The football team not only defeated the cross-town rival Cardinals in their final match up, they went on to win the Division II Super Bowl.

The girls' volleyball team finished the season 10-2. The boys' volleyball team finished 11-1. The track team went to the state finals and placed 2nd overall (first time for Westminster High). And let's not forget the Raiders baseball team who just had their best season ever with a 16-1 record.

Congratulations to all team members, coaches, and the very talented athletic director, Coach Bill Barnes. GO RAIDERS!!!

IMPORTANT DATES IN MAY
Check the school's website for upcoming activities Ⓖ

A Farewell Message
Reported by Megan Cloutier, Junior

As the time nears for seniors to leave, I've been walking around talking to students, faculty, and staff. I wanted to get their words of advice to pass on to the graduating class. It's an exciting, yet sometimes scary time for seniors as they embark on their new journey. The faculty, staff, and junior class would like to leave you with the following words of wisdom:

- Follow your passion.
- Dedicate yourself to success.
- Remember those who have helped you along the way.
- Always make time for your family and friends.
- Dream big!

When September Rolls Around

Even though it's May, before you know it, we will all be back here ready for another school year. Announcements are being put up on the video monitors around the school. The varsity teams are holding sign-ups and various clubs are looking for volunteers. GET INVOLVED!

May Cafeteria Specials

May 2 – Make your own sub
May 16 – Salad sensations
May 23 – Make your own sundae

Knowledge College Letterhead

Formatting Business Letterhead

Overview

A business's letterhead provides a professional representation of the business or organization. It serves as an identifier, or a signature, and includes important contact information such as the company's address, phone number, fax number, and website. The logo is the most important element on an letterhead, so it is most often the largest item.

An example of what your finished document should look like has been provided. Refer to this document for visual guidance as you complete the instructions.

In this lesson, you will create personalized business letterhead for Elizabeth Tutor, Academic Dean at Knowledge College. This letterhead will be used in all correspondence with students and their families, vendors, and staff.

New Skills / TEKS

Creating Business Letterhead

TEKS: 6.C.i, 6.C.ii, 6.G.i, 6.G.ii

Instructions

1. Create a new word processing document.

2. Save the document as **LETTERHEAD**.

3. Set the top margin at 2", allowing enough space to create the college's entire masthead (the top portion of the letterhead). Set the left, right, and bottom margins at 1".

4. Change the font to Arial, 12 point.

5. Download and save the Knowledge College logo from the Logos folder on the BIM Companion Website: **www.MyCompanionSite.com**.

6. Insert the Knowledge College logo in the header and resize it so it is in proportion with the rest of the information in the header section, as shown in **Figure 5.28-A**. See icon **A**.

   HINT: Use the wrap text feature as needed to adjust the placement of the logo.

7. While still in the header, to the left of the logo, insert a text box that has no border and type the text, using Arial, 10 point, left aligned as shown in **Figure 5.28-A**. See icon **B**.

   HINT: Within the text box, change the line spacing to single space with no additional spacing before or after the paragraphs.

8. Italicize the email address and remove the hyperlink if necessary as shown in **Figure 5.28-A**.

9. While still in the header, to the right of the logo, insert a text box that has no border along the right margin. Type the text using Arial, 10 point, right aligned as shown in **Figure 5.28-A**. See icon **C**.

    HINT: Within the text box, change the line spacing to single space with no additional spacing before or after the paragraphs.

10. Italicize the phone and fax numbers as shown in **Figure 5.28-A**.

11. Top align both text boxes as shown in **Figure 5.28-A**.

12. In the footer, type the text using Arial, 12 point, italic, and center aligned as shown in **Figure 5.28-A**. See icon **D**.

13. On the first line of the document, type your first and last name.

14. Carefully proofread your work for accuracy.

15. Be sure any changes have been saved.

16. Print the document if required by your instructor.

Figure 5.28-A

Elizabeth Tutor
Academic Dean
etutor@knowledgecollege.edu
www.knowledgecollege.edu

Administration Building
9382 Intellect Drive
College Park, MD 20740
Phone: 240-555-0404
Fax: 240-555-3456

KNOWLEDGE
COLLEGE

"Practical Learning for Serious Students"

Business Card

Creating a Business Card

Overview

Business cards provide an easy way to share contact information with current and potential customers. Given their small size, it's important to carefully consider the design of a business card. The space must be used wisely and highlight the most important information, including the person's name and job title, the company name and logo, its address and telephone number, and its email and website addresses.

Remember to keep plenty of white space to maximize readability. The style of the card should match the style of the business's logo. Business cards look best if only one or two fonts are used.

In this lesson, you will design a professional business card that will help project an image for a restaurant called Farm to Tables.

New Skills / TEKS

Creating a Business Card

TEKS: 6.A.i, 6.C.i, 6.C.ii, 6.F.i

Instructions

IMPORTANT NOTE: In this project, you will be provided with the content to include. The layout, design, and fonts for this document are left for you to decide.

1. Create a new word processing document.

2. Save the document as **CARD**.

3. Insert a header that has your name left aligned, and hit ENTER.

4. Below your name in the header, type the activity number and title "5.29 Business Card." Close the header.

5. Insert a rectangle that measures 3.5" wide and 2" high with no fill and a 1 point black border and position in the center of your page.

6. Download and save the Farm to Tables logo from the Logos folder on the BIM Companion Website: **www.MyCompanionSite.com**.

7. Within the rectangle, place the following information on the business card:

   a. The Farm to Tables logo

   b. Employee name: Ophelia McDonald

   c. Employee's title: Owner

    d. Business contact information:

       2314 Commercial Drive

       Lamont, CA 93241

       Phone: 1-661-555-0313

       Website: www.farmtotables.com

       Email: Ophelia@farmtotables.com

    e. Additional graphic images and/or border (optional)

    HINT: Use the wrap text feature as needed to adjust the placement of the elements.

8. Format the size and placement of the text and other elements on the business card so that they are in proportion with one another and project a professional image.

9. Carefully proofread your work for accuracy.

10. Be sure any changes have been saved.

11. Print the document if required by your instructor.

Promotional Flyer

Designing a Business Flyer

Overview

A flyer is a one-sided, one-page document that typically communicates a single message. Flyers are often used to announce events, advertise a product or service, or promote a cause. The primary objective of a flyer is to capture the reader's attention; to achieve this goal, the flyer must be visually appealing.

In this lesson, you will recreate and add design elements to a promotional flyer to encourage potential customers to visit a restaurant and try three new menu items.

New Skills / TEKS

Creating and Designing a Flyer • Selecting a Shadow and Dash Style

TEKS: 6.B.i, 6.C.i, 6.C.ii, 6.F.i

Instructions

1. Create a new word processing document.

2. Save the document as **FLYER**.

3. Insert a header that has your name left aligned, and hit ENTER.

4. Below your name in the header, type the activity number and title "5.30 Promotional Flyer." Close the header.

5. Set the page margins as follows: Top and Bottom to 1", Left and Right to 0.8".

6. On the first line of the document, type the name of the restaurant with a green text color of your choice, using Arial, 36 point, and bold as shown in **Figure 5.30-A**. See icon **Ⓐ**.

7. Insert an appropriate clip art image (i.e., a salad) that helps illustrate the message. Resize the image to 3" wide by 2" high (approximately) and position as shown in **Figure 5.30-A**. See icon **Ⓑ**.

   HINT: Use the wrap text feature as needed to adjust the placement of the image.

8. Create a text box that is 3" wide by 1" high with a red fill and a .5 black border. Select a shadow style (optional). Using Arial, 18 point, bold, and center aligned, type the text and position as shown in **Figure 5.30-A**. See icon **Ⓒ**.

   HINT: In each text box, set the line spacing to single space with no additional spacing before or after the paragraph.

9. Create a text box that is 3" wide by 1.7" high. Select a dashed line style and gray fill. Using Arial, 16 point, bold, and center aligned, with the last line using 12 point, bold, and center aligned, type the text and position as shown in **Figure 5.30-A**. See icon **Ⓓ**.

10. Create a text box with no border. Type the text using Arial, 18 point, italic, center aligned, and position as shown in **Figure 5.30-A**. See icon **E**.

11. Create a text box with no border and type the text using Arial, 12 point, and left aligned. Insert bullets, bold the name of each menu item, and position as shown in **Figure 5.30-A**. See icon **F**.

    NOTE: Make sure there is a blank line in between each menu item and description as shown in **Figure 5.30-A**.

12. Create a text box with no border and type the text using Arial, 12 point, bold, left aligned, and position as shown in **Figure 5.30-A**. See icon **G**.

13. Carefully proofread your work for accuracy.

14. Be sure any changes have been saved.

15. Print the document if required by your instructor.

Figure 5.30-A

A # Farm to Tables

B

C

Come Try Our
New Menu Items!!

D

**Try one of our new menu
items and get a FREE
delicious homemade
cookie and drink...**

Limit one per customer.

E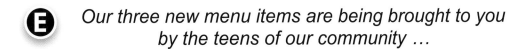

*Our three new menu items are being brought to you
by the teens of our community …*

- **Steamed Veggie Platter:** A nutritious and tasty main entrée for our vegetarian guests, the Steamed Veggie Platter includes a medley of locally grown seasonal vegetables from the McDonald farm. Usually served with butter or shredded cheese, a vegan option is also available.

F

- **Granny's Sweet Potato Pie:** This custard-style pie may initially make you think of pumpkin pie, but one taste will change your mind. Based on an old family recipe, you'll love the touch of honey and ginger that causes you to savor every bite. What a great way to finish any meal!

- **Fresh Kale and Apple Salad:** Turn anyone from a kale 'hater' into a kale 'lover' in just a few bites with this crunchy salad that features crisp apples and a lemon-garlic dressing that's to die for. The perfect accompaniment to any of our entrées.

G **Call ahead orders for take-out: 661-555-0313
We are located across from the public library.**

Resume

Recreating a Resume

Overview

A resume is a document that highlights an individual's work and educational experience, and is one of the most important documents that you will ever produce. Resumes are sent to prospective employers who use the contents of the resume to decide whether to interview an applicant. They may also be included with requests for funding or other queries where a person's experience and expertise will impact a decision made by someone else. Therefore, it is important that resumes are formatted professionally, contain no grammatical or spelling errors, and are formatted (usually) to fit on one page.

In this lesson, you will recreate and format a sample resume for a potential job candidate.

New Skills / TEKS

Creating and Formatting a Resume

TEKS: 6.A.i, 6.B.i, 6.C.i, 6.C.ii, 6.E.ii, 6.F.i

Instructions

1. Create a new word processing document.
2. Change the line spacing to single with no additional spacing before or after the paragraphs.
3. Save the document as **RESUME**.
4. Insert a header that has your name left aligned, and hit ENTER.
5. Below your name in the header, type the activity number and title "5.31 Resume." Close the header.
6. Change the font to Times New Roman, 12 point.
7. Set a left aligned tab at 1.5" and a right aligned tab at 6".
8. Starting on the first line of the document, type the resume as shown in **Figure 5.31-A**.

   HINT: Use the Tab key to align the text as shown. Use a 1.5" hanging indent in the OBJECTIVE paragraph.
9. Apply the following formatting changes to the text:
   a. Center align the name, address, phone and fax numbers, and email address.
   b. Change the font size of the name to 16 point and bold.
   c. Change the font size of the address, phone, fax, and email address to 14 point.
   d. Insert a bullet between the phone and fax numbers (insert one space before and after the bullet).

    e. Insert a 1 point, black top border (horizontal line) below the email address.

    f. Bold the headings OBJECTIVE, EDUCATION, WORK EXPERIENCE, COMMUNITY SERVICE, SKILLS, and REFERENCES.

    g. Bold the places of employment listed in the WORK EXPERIENCE section of the resume.

    h. Italicize the job titles listed in the WORK EXPERIENCE section of the resume.

    i. Format each list of job duties (found under each job title) as a bulleted list using a standard bullet style.

10. Carefully proofread your work for accuracy.

11. Be sure any changes have been saved.

12. Print the document if required by your instructor.

Figure 5.31-A

Andrea Mae Scott
750 E Grove Street
Fresno, CA 93717
Phone: 619-555-1234 Fax: 619-555-4567
amscott@info.net

OBJECTIVE:	An internship position in a busy, mixed animal practice that will provide support, mentoring, and guidance to allow me to continue my education to become a veterinarian.
EDUCATION:	Fresno High School Expected Diploma, June 2016
	Related Coursework: Computer Science, Physics, Biology, AP Calculus

WORK EXPERIENCE:	Pet City Grooming 90 W Collar Road Fresno, CA 93701	Fall 2015–Present
	Assistant Groomer Bathe animals Brush hair and teeth	
	Fresno Chaffee Zoo 894 W Belmont Ave Fresno, CA 93728	Summer 2015
	Assistant Zookeeper Provided tours for visiting groups and schools Fed and watered animals	
	Philly Steak Subs 312 W Ballentyne Street Fresno, CA 93717	Summer 2014
	Meat Department Assistant Wrapped, labeled, and priced packages	
COMMUNITY SERVICE:	Fresno Animal Shelter Central Animal Hospital	2013–Present
SKILLS:	CPR and First Aid	
REFERENCES:	Furnished upon request.	

Social Media Today

Creating an MLA Report

Overview

The Modern Language Association (MLA) is an authority on how to prepare and format scholarly manuscripts, reports, and research papers. MLA style is widely used in high schools, colleges, and professional publications.

In this lesson, you will format the provided text as a report using proper MLA style.

New Skills / TEKS

Formatting a Report in MLA Style

TEKS: 6.A.i, 6.B.i, 6.C.i, 6.C.ii, 6.E.iii, 16.F.i

Instructions

1. Create a new word processing document.

2. Save the document as **REPORT**.

3. Change the font to Times New Roman, 12 point.

4. Set up the document in proper MLA report style as follows:

   a. Set the page margins to 1" on all sides.

   b. Insert a header that includes your last name followed by the page number. Right align the text in the header. Be sure the font is Times New Roman, 12 point.

   c. Use only one space after periods and other punctuation marks (optional).

   d. Change the line spacing to double space with no additional spacing before or after paragraphs.

5. Starting on the first line of the document, do the following:

   a. Type your first and last name (left aligned), then hit ENTER.

   b. Type your instructor's name (left aligned), then hit ENTER.

   c. Type the title of the course you have enrolled in (left aligned), then hit ENTER.

   d. Type the current date (left aligned), then hit ENTER.

6. Type the title of the report as shown in **Figure 5.32-A**. Center align the title, then hit ENTER.

7. Type the body of the report as shown in **Figure 5.32-A**.

   HINT: Your report should be double spaced.

8. Insert a page break (CTRL+ENTER) after the last paragraph in the report (before the "Works Cited" text).

9. Type the "Works Cited" page as follows (be sure that it starts on a new page in the document):

   a. Center align the text "Works Cited," then hit ENTER.

   b. Type and format the text under the title exactly as shown in **Figure 5.32-B**.

10. Carefully proofread your work for accuracy.

11. Be sure any changes have been saved.

12. Print the document if required by your instructor.

Figure 5.32-A

Social Media Today

      Social media is a form of online communication using web-based tools such as blogs, social networking sites, online communities, and virtual game worlds. Users can send messages and share pictures, news, and status updates with friends, family, and even strangers. Social media tools, such as Facebook and Twitter, have drastically changed how we communicate. The World Wide Web has opened a cyber sphere so big that the social media tools available are endless. Social media keeps people connected and up-to-date on what is happening in the world. The use of social media tools makes interacting in real time possible without actually being face-to-face with another person.

      Even a friend home sick can experience the excitement of a homecoming game through tweets, status updates, and photo sharing without actually being at the game in person. Businesses also use social media to reach customers and many people rely on social media for real-time news.

      Social networking allows us to connect with others online through status updates, wall posts, and sharing pictures and videos. These sites are formed around user profiles, allowing users to share information like favorite movies or music. Blogging is like an online journal. Bloggers can write about a trip they took, day-to-day life, or offer advice on different topics. Many blogs are public, though some may require registration to read.

      We use social media primarily for personal, academic, and professional purposes. Social media offers convenience for many personal uses. These may include writing a blog, chatting with friends who live far away, or keeping friends updated with status posts on websites like Facebook. Social media is a powerful tool when it comes to academics and research. From Googling information for a report to researching websites, social media puts the world at our fingertips in seconds. Social media isn't only for fun and school; it also has professional uses such as networking or product advertising or endorsement. Social media provides a platform for creative expression and exchange of ideas.

      Overuse of social media websites can have a negative effect on real-life relationships. Sometimes using social media sources can become more important than investing time in everyday relationships with friends and family. It can cause personal relationships to deteriorate and result in someone valuing online connections more than face-to-face connections. The Internet allows people to be anonymous, giving them freedom to post hurtful comments without assuming responsibility. Use of social media for cyber bullying is dangerous because it can spread negative messages quickly.

      Sharing too much personal information puts people at risk. Revealing personal information online, such as a home address or online passwords, is dangerous and can allow people to hack into personal accounts, gain access to financial information, or send messages under a stolen identity. Inappropriate pictures or comments may be seen by prospective employers. As with any online communication, social media should be used with caution and responsibility.

Figure 5.32-B

Works Cited

Mulka, Lisa. *Cyber Literacy for the Digital Age*. Warwick: B.E. Publishing, 2014. Print.

Knowledge College Majors

Using Online Word Processing Software

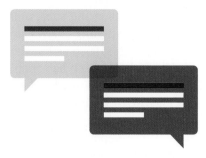

Overview

The ability to collaborate and share using online word processing software offers a variety of advantages for users. Text can be inserted and edited by multiple people in order to evenly distribute the workload. In addition, comments can be shared on the document to allow for fast and convenient communication.

In this lesson, you will collaborate with a partner to create a list of majors at Knowledge College and the potential careers in those fields.

New Skills / TEKS

Creating, Editing, and Sharing an Online Word Processing Document • Collaborating Using Online Word Processing Software

TEKS: 6.B.i, 6.C.i, 6.C.ii, 6.F.i, 6.I.i, 6.I.ii, 6.I.iii

Instructions

IMPORTANT NOTE BEFORE YOU BEGIN: To complete this lesson, you must be assigned a partner with whom you will collaborate. Once partners have been assigned, determine who will take on the role of Student A and who will take on the role of Student B. As you complete this lesson, refer to **Figure 5.33-A** for visual guidance.

STUDENT A

1. Using Google Docs, or a similar online word processing application, create a new document.

2. Rename or save the document as **MAJORS**.

3. Share the document with Student B and assign the "Can edit" permission.

4. In the header of the document, type your and your partner's first and last names right aligned, then hit ENTER.

5. Below the names in the header, type the activity number and title "5.33 Knowledge College Majors" right aligned. Close the header.

6. Download and save the Knowledge College logo from the Logos folder on the BIM Companion Website: **www.MyCompanionSite.com**.

7. Insert the Knowledge College logo at the top of the document.

   HINT: Use the wrap text feature as needed to adjust the placement of the logo.

8. Resize and center align the logo as shown in **Figure 5.33-A**. See icon **Ⓐ**.

9. Once Student B has inserted a 2 column by 4 row table, type the text in the **left** column using Arial, 12 point as shown in **Figure 5.33-A**. See icon **Ⓑ**.

10. Shade the career that is of most interest to you in the color of your choice.

STUDENT B

1. Retrieve and open the **MAJORS** document from your "Shared with me" drive (if applicable).

2. Once Student A has inserted and resized the Knowledge College logo, insert a 2 column by 4 row table and position as shown in **Figure 5.33-A**. See icon **Ⓒ**.

3. Type the text in the **right** column using Arial, 12 point as shown in **Figure 5.33-A**. See icon **Ⓓ**.

4. Bold the text of each major in the left and right columns, and format each list of related careers using standard bullets as shown in **Figure 5.33-A**.

5. Insert a row above row 1 that is merged and centered with the text, "What Can I Do with My Major?" and change the font to Arial, 18 point, and bold as shown in **Figure 5.33-A**. See icon **Ⓔ**.

6. Shade the career that is of most interest to you in the color of your choice.

STUDENTS A AND B

1. Carefully proofread your work for accuracy.

2. Use the Comment feature to collaborate and inform each other that you have completed your portion of the lesson.

3. When the lesson is complete, print preview the document. It should look similar to **Figure 5.33-A**.

4. Use the Comment feature to communicate and decide which of you will share the document with your instructor.

5. Share or print the document if required by your instructor.

Figure 5.33-A

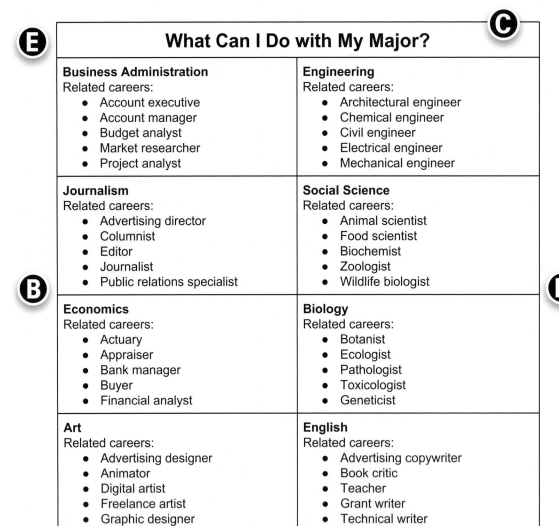

KNOWLEDGE COLLEGE

What Can I Do with My Major?

Business Administration
Related careers:
- Account executive
- Account manager
- Budget analyst
- Market researcher
- Project analyst

Engineering
Related careers:
- Architectural engineer
- Chemical engineer
- Civil engineer
- Electrical engineer
- Mechanical engineer

Journalism
Related careers:
- Advertising director
- Columnist
- Editor
- Journalist
- Public relations specialist

Social Science
Related careers:
- Animal scientist
- Food scientist
- Biochemist
- Zoologist
- Wildlife biologist

Economics
Related careers:
- Actuary
- Appraiser
- Bank manager
- Buyer
- Financial analyst

Biology
Related careers:
- Botanist
- Ecologist
- Pathologist
- Toxicologist
- Geneticist

Art
Related careers:
- Advertising designer
- Animator
- Digital artist
- Freelance artist
- Graphic designer

English
Related careers:
- Advertising copywriter
- Book critic
- Teacher
- Grant writer
- Technical writer

Unit 6
Databases

TEKS

7.A.i, 7.B.i, 7.C.i, 7.D.i,
7.D.ii, 7.E.i, 7.F.i, 7.G.i,
8.A.i, 8.B.i, 9.A.i, 10.A.i,
10.B.i, 10.C.i, 10.D.i

What is a Database?

Every time you use Google to find something, chances are the search results you see on screen were retrieved from a database. A **database** is a collection of information (data) that is stored on a computer in an organized format so that the information can be easily accessed, managed, and updated.

Think of a database like an electronic filing cabinet. Although you may not realize it, you probably access multiple databases every day: the contacts in your cell phone, using a map app, or accessing iTunes to download a song. All of the information that you're accessing is stored using a database management system (DBMS). Just about every business and organization, large and small alike, use databases to manage and store information.

Why Learn Databases?

For any type of business or organization, databases are the primary tool for storing, managing, and analyzing information. Without databases, we wouldn't have search engines, phone directories, or even the ability to use a website to order a pizza. Whether serving the needs of large Internet search engines, like Google, or simply being used by your school to track students, classes, and grades, databases play a vital role in today's high tech world.

The amount of data that needs to be stored and managed is only increasing. Given the explosive growth of everything from smartphones or phablets, to wearable fitness trackers to GPS tracking devices, more and more data is being collected and shared. Understanding databases and the information and data they provide is an essential workplace skill to have.

Structure of a Database

A database is structured by storing and organizing interrelated information into one or more tables. Similar in format to a spreadsheet, a **table** uses columns and rows to store data in a **cell**, or the intersection of a column and row.

Tables contain a series of **records**. Each record contains data segments called **fields**. For example, a record for a business's customer might contain fields such as first name, last name, street address, city, state, and zip code. Each field within a database is required to have a data type. A **data type** is the term used to determine what format each field in the database structure is defined as. While there are a variety of data type format options, some of the most common are listed in **Figure 6.0-A**.

Figure 6.0-A

Common Data Types	
Long and Short Text	Short text is used for storing non-numeric data that is brief, generally under 256 characters. Long text is used for longer segments of text, more than 256 characters.
Number	Number fields are used for storing numbers, and can be formatted in a variety of ways such as currency, percentages, or decimals.
Yes/No	The Yes/No data type is used to determine if the data in that field has "yes" or "no" answers. Yes/No is actually a special form of the number data type, where only two numbers are used: 0 (for "no") and 1 (for "yes").
Date/Time	The Date/Time data type is used to display data in the form of a date, time, or both. Date/Time is also a special form of the number data type.
Object	The Object data type is used for formatting fields that contain data that cannot be entered by a keyboard, such as an image or sound file.

To illustrate how data types are utilized in a database, let's take a look at how a database record would be structured to collect and organize data required for students in a high school in **Figure 6.0-B**.

Figure 6.0-B

Field Name	Data Type
Student ID #	Number
First Name	Text
Last Name	Text
Address	Text
City	Text
State	Text
Zip	Text
Phone	Number
Email	Text
Username	Text
Password	Text
Y.O.G.	Date
Student Picture	Object
Gender	Text
Member of a Club	Yes/No

Databases Tools

We all use different tools to find the information we want. From search engines to apps, today's technology allows us to find information quickly by using multiple sources. Behind all of these tools are databases that must be accurate, reliable, and managed.

Database Management Systems (DBMS)

The tool that manages all of that information is known as a database management system (DBMS). Used by just about every business and organization, a database management system (DBMS) is a computer software application that enables users and applications to interact with a database to capture, store, retrieve, and analyze data. To be front-runners in their respective industries, database management systems (DBMS) have become a primary technology tool that businesses rely on.

A good example of a technology that utilizes the power of a DBMS is a mobile phone. The software on your phone accesses the contacts database so that data records (your contacts) can be displayed, utilized, edited, or deleted. DBMS packages generally provide an interface to view and change the design of the database, create queries, and develop reports. To further explain what a DBMS is, let's take a look at a real-world example of how Apple's iTunes.com uses a database management system.

In order for songs to be viewed on screen and played for users, the iTunes application needs to access one or more databases. Back at Apple, the iTunes database is managed by a multitude of technical staff, using a dedicated DBMS. Some employees use the database application to add new records, in other words, new artists and their songs. Others manage these records by inputting more data, such as a song's genre.

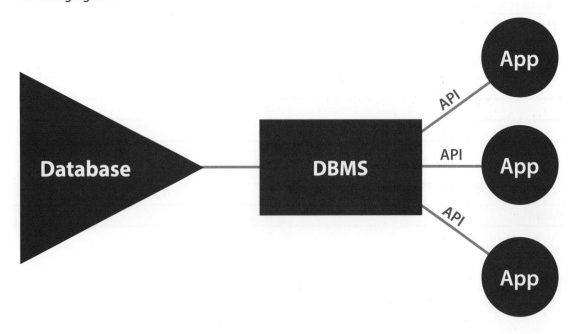

Determining Database Software

There are two categories of database software:

Desktop database software is typically utilized by home users and small businesses. Examples include Microsoft Access, My Database, and FileMaker Pro.

Enterprise level database software is used by large companies and organizations that need to manage and share information across many platforms, among a large number of users, and across distant geographical locations, even worldwide. Examples include Oracle, Microsoft SQL Server, and IBM DB2.

Selecting Database Software

In order to determine what database software and system to use, businesses must define what their data requirements are. As a starting point, all businesses need to answer the following questions:

1. What type of information needs to be collected?
2. Will the data need to be accessed and shared by multiple users, and if so, by how many?
3. How many users can the database system accommodate at one time?
4. Will customers need to access the data?
5. Will data need to be served on a website? If so, does the database software support that technology?
6. Can the database software integrate with other business applications?

Working with Microsoft Access

To complete the hands-on lessons included in this unit, you will need to use **Microsoft Access**, a DBMS application produced by Microsoft Corporation. MS Access is one of the most popular database applications. Commonly used by both businesses and individuals, MS Access enables users to create custom databases and contains a variety of tools to manage their data. Like most DBMS systems, MS Access comes equipped with a variety of features to access, format, and retrieve information, including:

- Creating visual forms for easy data entry
- Searching and browsing abilities
- Connecting to websites and external applications
- Queries
- Generating reports
- Sorting data
- Filtering data
- Importing and exporting data

Database Relationships

Relationships Between Tables

A database can be made up of one or many tables. When a database contains more than one table, often the tables will have identical fields, forming a table relationship. A relationship works by matching data in key columns, usually columns with the same name in both tables. The database relationships keep users from redundant data entry. To demonstrate the concept of table relationships, read the following scenario:

Libraries use databases to store information about books and publishers. Let's say the local library creates a database containing just one table called Book Titles which includes fields such as book title, date of publication, publisher's name, and publisher's phone number. In this one-table database, a redundancy would occur. Since many books have the same publisher, the publisher's name and phone number would need to be entered multiple times. A better solution would be for the library to create a separate table called Publisher Contact Information, which could include the publisher's name, address, city, state, zip code, as well as phone number. An identical field (the publisher's name, for example), shared by both of the tables (Book Titles and Publisher Contact Information) would create a table relationship. This relationship would make it **unnecessary** to enter the publisher's phone number in the Book Titles table.

Relationships Between Databases

A company may have one or many databases in their DBMS. When there is more than one database within a DBMS, they typically have pieces of data that are shared or related. Databases that are related to each other are referred to as **relational databases**. Browsing a website that sells technology equipment, for instance, may have a catalog database so that users can search for products, and a separate technical support database so that users can search for answers to technical support questions about a specific product. The website itself is not the database. However, as users are browsing and searching for products, the website is communicating with each database. While the two databases are separate, they have a relationship to each other—in this case, the product field.

Since a relational database is a collection of data organized as a set of related tables, its data can be accessed or reassembled in various ways without having to reorganize the database tables themselves. To illustrate relational databases, let's look at a popular college information website:

CollegeBoard.org is used by millions of potential college applicants to help find information about colleges. For example, let's say a high school student wanted to find which colleges offer physical therapy as a major and are located in warm climates. To find the answer, CollegeBoard.org first would look in its "college database" for institutions that offer physical therapy. Next, it would look in a "geographical location" database for a location with a warm climate. Then it would reference this location with the locations of its "physical therapy colleges." The records of colleges with warm climate locations would be returned as the answer.

Analyzing and Retrieving Data

Information isn't very useful if we don't do anything with it. Databases aren't just a great tool for storing information, they also make information useful. The process of studying information to make it useful is known as **data analysis**. The process of accessing data is known as data retrieval. Database software applications provide commands that allow data to be filtered and retrieved. While it may sound like a technical term only used by "business people," we all analyze data.

Asking the Right Questions to Find the Right Answers

Analyzing and retrieving data is essentially asking questions. In fact, a request for a specific answer, or list of records, from a database is called a **query**. From reading the sports statistics page, to tracking the progress of a diet, looking at data helps us make decisions based on the answers to questions we ask. How much weight have I lost this month? Do I need to adjust my diet? How are the players on my Fantasy Football team performing? Should I trade some players to improve my team?

To illustrate the importance of analyzing data, let's look at the following scenario:

Choosing what college to attend is one of the biggest decisions many of you will make. A decision of this magnitude requires a lot of thought. To help you make a well-informed choice, you can count on data analysis for some help. Using real data, you need to get the answers to these, and many other questions:

What is the school population?

What is the cost of tuition and room and board?

What is the ratio of females to males?

What are the minimum G.P.A. and S.A.T. requirements?

What are the job placement percentages for graduating students?

Where do you find the answers to these questions? A quick Google search might land you at a blog where you can read student reviews about the college you want to attend. But, who are these students? What blog is it? With more research, you might find that the links you clicked on were to sites authored by those who possess minimal or no credentials. After sifting through additional information, you realize that data provided by sites like Cappex.com and CollegeBoard.org offer much more reliable data on all aspects of attending college. Your decision becomes clearer as you ask questions and find answers—in other words, as you do data analysis.

How Businesses Use Data

Businesses regularly analyze data to help them make strategic decisions. For instance, let's say a national fast food company is considering launching a new type of cheeseburger infused with barbeque sauce. Before making any decisions, they advertise the new burger in only a handful of stores. After the testing phase is completed, the company would then analyze the sales data to decide whether or not to market the new burger in all of its locations.

In a world flooded with information pouring in from the web, cell phones, and social media, we can't trust or believe everything we read or hear. When analyzing data, the same holds true. Imagine if you were asked to write a report titled "The Top Ten Athletes of All Time." In the report, you decide to include statistics on each athlete. When your teacher passes out the graded reports, you read the comment "Many of the statistics you included were inaccurate."

To avoid inaccurate or incomplete information, there are a series of simple principles to follow when conducting a data analysis.

1. **Define your questions**

   Before you begin the analysis, know the questions you're trying to answer and what you're trying to accomplish. What is it that you want the data (information) to tell you?

2. **Identify and know your sources**

   Where will you get the information from? Are the sources credible?

3. **Collect the data**

   With your questions and sources clearly defined, you can now gather all the data you will need to analyze.

4. **Analyze the data**

   Keep an unbiased opinion, study the data from several different angles.

5. **Interpret the results**

   Summarize and display the data.

Data Warehouses

How does the data we have today compare with the same set of data from this time last month, or last year? The concept of a data warehouse helps meet this need to compare different sources or periods of data.

Today, businesses are able to collect and store massive amounts of data, from multiple and often unconnected sources. However, databases that store this information may not always be optimized for processing large amounts of data and the continuous retrieval of reports by employees, customers, and other information requests. The primary purpose of a **data warehouse** is to manage large amounts of stored data from multiple sources so it can be stored and accessed by a centralized system. A data warehouse essentially creates a copy of much of the data that is spread out across sources, and over time, allows businesses easy access to their data to make informed decisions.

Benefits of Data Warehouses

Organizations find data warehouses beneficial for a number of reasons:

1. A data warehouse helps an organization better see what data it is collecting, as well as what data it should or should not be collecting.

2. A data warehouse offers a centralized view of all data across a system, making it possible to see how clean, or consistent, the data is.

3. Once the data is consistent, an organization can work off of one clean version of their data for better analysis of accurate information.

4. With a data warehouse, "snapshots" can be taken of data over time, enabling an analysis of historical trends—this is known as data mining.

Data Mining

In the business world, data mining can help businesses predict certain behaviors about their customers and products, including:

- Characteristics of typical customers
- Predictions about customer loyalty
- Purchasing patterns—items or services that are likely to be purchased at the same time
- Warning indicators of fraudulent purchases
- Best features for interactive business websites
- Identifying customers to target for specific ad campaigns

By being aware of these predictions, companies can use them to focus their marketing efforts, make decisions about when to introduce a product to customers, as well as decide to focus on a particular type of customer for certain types of products.

To do this, a company needs to purchase and use **data mining** tools that generate this sort of predictive business information. Larger companies may decide to use dedicated data mining tools such as SAS Enterprise Miner from SAS or Oracle Advanced Analytics by Oracle. These tools are designed to analyze huge volumes of data and can be customized to work with the unique needs of larger companies. These tools are also capable of performing more advanced data mining techniques that require a significant amount of data preparation and computing power. Smaller businesses can also use data mining tools that are now offered with desktop databases such as Microsoft Access or even as a plug-in for Microsoft Excel.

Data mining does not use one single technique to produce predictive information. Some of the different techniques include:

1. **Clustering**

   Used to group customer and/or products into pre-defined "clusters" based on their characteristics. The behavior of customers and products can then be predicted based on which cluster they're in.

2. **Nearest Neighbor Classification**

   The process of classifying business information based on how "near" or similar the information is to its "neighbor." Defining the nearest neighbor is dependent on how a business views its customers and product relationships.

3. **Decision Trees**

   Uses a series of questions to narrow down and segment the business information into a predictable result.

4. **Neural Network**

   A highly accurate predictor of business behavior by using complex computer analysis.

Databases Are Powerful Tools for Using Information Successfully

A database literally puts information at your fingertips. The electronic storage of data records makes it easy and fast to search, retrieve, and organize information in countless ways. Managing information with a database enables users to identify how information relates to other information in ways not possible with paper or spreadsheets.

Databases save businesses time and money by making information easily accessible, efficiently analyzed, and used to make effective decisions. Understanding database basics and having a familiarity working with database tools are skills valued by businesses across every field.

SOFTWARE NOTES

If you encounter a skill or feature that is not available in the software version you are using, use an equivalent feature or adjust your document accordingly.

It is important to note that all of the lessons in this unit are written in a generic format and in most cases, the skills required can be achieved using any version of Microsoft Access.

A LOOK AHEAD TO YOUR FINAL ASSESSMENT

❝Pitch It!™

As a final assessment (Unit 10), you will be divided into teams and "pitch" a new product idea to your instructor. This assessment will give you exciting, first-hand knowledge of how databases can be used as a tool for creating and organizing information. Pay close attention to the skills you will be learning in this unit, as you will draw on them again in the "Pitch It!" final assessment.

Unit 6 Review

1. Visit **www.MyCompanionSite.com**.

2. Download and complete the **Unit 6 Review** worksheet.

3. Submit your completed worksheet to your instructor.

My CompanionSite.com

Address Book

Creating Your First Database

Overview

In this lesson, you will create your first database! The first step after you create the actual database file will be to create a database structure for the first table that will be added to the database. Once the structure is created for the table, you will use the table's datasheet view to easily enter data into the database fields, similar to the way that data is entered into a spreadsheet.

In this lesson, you will create a new database and use it to store the data for a personal address book.

New Skills / TEKS

Creating a Blank Database • Naming and Saving a Database • Defining the Structure of a Database • Selecting Data Types • Naming and Creating Fields • Naming and Saving a Table • Adjusting Column Widths • Printing a Table • Closing a Database

TEKS: 7.D.i, 7.D.ii, 7.E.i, 8.A.i, 8.C.i

Instructions

1. Using Microsoft Access, create a new database file.

2. Name and save the database file as **ADDRESSES**.

3. Set up the database table using the field names and data types provided below.

    NOTE: Most versions of Access include an ID field to the left of Field 1 in each database file. This is how the program assigns a unique number to each record in the database table.

Database Structure	
Field Name	**Data Type**
First Name	Text or Short Text
Last Name	Text or Short Text
School/Institution	Text or Short Text
Address Line 1	Text or Short Text
City	Text or Short Text
State	Text or Short Text
ZIP Code	Text or Short Text

4. Enter the data as shown in **Figure 6.1-A**.

5. Name and save the table as **FRIENDS**.

6. Adjust the column widths so that all data displays properly.

7. Resave the table.

8. Carefully proofread your work for accuracy.

9. Print a copy of the table if required by your instructor.

10. Save and close the database file.

Figure 6.1-A

ID	First Name	Last Name	School/Institution	Address Line 1	City	State	ZIP Code
1	Nancy	Brown	Argonne High	1421 Newhall St.	Argonne	WI	54511
2	Peter	Smith	Argonne High	874 Albany Ave.	Argonne	WI	54511
3	Arlene	Landers	Speedy Deli	776 East First St.	Argonne	WI	54511
4	Albert	Rosen	Argonne High	1111 North A St.	Argonne	WI	54511
5	Lily	Field	Speedy Deli	654 South Main St.	Argonne	WI	54511
6	Ahmet	Zehra	Argonne Public Library	12 Oak St.	Argonne	WI	54511
7	Thomas	Ogden	Argonne High	116 Hoover St.	Argonne	WI	54511
8	Nicole	Bell	Presto Pizza	1010 Lake St.	Argonne	WI	54511
9	Julie	Doubek	Argonne High	2734 Center St.	Argonne	WI	54511
10	Kurt	Gould	Argonne High	541 Cook St.	Argonne	WI	54511

Address Book 2

Working with an Existing Database

Overview

Databases are used to keep track of many different kinds of information. One of the great features of an existing database is that you can add new information as you need to, add new fields and modify old ones to keep track of additional information, and delete fields that are no longer important to you. In other words, you don't have to start over as your needs change.

In this lesson, you will use the existing Address Book database you created in **Lesson 6.1**. The ten people listed in that database are members of the Argonne School-Business Partnership. You will make a new database for recording when each member joined the partnership, and record whether the members have paid their dues for the year.

New Skills / TEKS

Opening an Existing Database • Adding New Fields • Using New Data Types • Formatting a Date/Time Field • Formatting a Yes/No Field

TEKS: 7.D.i, 7.D.ii, 7.E.i, 8.A.i, 8.C.i

Instructions

1. Open the **ADDRESSES** database file previously created in **Lesson 6.1**.
2. Name and save the database file as **PARTNERSHIP**.
3. Rename the **FRIENDS** table as **MEMBERS**.
4. Add two new fields to the database structure.
5. Name the first new field Date Joined. Identify the data type as Date or Date & Time (default format).
6. Name the second new field Dues Paid. Identify the data type as Yes/No.
7. Save the table as **MEMBERS**.
8. Enter the Date Joined and Dues Paid data as shown in **Figure 6.2-A**.
9. Adjust the column widths so that all data displays properly.
10. Resave the table.
11. Carefully proofread your work for accuracy.
12. Print a copy of the table if required by your instructor.
13. Save and close the database file.

Figure 6.2-A

ID	First Name	Last Name	School/Institution	Address Line 1	City	State	ZIP Code	Date Joined	Dues Paid
1	Nancy	Brown	Argonne High	1421 Newhall St.	Argonne	WI	54511	9/26/2015	☑
2	Peter	Smith	Argonne High	874 Albany Ave.	Argonne	WI	54511	9/5/2014	☑
3	Arlene	Landers	Speedy Deli	776 East First St.	Argonne	WI	54511	10/3/2014	☐
4	Albert	Rosen	Argonne High	1111 North A St.	Argonne	WI	54511	9/15/2015	☐
5	Lily	Field	Speedy Deli	654 South Main St.	Argonne	WI	54511	9/13/2015	☑
6	Ahmet	Zehra	Argonne Public Library	12 Oak St.	Argonne	WI	54511	2/21/2015	☐
7	Thomas	Ogden	Argonne High	116 Hoover St.	Argonne	WI	54511	9/30/2014	☐
8	Nicole	Bell	Presto Pizza	1010 Lake St.	Argonne	WI	54511	9/14/2014	☑
9	Julie	Doubek	Argonne High	2734 Center St.	Argonne	WI	54511	9/5/2014	☑
10	Kurt	Gould	Argonne High	541 Cook St.	Argonne	WI	54511	12/7/2015	☑

Colleges

Working with Interactive Data Types

Overview

Databases can store information in various forms. For example, sometimes you will need to display numbers as currency. Database fields can also store information in the form of links to websites, called hyperlinks.

In this lesson, you will create a database to compare information about ten of the largest public universities in the U.S. in terms of enrollment and tuition. You will also include links to the websites in the database.

New Skills / TEKS

Formatting Currency Fields • Using Hyperlinks • Formatting Number Fields

TEKS: 7.D.i, 7.D.ii, 7.E.i, 8.A.i, 8.C.i

Instructions

1. Using Microsoft Access, create a new database file.

2. Name and save the database file as **COLLEGES**.

3. Set up the database table using the field names and data types provided below.

Database Structure	
Field Name	**Data Type**
Rank	Text or Short Text
College Name	Text or Short Text
Location	Text or Short Text
2015 Undergraduate Enrollment	Number (Standard Format and 0 Decimal Places)
Tuition for State Residents	Currency
Website	Hyperlink

4. Name and save the table as **COLLEGE INFORMATION**.

5. Enter the data as shown in **Figure 6.3-A**.

6. Test one or two of the hyperlinks to ensure they work properly.

7. Adjust the column widths so that all data displays properly.

8. Resave the table.

9. Carefully proofread your work for accuracy.

10. Print a copy of the table if required by your instructor.

11. Save and close the database file.

Figure 6.3-A

ID	Rank	College Name	Location	2015 Undergraduate Enrollment	Tuition for State Residents	Website
1	1	University of Central Florida	Orlando, FL	52532	6368	www.ucf.edu
2	2	Texas A&M University	College Station, TX	47093	9180	www.tamu.edu
3	3	Ohio State University	Columbus, OH	44741	10037	www.osu.edu
4	4	Pennsylvania State University	University Park, PA	40541	17514	www.psu.edu
5	5	Arizona State University	Tempe, AZ	39968	10127	www.asu.edu
6	6	University of Texas at Austin	Austin, TX	39523	9830	www.utexas.edu
7	7	Michigan State University	East Lansing, MI	38786	13560	www.msu.edu
8	8	University of Minnesota	Minneapolis/St. Paul, MN	34351	13560	www.umn.edu
9	9	University of Florida	Gainesville, FL	33720	6313	www.ufl.edu
10	10	University of South Florida	Tampa, FL	31067	6410	www.usf.edu

Favorite U.S. Roller Coasters

Changing Data Types and Formatting Fields

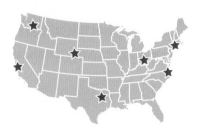

Overview

Sometimes you create a database and then discover some new information to add. Or, after setting up a database, you decide that you want to include additional or different facts. This may mean changing how numbers are displayed in the database, or that a field needs to be deleted and replaced with a new one. Databases are used so frequently because of such versatility.

In this lesson, you will create a database to show the top 15 favorite roller coasters in the United States using information found in the fan-generated list Coaster Buzz 100 from www.coasterbuzz.com. You will also delete and add fields to modify the information stored in the database.

New Skills / TEKS

Deleting Fields

TEKS: 7.D.i, 7.D.ii, 7.E.i, 8.A.i, 8.C.i

Instructions

1. Using Microsoft Access, create a new database file.

2. Name and save the database file as **COASTERS**.

3. Set up the database table using the field names and data types provided below.

Database Structure	
Field Name	**Data Type**
Rank	Text or Short Text
Coaster Name	Text or Short Text
Amusement Park and Location	Text or Short Text
Height (ft)	Number (Standard Format and 0 Decimal Places)
Year Opened	Text or Short Text
Coaster Type	Text or Short Text

4. Enter the data as shown in **Figure 6.4-A**.

5. Name and save the table as **FAVORITE COASTERS**.

6. Adjust the column widths so that all data displays properly.

7. Resave the table.

8. Delete the Coaster Type field.

9. Add a new field after the Height (ft) field. Name the new field Height (m). Identify the data type as Number.

10. Enter the data as shown in **Figure 6.4-B** into the new field.

11. Adjust the column widths so that all data displays properly.

12. Resave the table.

13. Carefully proofread your work for accuracy.

14. Print a copy of the table if required by your instructor.

15. Save and close the database file.

Figure 6.4-A

ID	Rank	Coaster Name	Amusement Park and Location	Height (ft)	Year Opened	Coaster Type
1	1	Fury 325	Carowinds, Charlotte, NC	325	2015	Steel
2	2	El Toro	Six Flags Great Adventure, Jackson, NJ	188	2006	Wood
3	3	Millennium Force	Cedar Point, Sandusky, OH	310	2000	Steel
4	4	The Voyage	Holiday World, Santa Claus, IN	173	2006	Wood
5	5	Boulder Dash	Lake Compounce, Bristol, CT	145	2000	Wood
6	6	Ravine Flyer II	Waldameer Park, Erie, PA	80	2008	Wood
7	7	Outlaw Run	Silver Dollar City, Branson, MO	107	2013	Wood
8	8	Banshee	Kings Island, Mason, OH	167	2014	Steel
9	9	Goliath	Six Flags Great America, Gurnee, IL	165	2014	Hybrid
10	10	Bizarro	Six Flags New England, Agawam, MA	208	2009	Steel
11	11	Maverick	Cedar Point, Sandusky, OH	105	2014	Steel
12	12	Phoenix	Knoebels, Elysburg, PA	78	1947	Wood
13	13	Intimidator	Carowinds, Charlotte, NC	232	2010	Steel
14	14	Diamondback	Kings Island, Mason, OH	230	2009	Steel
15	15	Texas Giant (New)	Six Flags Over Texas, Arlington, TX	143	2011	Hybrid

Figure 6.4-B

ID	Coaster Name	Height (m)
1	Fury 325	99
2	El Toro	55
3	Millennium Force	94
4	The Voyage	52
5	Boulder Dash	44
6	Ravine Flyer II	24
7	Outlaw Run	32
8	Banshee	50
9	Goliath	50
10	Bizarro	63
11	Maverick	32
12	Phoenix	23
13	Intimidator	70
14	Diamondback	70
15	Texas Giant (New)	43

Address Book 3

Working with Text and Formats

Overview

In this lesson, you will modify the appearance of data as well as use two methods for directly modifying data within a table. As a basic database will generally lack visual appeal, you can apply formatting changes, such as font size and color, in order to improve its appearance. Additionally, there are many ways to change data values within a database. In this lesson, you will use two of them. First, you will edit text directly in a field within a table in your database identical to the way you would edit data in a spreadsheet. Second, you will use Find and Replace to search for and automatically change data values.

In this lesson, you will use an existing database and modify its appearance by making changes to the font style, alignment, color, size—even which font is displayed. You will also learn how to use the Find and Replace command and to rearrange data by sorting it in ascending or descending order.

New Skills / TEKS

Applying Bold and Italics • Changing Font and Font Size • Changing Alignment • Changing Font Color • Using Find and Replace • Sorting Ascending and Descending

TEKS: 7.D.i, 7.D.ii, 7.E.i, 8.A.i, 8.C.i, 8.C.iii

Instructions

1. Open the **PARTNERSHIP** database file previously created in **Lesson 6.2**.
2. Name and save the database file as **PARTNERSHIP2**.
3. Rename the **MEMBERS** table as **NEW FORMATTING** and open the table.
4. Change the font style to bold and italic.
5. Change the font to Arial and the font size to 12 point.
6. Change the font color to dark blue, 4.
7. Change the alignment of the ID field to center.
8. Change the School/Institution for Nancy Brown to Springfield High School.
9. Using the Find and Replace feature, find the name Peter in the entire table and replace it with Paul.
10. Using the Find and Replace feature, find the name Nicole in the entire table and replace it with Nikki.
11. Sort the Last Name field in ascending order.

    NOTE: All table records move together when sorting a single column.
12. Sort the School/Institution field in descending order.

13. Adjust the column widths so that all data displays properly.

14. Resave the table.

15. Carefully proofread your work for accuracy.

16. Print a copy of the table if required by your instructor.

17. Save and close the database file.

Sales at the School Store

Working in Design View

Overview

School stores are a source of income for the associated student body. Your principal has asked you to create a database to store information about a sampling of 20 items currently being sold in the store. This information will be used to monitor sales.

In this lesson, you will create a database structure in Design View and enter data about a sampling of items sold in the school store in Datasheet View.

New Skills / TEKS

Creating Tables Using Design View

TEKS: 7.D.i, 7.D.ii, 7.E.i, 8.A.i, 8.C.i

Instructions

1. Using Microsoft Access, create a new database file.

2. Name and save the database file as **STORE**.

3. Create a new table in Design View.

4. Name and save the table as **STORE SALES**.

5. Set up the database table using the field names and data types provided below.

Database Structure	
Field Name	**Data Type**
Product Category	Text or Short Text
Product	Text or Short Text
Price	Currency
Units Sold	Number

6. In Datasheet View, enter the data as shown in **Figure 6.6-A**.

   HINT: You will be prompted to save the table once again. Click Yes.

7. Adjust the column widths so that all data displays properly.

8. Resave the table.

9. Carefully proofread your work for accuracy.

10. Print a copy of the table if required by your instructor.

11. Save and close the database file.

Figure 6.6-A

ID	Product Category	Product	Price	Units Sold
1	Clothing	Varsity Jacket	164.99	5
2	Supplies	Folders (25 Pack)	7.89	10
3	School Keepsakes	Class Ring	255.00	3
4	Miscellaneous	Backpack	21.44	2
5	Electronics	32 GB Flash Drive	12.97	15
6	Electronics	Graphing Calculator	124.33	1
7	Supplies	Black Pens (12-Pack)	9.00	5
8	School Keepsakes	Class Tag	288.00	1
9	Miscellaneous	Hand Sanitizer	2.97	10
10	Clothing	Hooded Sweatshirt	36.99	4
11	Electronics	Ear Buds	13.95	5
12	Miscellaneous	Adjustable Cap	20.39	2
13	Clothing	T-Shirt	19.99	6
14	Electronics	Bluetooth Headset	14.75	3
15	School Keepsakes	Water Bottle	16.95	5
16	Supplies	Colored Pencils (set of 24)	19.79	7
17	Miscellaneous	Tissues (3-Pack)	3.45	10
18	Clothing	Sweatpants	24.99	4
19	School Keepsakes	Senior Memory Book	23.50	4
20	Supplies	5-Subject Spiral Notebook (2-Pack)	5.67	12

Income

Editing Field Properties

Overview

In this lesson, you will edit field properties from within Design View so that entered data matches the correct data value format. For example, you can define a field that is intended to be used for pricing information as Currency and then limit the number of decimal values so that it only shows whole dollars and no cents. Also in this lesson, you will export data from your database to an external file. Databases offer numerous options for importing and exporting data in a database. One of these options is to simply export a table from within the database to an external Excel file. You will see that tables in a database are just like a standalone spreadsheet file.

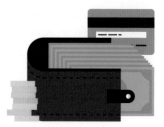

In this lesson, you will create a database structure in Design View and enter data about the median household income in 20 states for some recent years in Datasheet View. You will then export a table for use outside the database.

New Skills / TEKS

Adding a Field Description • Setting a Field Size • Inserting/Deleting Fields • Moving Fields • Naming and Creating Fields in Design View • Exporting a Table from a Database

TEKS: 7.D.i, 7.D.ii, 7.E.i, 8.A.i, 8.C.i

Instructions

1. Using Microsoft Access, create a new database file.
2. Name and save the database file as **INCOME**.
3. Create a new table in Design View.
4. Name and save the table as **MEDIAN INCOME**.
5. Set up the database table using the field names and data types provided below.

Database Structure		
Field Name	**Data Type**	**Description**
Rank	Text or Short Text	Median Household Income
State	Text or Short Text	Median Household Income
2012 Income	Currency	Median Household Income
2010 Income	Currency	Median Household Income
2009 Income	Currency	Median Household Income

6. Make the following field property changes:

   a. Change the Decimal Places of the Currency fields (2012 Income, 2010 Income, and 2009 Income) to 0.

   b. Change the Field Size of the State field to 2.

7. Insert a row above the 2009 Income field and name the new field 2014 Income. Change the data type to Currency, the Decimal Places to 0, and enter Median Household Income in the Description area.

8. Delete the row containing the 2012 Income field.

9. Move the 2014 Income field above the 2010 Income field.

10. Resave the table.

11. In Datasheet View, enter the data as shown in **Figure 6.7-A**.

    NOTE: Key the first state as Maryland. Notice that Access stops you from continuing to type after you enter the first two letters. This is because you changed the field size to 2. Be sure to type the two-letter state abbreviation when entering the states in your table.

12. Adjust the column widths so that all data displays properly.

13. Resave the table.

14. Export the Median Income table as an Excel spreadsheet.

    NOTE: Preserve formatting and layout of the data when exporting.

15. Carefully proofread your work for accuracy.

16. Print a copy of the table if required by your instructor.

17. Save and close the database file.

Figure 6.7-A

ID	Rank	State	2014 Income	2010 Income	2009 Income
1	1	MD	70004	69272	70545
2	2	AK	69825	68342	70378
3	3	CA	67458	67034	71595
4	4	CT	65753	66953	68460
5	5	DC	65124	63098	57214
6	6	MA	64859	62081	61401
7	7	NH	64712	63557	62731
8	8	VA	62881	61330	58233
9	9	HI	62814	59290	57936
10	10	MN	61814	58931	57021
11	11	NJ	60287	69860	79989
12	12	DE	57954	58548	60078
13	13	WA	57835	54616	52288
14	14	WY	56322	55430	56993
15	15	UT	55869	55117	56633
16	16	CO	55387	54659	56033
17	17	NY	55246	54119	55701
18	18	RI	53636	53966	56235
19	19	IL	53234	53341	56361
20	20	VT	52776	52664	53207
21		US	50502	50221	52029

Concerts

Applying Filters

Overview

Have you ever attended a live performance of one of your favorite musical performers? Concerts not only provide a completely different listening experience for fans, but can also be very lucrative for performers. The following information, found at pollstarpro.com, shows how much money musicians had earned by mid-year 2015.

In this lesson, you will create a database structure in Design View and enter data about the top grossing concerts at the mid-year mark in 2015 in Datasheet View. You will then apply a filter to see how many concerts exceeded a certain attendance mark.

New Skills / TEKS

Changing Data Types • Applying a Selection Filter • Using Toggle Filter • Formatting Number View

TEKS: 7.D.i, 7.D.ii, 7.E.i, 8.A.i, 8.C.i, 8.D.ii, 9.A.i

Instructions

1. Using Microsoft Access, create a new database file.
2. Name and save the database file as **CONCERTS**.
3. Create a new table in Design View.
4. Name and save the table as **TOP TOURS**.
5. Set up the database table using the field names and data types provided below.

Database Structure	
Field Name	**Data Type**
Rank	Text or Short Text
Artist	Text or Short Text
Number of Shows	Number
Total Tickets	Number
Gross in Millions of $	Text or Short Text

6. Make the following field property changes to the Number fields:
    a. Use the Format drop-down arrow and select Standard.
    b. Change the Decimal Places to 0.

7. Resave the table.

8. In Datasheet View, enter the data as shown in **Figure 6.8-A**.

9. Adjust the column widths so that all data displays properly.

10. Resave the table.

11. To retrieve data from the table, create a Selection Filter showing the tickets sold amounts that are Greater Than or Equal To 258,787.

12. Click on the Toggle Filter to see the original table and click again to see the filtered results.

13. Resave the table.

14. Carefully proofread your work for accuracy.

15. Print a copy of the table if required by your instructor.

16. Save and close the database file.

Figure 6.8-A

ID	Rank	Artist	Number of Shows	Total Tickets	Gross in Millions of $
1	1	The Rolling Stones	10	452041	80.7
2	2	Garth Brooks	74	1207109	79.9
3	3	Fleetwood Mac	41	525617	65.9
4	4	Kenny Chesney	33	691619	55.8
5	5	U2	21	372630	40.3
6	6	Maroon 5	30	452771	39.8
7	7	Neil Diamond	36	343439	37.7
8	8	Taylor Swift	10	309610	35.6
9	9	Elton John	35	232168	29.8
10	10	Bette Midler	26	223168	28.2
11	11	Cirque du Soleil - "Kurios"	156	298213	26.9
12	12	Luke Bryan	25	411633	25.9
13	13	Chris Brown	28	258787	25.4
14	14	Rush	22	287359	24.6
15	15	Eric Church	49	522260	24.4
16	16	Juan Gabriel	31	260878	24.1
17	17	Charlie Wilson	47	256945	23.4
18	18	Ed Sheeran	34	391369	23.4
19	19	Cirque du Soleil - "Varekai"	163	389891	23.4
20	20	New Kids On The Block	45	267141	21.9
21	21	Bob Seger & The Silver Bullet Band	27	250143	21.8
22	22	Billy Joel	13	242768	21.4
23	23	Kevin Hart	48	300805	20.9
24	24	Romeo Santos	24	236622	17.6
25	25	Shania Twain	15	191517	17.0

Multiple Oscar Winners

Editing Records

Overview

The Academy Awards is an annual ceremony hosted by the Academy of Motion Picture Arts and Sciences. Its purpose is to recognize excellence in a variety of categories, including Best Actor, Best Actress, Best Supporting Actor, and Best Supporting Actress. Forty performers have won two or more of these awards. The information for this database, found at Wikipedia.org, lists ten of these performers.

In this lesson, you will create a database structure in Design View and enter the names of 10 performers who have won two or more Oscars in Datasheet View.

New Skills / TEKS

Using Cut, Copy, and Paste

TEKS: 7.D.i, 7.D.ii, 7.E.i, 8.A.i, 8.C.i

Instructions

1. Using Microsoft Access, create a new database file.
2. Name and save the database file as **OSCARS**.
3. Create a new table in Design View.
4. Name and save the table as **MULTIPLE OSCARS**.
5. Set up the database table using the field names and data types provided below.

Database Structure	
Field Name	**Data Type**
First Name	Text or Short Text
Last Name	Text or Short Text

6. Resave the table.
7. In Datasheet View, enter the data as shown in **Figure 6.9-A** as follows:
   a. Key the first record, *Katharine Hepburn*.
   b. Copy and paste that record three times.
   c. Key the fifth record, *Daniel Day-Lewis*. Copy and paste that record two times.
   d. Key the eighth record, *Bette Davis*. Copy and paste that record one time.
   e. Continue this process until you have keyed (or copied and pasted) the remaining records shown.

8. You want to keep only the names of the people who have won three or more Oscars.

   a. Cut records 8 and 9.

   NOTE: You will see a message warning that you are about to delete 2 record(s). Click Yes. Notice that the ID numbers are also deleted.

   b. Cut records 10 and 11, 15 and 16, 20 and 21, 22 and 23.

9. Adjust the column widths so that all data displays properly.

10. Resave the table.

11. Carefully proofread your work for accuracy.

12. Print a copy of the table if required by your instructor.

13. Save and close the database file.

Figure 6.9-A

ID	First Name	Last Name
1	Katharine	Hepburn
2	Katharine	Hepburn
3	Katharine	Hepburn
4	Katharine	Hepburn
5	Daniel	Day-Lewis
6	Daniel	Day-Lewis
7	Daniel	Day-Lewis
8	Bette	Davis
9	Bette	Davis
10	Spencer	Tracy
11	Spencer	Tracy
12	Walter	Brennan
13	Walter	Brennan
14	Walter	Brennan
15	Marlon	Brando
16	Marlon	Brando
17	Jack	Nicholson
18	Jack	Nicholson
19	Jack	Nicholson
20	Dustin	Hoffman
21	Dustin	Hoffman
22	Tom	Hanks
23	Tom	Hanks
24	Meryl	Streep
25	Meryl	Streep
26	Meryl	Streep

Winter Olympics and Paralympics

Working with Queries

Overview

A key aspect of databases is the way in which data can be retrieved using what are called queries. Queries enable you to retrieve, filter, summarize, and perform calculations on retrieved data. When you create a simple query, you select which tables you want the data to come from and also which fields from within those tables. You can also select the results of another query to be used as input to a query. In this lesson, you will create and run a query and also sort the results of the query. Additionally in this lesson, you will see how two tables appear within the same database.

In this lesson, you will create a database that holds information about medal winners for the 2014 Winter Olympics and Paralympics and categorize the data by creating two tables within one database file. You will use the information in one table to create a query on the data. A query is a way to search for and compile data in a database.

New Skills / TEKS

Using Multiple Tables • Using the Query Wizard • Running a Query • Sorting Query Results

TEKS: 7.D.i, 7.D.ii, 7.E.i, 8.A.i, 8.C.i, 9.A.ii, 9.B.i

Instructions

1. Using Microsoft Access, create a new database file.

2. Name and save the database file as **OLYMPICS**.

3. Set up the database table using the field names and data types provided below.

Database Structure	
Field Name	**Data Type**
Rank	Number
Country	Text or Short Text
Gold	Number
Silver	Number
Bronze	Number
Total	Number

4. Enter the data as shown in **Figure 6.10-A**.

5. Name and save the table as **OLYMPIC MEDALS**.

6. Adjust the column widths so that all data displays properly.

7. Resave and close the table.

8. Create another table by copy/pasting the **OLYMPIC MEDALS** table (structure only).

9. Name and save the table as **PARALYMPIC MEDALS**.

10. Enter the data as shown in **Figure 6.10-B**.

11. Adjust the column widths so that all data displays properly.

12. Resave and close the table.

13. Using the Query Wizard and the **OLYMPIC MEDALS** table, create a query that shows only the rank, country, and number of Gold medals, then run the query.

14. Save the query as **OLYMPIC GOLD**.

15. Sort the query result to show the number of Gold medals in ascending order (lowest to highest).

16. Carefully proofread your work for accuracy.

17. Print a copy of the tables if required by your instructor.

18. Save and close the database file.

Figure 6.10-A

ID	Rank	Country	Gold	Silver	Bronze	Total
1	1	Russia	13	11	9	33
2	2	Norway	11	5	10	26
3	3	Canada	10	10	5	25
4	4	United States	9	7	12	28
5	5	Netherlands	8	7	9	24
6	6	Germany	8	6	5	19
7	7	Switzerland	6	3	2	11
8	8	Belarus	5	0	1	6
9	9	Austria	4	8	5	17
10	10	France	4	4	7	15
11	11	Poland	4	1	1	6
12	12	China	3	4	2	9
13	13	South Korea	3	3	2	8
14	14	Sweden	2	7	6	15
15	15	Czech Republic	2	4	2	8
16	16	Slovenia	2	2	4	8
17	17	Japan	1	4	3	8
18	18	Finland	1	3	1	5
19	19	Great Britain	1	1	2	4
20	20	Ukraine	1	0	1	2
21	21	Slovakia	1	0	0	1
22	22	Italy	0	2	6	8
23	23	Latvia	0	2	2	4
24	24	Australia	0	2	1	3
25	25	Croatia	0	1	0	1
26	26	Kazakhstan	0	0	1	1

Figure 6.10-B

ID	Rank	Country	Gold	Silver	Bronze	Total
1	1	Russia	30	28	22	80
2	2	Germany	9	5	1	15
3	3	Canada	7	2	7	16
4	4	Ukraine	5	9	11	25
5	5	France	5	3	4	12
6	6	Slovakia	3	2	2	7
7	7	Japan	3	1	2	6
8	8	United States	2	7	9	18
9	9	Austria	2	5	4	11
10	10	Great Britain	1	3	2	6
11	11	Norway	1	2	1	4
12	12	Sweden	1	2	1	4
13	13	Spain	1	1	1	3
14	14	Netherlands	1	0	0	1
15	15	Switzerland	1	0	0	1
16	16	Finland	0	1	0	1
17	17	New Zealand	0	1	0	1
18	18	Belarus	0	0	3	3
19	19	Australia	0	0	2	2

James Bond Movies

Specifying Criteria in Query Design

Overview

The year 2015 brought the release of the 24th official James Bond movie, *Spectre*. (There have also been three unofficial James Bond movies.) Some younger people may be surprised to learn that many other actors besides Daniel Craig have played James Bond in previous movies. The famous British Secret Service agent has now been played by six different actors spanning over four decades. Bond movies are famous for their thrills, exotic locations, gadgets, and villains.

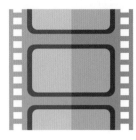

In this lesson, you will make a database and use it to create multiple queries about the different Bond eras using the Query Design View.

New Skills / TEKS

Using Query Design View • Viewing Queries

TEKS: 7.D.i, 7.D.ii, 7.E.i, 8.A.i, 8.C.i, 9.B.i

Instructions

1. Using Microsoft Access, create a new database file.

2. Name and save the database file as **BOND MOVIES**.

3. Create a new table in Design View.

4. Name and save the table as **ALL BOND MOVIES**.

5. Set up the database table using the field names and data types provided below.

Database Structure	
Field Name	**Data Type**
Year Released	Text or Short Text
Film Title	Text or Short Text
Actor	Text or Short Text

6. In Datasheet View, enter the data as shown in **Figure 6.11-A**.

7. Adjust the column widths so that all data displays properly.

8. Carefully proofread your work for accuracy.

9. Print a copy of the table if required by your instructor.

10. Resave and close the **ALL BOND MOVIES** table.

11. Use the Query Design View with the **ALL BOND MOVIES** table to create three new queries as follows:

    a. Query 1 will display a list of all the Bond movies and the years they were released (show the Year Released and Film Title fields only). Save the query as **YEAR TITLE**.

    b. Query 2 will display all Bond movies sorted from oldest to newest (show all three available fields in the query result). Save the query as **BY YEAR**.

    c. Query 3 will display all Bond movies starring Sean Connery (show all three available fields in the query result). Save the query as **CONNERY MOVIES**.

12. Print the query results if required by your instructor.

13. Save and close the database file.

Figure 6.11-A

JAMES BOND MOVIES DATA TO INPUT							
Record # 1			**Record # 9**			**Record # 17**	
Year Released	1962		Year Released	1989		Year Released	1979
Film Title	Dr. No		Film Title	License to Kill		Film Title	Moonraker
Actor	Sean Connery		Actor	Timothy Dalton		Actor	Roger Moore
Record # 2			**Record # 10**			**Record # 18**	
Year Released	1973		Year Released	1997		Year Released	2002
Film Title	Live and Let Die		Film Title	Tomorrow Never Dies		Film Title	Die Another Day
Actor	Roger Moore		Actor	Pierce Brosnan		Actor	Pierce Brosnan
Record # 3			**Record # 11**			**Record # 19**	
Year Released	2012		Year Released	1964		Year Released	1967
Film Title	Skyfall		Film Title	Goldfinger		Film Title	You Only Live Twice
Actor	Daniel Craig		Actor	Sean Connery		Actor	Sean Connery
Record # 4			**Record # 12**			**Record # 20**	
Year Released	1987		Year Released	1969		Year Released	2015
Film Title	The Living Daylights		Film Title	On Her Majesty's Secret Service		Film Title	Spectre
Actor	Timothy Dalton		Actor	George Lazenby		Actor	Daniel Craig
Record # 5			**Record # 13**			**Record # 21**	
Year Released	1995		Year Released	1977		Year Released	1981
Film Title	GoldenEye		Film Title	The Spy Who Loved Me		Film Title	For Your Eyes Only
Actor	Pierce Brosnan		Actor	Roger Moore		Actor	Roger Moore
Record # 6			**Record # 14**			**Record # 22**	
Year Released	2006		Year Released	1999		Year Released	1971
Film Title	Casino Royale		Film Title	The World Is Not Enough		Film Title	Diamonds Are Forever
Actor	Daniel Craig		Actor	Pierce Brosnan		Actor	Sean Connery
Record # 7			**Record # 15**			**Record # 23**	
Year Released	1963		Year Released	2008		Year Released	1983
Film Title	From Russia With Love		Film Title	Quantum of Solace		Film Title	Octopussy
Actor	Sean Connery		Actor	Daniel Craig		Actor	Roger Moore
Record # 8			**Record # 16**			**Record # 24**	
Year Released	1974		Year Released	1965		Year Released	1985
Film Title	The Man With the Golden Gun		Film Title	Thunderball		Film Title	A View to a Kill
Actor	Roger Moore		Actor	Sean Connery		Actor	Roger Moore

Cars

Creating a Form

Overview

One of the more beneficial uses of databases is the ability to create and use forms as a method of inputting data into the database as well as more easily viewing data records. Forms allow you to display data in a number of different form views, such as in columnar or tabular format among others. When you create a form, you select which tables or queries you want to use for the data in the form as well as the type of view for the form. Formatting of fields and the placement of fields on a form can also be modified. Also in this lesson, you will create a query that, in addition to showing and sorting data in selected fields, will use criteria to determine if a data record will be displayed in the result.

In this lesson, you will create a database that will be used to hold data about the top 20 best-selling cars for 2015 and use that information to create a report on the cars with the highest growth in sales from 2014 to 2015.

New Skills / TEKS

Using Criteria to Filter Records • Using the Form Wizard

TEKS: 7.D.i, 7.D.ii, 7.E.i, 8.A.i, 8.C.i, 8.C.ii, 9.B.i

Instructions

1. Using Microsoft Access, create a new database file.
2. Name and save the database file as **CARS**.
3. Set up the database table using the field names and data types provided below.

Database Structure	
Field Name	**Data Type**
Rank	Number
Best-Selling Car	Text or Short Text
2015 Sales	Number
2014 Sales	Number
% Change	Number

4. Name and save the table as **BEST-SELLING CARS**.

5. Change the Field Properties for the % Change field as follows:

    a. Change the Field Size to Double.

    b. Change the Format to Percent.

    c. Change the Decimal Places to 1.

6. Enter the data as shown in **Figure 6.12-A**.

7. Adjust the column widths so that all data displays properly.

8. Carefully proofread your work for accuracy.

9. Resave and close the table.

10. Create a query using the **BEST-SELLING CARS** table to show only cars with a % Change greater than 0.

11. Save the query as **HIGHEST SALES CARS**.

12. Using the Form Wizard and the **HIGHEST SALES CARS** query, create a Columnar Form to show only the Rank, Best-Selling Car, and % Change fields.

13. Save the form as **GREATEST SALES GROWTH**.

14. Click on the record arrows at the bottom of the screen to scroll through the forms one-by-one.

15. Print a copy of the form page(s) if required by your instructor.

16. Save and close the database file.

Figure 6.12-A

ID	Rank	Best-Selling Car	2015 Sales	2014 Sales	% Change
1	1	Toyota Camry	326330	334978	-2.6
2	2	Honda Accord	264814	304382	-13
3	3	Honda Civic	249749	253430	-1.5
4	4	Toyota Corolla	278742	258805	7.7
5	5	Ford Fusion	231475	240585	-3.8
6	6	Nissan Altima	262424	256935	2.1
7	7	Hyundai Elantra	193962	176403	10
8	8	Nissan Versa	109832	110272	-0.4
9	9	Chevrolet Malibu	147161	148574	-1
10	10	Hyundai Sonata	157680	164934	-4.4
11	11	Subaru Outback	108419	97266	11.5
12	12	Nissan Sentra	154270	141216	9.2
13	13	Chevrolet Cruze	177970	208114	-14.5
14	14	Kia Soul	112683	115579	-2.5
15	15	Ford Focus	163864	176156	-7
16	16	Kia Optima	118301	122646	-3.5
17	17	Chrysler 200	147073	75142	95.7
18	18	Toyota Prius	89812	110455	-18.7
19	19	Ford Mustang	96225	59831	60.8
20	20	Chevrolet Impala	85466	107162	-20.2

Entertainment Data Warehouse

Creating a Report

Overview

Your company maintains a number of entertainment-related databases containing a large amount of historical and current entertainment information, from movies to songs to books. You have been asked to start building a data warehouse containing the company's entertainment information so that reports and other data analysis activities can be performed. In this lesson, you will populate the data warehouse by importing data from another database. Importing data into a database is simply a matter of selecting which table you would like to import from the other database. Since one of the primary purposes of a data warehouse is for it to be used for data reporting, you'll create and print a report as part of this lesson. When you create a report, you select which tables or queries you want to use as data for the report and then any grouping, sorting, and layout you would like to have applied to the report data output. By using design view, you can apply further customization to generate and print impressive, professional-looking reports.

In this lesson, you will build a data warehouse containing entertainment data. You will then use the data warehouse to create and run a report showing performers who have won Entertainer of the Year more than once from 2000 through 2015.

New Skills / TEKS

Using Find Duplicates Query • Using the Report Wizard • Using the External Data Wizard

TEKS: 7.D.i, 7.D.ii, 7.E.i, 8.A.i, 8.B.i, 8.D.i, 8.D.ii, 9.B.i, 9.C.i, 9.C.ii

Instructions

1. Using Microsoft Access, create a new database file.
2. Name and save the database file as **AWARDS**.
3. Set up the database table using the field names and data types provided below.

Database Structure	
Field Name	**Data Type**
Award Year	Text or Short Text
Entertainer of the Year	Text or Short Text
Male Vocalist of the Year	Text or Short Text
Female Vocalist of the Year	Text or Short Text
Song of the Year	Text or Short Text

4. Enter the data as shown in **Figure 6.13-A**.

5. Name and save the table as **AWARD WINNERS**.

6. Adjust the column widths so that all data displays properly.

7. Carefully proofread your work for accuracy.

8. Save and close the **AWARDS** database file.

9. Using Microsoft Access, open the database file **CONCERTS** created in **Lesson 6.8**.

10. Name and save the database as **ENTERTAINMENT DATA WAREHOUSE**.

11. Import the **AWARD WINNERS** table from the **AWARDS** database into the **ENTERTAINMENT DATA WAREHOUSE** database using the External Data wizard.

    NOTE: When using the External Data wizard, be sure to select the TABLES tab to see the available tables in the **AWARDS** database for importing.

12. The **ENTERTAINMENT DATA WAREHOUSE** is now ready to be used to generate and run reports.

13. Using the Query Wizard, Find Duplicates Query Wizard, and the **AWARD WINNERS** table, create a query to show only performers who have won Entertainer of the Year more than once.

14. Then, select Entertainer of the Year from the list of fields that may have duplicate data and move the field to the Duplicate-value fields box.

15. Then, select Award Year as an additional field to display and move the field to the Additional query fields box.

16. Save the query as **ENTERTAINERS OF THE YEAR**.

17. Sort the Year field in ascending order (A to Z).

18. Print a copy of the table if required by your instructor.

19. Using the Report Wizard and the **AWARD WINNERS** table, create a report using the following parameters:

    a. Select all fields (not including the ID field)

    b. No grouping

    c. Sort by Award Year (Ascending)

    d. Set layout to Tabular

20. Save the report as **AWARD WINNERS BY YEAR**.

21. Print a copy of the report and both tables in the data warehouse if required by your instructor.

22. Save and close the database file.

Figure 6.13-A

ID	Award Year	Entertainer of the Year	Male Vocalist of the Year	Female Vocalist of the Year	Song of the Year
1	2015	Luke Bryan	Chris Stapleton	Miranda Lambert	"Girl Crush"
2	2014	Luke Bryan	Blake Shelton	Miranda Lambert	"Follow Your Arrow"
3	2013	George Strait	Blake Shelton	Miranda Lambert	"I Drive Your Truck"
4	2012	Blake Shelton	Blake Shelton	Miranda Lambert	"Over You"
5	2011	Taylor Swift	Blake Shelton	Miranda Lambert	"If I Die Young"
6	2010	Brad Paisley	Blake Shelton	Miranda Lambert	"The House That Built Me"
7	2009	Taylor Swift	Brad Paisley	Taylor Swift	"In Color"
8	2008	Kenny Chesney	Brad Paisley	Carrie Underwood	"Stay"
9	2007	Kenny Chesney	Brad Paisley	Carrie Underwood	"Give It Away"
10	2006	Kenny Chesney	Keith Urban	Carrie Underwood	"Believe"
11	2005	Keith Urban	Keith Urban	Gretchen Wilson	"Whiskey Lullaby"
12	2004	Kenny Chesney	Keith Urban	Martina McBride	"Live Like You Were Dying"
13	2003	Alan Jackson	Alan Jackson	Martina McBride	"Three Wooden Crosses"
14	2002	Alan Jackson	Alan Jackson	Martina McBride	"Where Were You (When the World Stopped Turning)"
15	2001	Tim McGraw	Toby Keith	Lee Ann Womack	"Murder on Music Row"
16	2000	Dixie Chicks	Tim McGraw	Faith Hill	"I Hope You Dance"

Graduation Announcements

Creating Mailing Labels

Overview

It turns out that helping your mother convert her paper address book into a database is going to help you! Graduation is just a couple of months away and it's time to get announcements ready to mail to relatives and friends.

In this lesson, you will use the Friends and Relatives database you created to generate mailing labels for your announcements by creating address queries for each table and combining them to make the labels.

New Skills / TEKS

Using the Label Wizard

TEKS: 7.D.i, 7.D.ii, 7.E.i, 8.A.i, 8.C.i, 9.B.i

Instructions

1. Using Microsoft Access, create a new database file.
2. Name and save the database file as **FRIENDS AND RELATIVES**.
3. Set up the database table using the data types and field names provided below.

Database Structure	
Field Name	**Data Type**
First Name	Text or Short Text
Last Name	Text or Short Text
Street Address	Text or Short Text
City	Text or Short Text
State	Text or Short Text
Zip Code	Text or Short Text
Telephone	Text or Short Text
Birthdate	Date

4. Name and save the table as **FRIENDS INFO**.
5. Enter the data as shown in **Figure 6.14-A**.
6. Adjust the column widths so that all data displays properly.
7. Carefully proofread your work for accuracy.
8. Resave and close the table.

9. Using Microsoft Access, create a new database file.

10. Name and save the database file as **GRADUATION**.

11. Import the **FRIENDS INFO** table you created in the database file named **FRIENDS AND RELATIVES** earlier in this lesson.

12. Create a query using the imported **FRIENDS INFO** table that displays the First Name, Last Name, Street Address, City, State, and Zip Code fields.

13. Save the first query as **FRIENDS ADDRESS**.

14. Proofread your work for accuracy.

15. Using the Label Wizard, create mailing labels and include the First Name, Last Name, Address, City, State, and Zip Code fields on the labels.

    NOTE: Use default values unless otherwise indicated.

    HINT: Arrange fields in a proper address format in the Label Wizard.

16. Sort the query result by Last Name.

17. Save the label report as **LABELS ADDRESS LIST**. Notice the "See the labels as they will look printed" button is selected.

18. Print a copy of the labels if required by your instructor.

19. Save and close the database file.

Figure 6.14-A

First Name	Last Name	Street Address	City	State	Zip Code	Telephone	Birthdate
John	Elliott	143 E. H St.	Upland	CA	91786	951 5551456	6/1/1950
Mary	Smith	982 Main Ave.	Baltimore	MD	21270	410 5559988	12/25/1949
DeWayne	Clark	8372 S. 1st St.	Upland	CA	91786	909 5550372	4/13/1945
Bill	Jones	94832 Nelson Rd.	Claremont	CA	91711	909 5552546	5/29/1956
Luisa	Hidalgo	730 Baseline Rd.	Claremont	CA	91711	951 5557635	8/30/1972
Fatima	Hakim	44 Township Dr.	Cincinnati	OH	45236	513 5554422	2/14/1938
Esther	Goldman	9373 W. 22nd St.	Upland	CA	91786	909 5558374	1/22/1952
Jorge	Sanchez	1025 Lilac Ln.	Upland	CA	91786	951 5551989	7/23/1963
Bette	Harrison	3522 Shiloh Dr.	Fischers	IN	46038	317 5553376	4/10/1974
Marie	LaRue	694 Wilson St.	Ontario	CA	91762	909 5550192	9/17/1980
Ralph	Taylor	2983 7th Ave.	Upland	CA	91786	909 5553355	5/2/1951
Steven	Wong	888 Hamilton St.	Ontario	CA	91762	909 5553874	11/10/1965

TechieTs.com

Determining the Database Requirements for a Business

Overview

TechieTs.com is a new startup company that manufactures T-shirts imprinted with technology-related themes to sell online. As the Database Specialist for this company, you will create an online catalog database containing information that is based on the TechieTs.com business requirements.

In this lesson, you will determine the company requirements for an online catalog database, design the database structure, and create the database.

New Skills / TEKS

Designing and Creating a Database Based on a Business's Requirements

TEKS: 7.D.i, 7.D.ii, 7.E.i, 7.G.i, 7.H.i, 8.A.i, 8.C.i

Instructions

1. Review the business requirements provided in **Figure 6.15-A**.
2. Using Microsoft Access, create a new database file.
3. Name and save the database file as **TECHIETS**.
4. Design and create the structure of the database by defining the fields, data types, and field descriptions based on the business requirements provided in **Figure 6.15-A**.
5. Create a table based on your database structure.
6. Name and save the table as **CATALOG**.
7. Create a form titled **CATALOG FORM** to use for entering data into the **CATALOG** table.
8. Open the **CATALOG FORM** and enter a minimum of 10 records containing fictitious, "but real" data.
9. Using the form, enter different T-shirts that your company will be selling.
10. Adjust the column widths so that all data displays properly.
11. Carefully proofread your work for accuracy.
12. Print a copy of the database if required by your instructor.
13. Save and close the database file.

Figure 6.15-A

TechieTs.com Database Business Requirements

You have landed your dream job as the Database Specialist for TechieTs.com, a new online startup company that manufactures and sells T-shirts imprinted with technology-based themes, such as Geeks Rock! and I Love Technology! Your primary duty is to design and maintain an online catalog database. You will determine the fields, database structure, and field descriptions for the database.

As you design the database structure, be sure to include fields for: **item number**, **message category** (cell phone, computer, social media, humor), **size** (S, M, L, XL - Adult, Youth, Toddler), **color** (provide color selections), **gender**, **price**, **description**, **website product link**, and **date** added to the catalog.

Unit 7
Spreadsheets

Part 1 Introduction to Spreadsheets

Hands-on Lessons:

What are Spreadsheets?

A spreadsheet is a document organized into rows and columns in which data can be manipulated and used in calculations. A spreadsheet will not only organize information, but will complete a variety of mathematical formulas for the user, such as calculating totals, averages, percentages, budgets, and complex financial and scientific formulas. Spreadsheet software was first developed to complete accounting tasks, but today it has countless purposes for both personal use and for business.

Spreadsheet software can be used for a simple table that organizes a weekly fundraiser schedule, or it can be used for a complex series of workbooks that arrange and calculate financial information for a major company. With spreadsheets, creating business models, graphs, charts, and reports becomes a quick and efficient task.

Why Learn Spreadsheets?

Along with word processing software and databases, spreadsheet software is commonly used by businesses. Spreadsheets simplify many complicated tasks. For instance, a student could use spreadsheet software to keep track of her grades in a course, or the manager of a small business could use it to keep track of salary expenses for his employees. With spreadsheets, users have the ability to enter data, perform calculations, analyze results, and display this information easily through graphs, charts, and infographics.

Using spreadsheet software requires you to add text and data using an input device, such as a keyboard. In this unit, you will not only improve your knowledge of spreadsheets, but by practicing proper touch typing techniques on the numeric keypad, you will improve your ability to input data efficiently and accurately.

Types of Spreadsheet Software

One of the most popular spreadsheet programs for businesses is Microsoft Excel because of its powerful features, which include sorting and filtering data and formatting numbers and graphs. Another option is Google Sheets, a free spreadsheets application in which users create and edit spreadsheets online. While Google Sheets may be more limited than Microsoft Excel in terms of its robust features, this application is the perfect tool for collaboration and sharing since multiple people can work simultaneously on the same spreadsheet. Before deciding which spreadsheet software to use, it is important to consider what kind of spreadsheet needs to be created and what features are required to create it.

The Most Popular Spreadsheet Software

 Microsoft Excel is a widely used spreadsheet software designed by Microsoft. Excel is a component of the Microsoft Office Suite, but can be used as a stand-alone product. Released in 1982, Excel allows users to organize, format, and calculate data with formulas broken up by rows and columns. Excel works with Windows and Macintosh operating systems.

 Numbers is a spreadsheet software that was developed by Apple, Inc. It is part of the iWork productivity suite, and runs on Apple's OS X and iOS operating systems. The first version of Numbers was released in 2007. Numbers uses what is known as a free-form "canvas" approach that demotes tables to one of many different media types placed on a page.

 Google Sheets is a free web-based application in which spreadsheets can be created, edited, and stored online. Files can be accessed from any computer with an Internet connection and a full-featured web browser. Google Sheets was released to the public in 2007, and is integrated with Google Drive.

Identifying Parts of a Standard Spreadsheet

A spreadsheet is where data is entered, organized, and calculated. Spreadsheets are divided into columns and rows. The intersection point of a column and row is a cell. Data is entered and stored in individual cells. The illustration in **Figure 7.0** below is from Microsoft Excel. Depending on the spreadsheet software being used, visual references will vary.

Figure 7.0

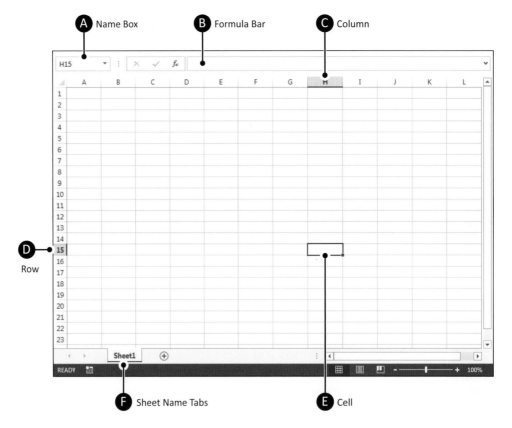

SPREADSHEET KEY

A Name Box
Displays the name or location of the active cell

B Formula Bar
Where data and formulas are entered and edited, which then appears in the active cell

C Column
Vertical cells that are labeled by letters

D Row
Horizontal cells that are labeled by numbers

E Cells
The intersection of a row and column which is identified by a letter and number

F Sheet Name Tabs
Can be added or deleted, renamed, and reordered

Hardware Requirements for Spreadsheet Applications

In this unit, you will create a series of spreadsheets that require the use of spreadsheet software. As with all software applications, there are certain hardware requirements necessary to complete this task.

Hardware refers to the physical elements of a computer, so in this case, in order for you to use spreadsheet software, you will need some type of computer to run the software, such as a desktop computer, tablet, or mobile phone. Some input devices that you would need include a mouse and a keyboard. Of course, if you are going to print any of your spreadsheets, you will need a printer. If the spreadsheet software requires access to the Internet, such as Google Sheets, then a router and Internet connection are required.

A LOOK AHEAD TO YOUR FINAL ASSESSMENT

Pitch It!

As a final assessment (Unit 10), you will be divided into teams and "pitch" a new product idea to your instructor. This assessment will give you exciting, first-hand knowledge of how spreadsheets can be used as a tool for creating and organizing information. Pay close attention to the skills you will be learning in this unit, as you will draw on them again in the "Pitch It!" final assessment.

SOFTWARE NOTES

If you encounter a skill or feature that is not available in the software you are using, use an equivalent feature or adjust your document accordingly.

Unless otherwise stated, use the default font of the spreadsheets software being used. For example, the default font in Microsoft Excel is Calibri, while the default font in Google Sheets is Arial.

It is important to note that all of the lessons in this unit are written in a generic format and in most cases, the skills required can be achieved using any type of spreadsheet software.

Generation What?

Creating Your First Workbook

Overview

Spreadsheet programs and applications are powerful tools that allow a user to enter data, perform calculations, analyze results, and display information in a variety of ways. Spreadsheet files are made up of worksheets that can be many pages. Data is organized in rows and columns, and cells can be referenced as part of mathematical calculations. Whether you are keeping a budget, creating an invoice, or formatting a financial report, spreadsheets make it easy to work with different kinds of data.

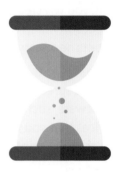

In this lesson, you will become familiar with your spreadsheet application interface while creating, saving, and printing your first spreadsheet file that showcases the various generation names, such as Millennials and Generation X.

New Skills / TEKS

Creating, Naming, and Saving a Workbook • Identifying Rows, Columns, and Cell Addresses • Previewing and Printing a Worksheet • Closing a Worksheet

TEKS: 6.B.ii

Instructions

1. Create a new spreadsheet.
2. Practice getting to know more about available options in the toolbars by clicking on various menus or drop-downs to see what you can find.
3. Use the default font and size of the spreadsheet software being used.
4. Type the data as shown in **Figure 7.1-A**. Notice how the cell address changes with each new entry.
5. Name and save the spreadsheet as **GENERATION**.
6. Carefully proofread your work for accuracy.
7. Be sure any changes have been saved.
8. Print preview and be sure that all cells containing data will be included in printing. Adjust the print area if necessary.
9. Print a copy of the spreadsheet if required by your instructor.
10. Save and close the spreadsheet.

Figure 7.1-A

	A	B	C	D
1	GENERATION WHAT?			
2				
3	Name	Born Start	Born End	Age in 2020
4	Millennial	1981	1997	23–39
5	X	1965	1980	40–50
6	Boomers	1946	1964	56–74
7	Silent	1928	1945	75–92
8	Greatest	1910	1927	93–110
9				
10	STUDENT NAME			

NBA Hall of Fame

Working with Columns and Rows

Overview

Inevitably, there will be times when the data you enter into your spreadsheet will be too large to fit in the default column width or row height. Changing font sizes and including large amounts of data within a single cell requires column and row resizing. Resizing columns and rows improves the appearance of your worksheet and makes it easier for you to manipulate data. Large amounts of text can be contained within a cell if the row is high enough and text wrapping is activated.

In this lesson, you will create a spreadsheet that showcases a roster of NBA Hall of Fame players, the year they were enshrined, their date of birth, and a highlight from their biography.

New Skills / TEKS

Resizing Rows and Columns • Centering Text Vertically in a Cell • Wrapping Text in a Cell • Setting the Print Area

TEKS: 6.B.ii

Instructions

1. Create a new spreadsheet.

2. Use the default font and size of the spreadsheet software being used.

3. Format the width of column A to 20 and column D to 35.

4. Format the height of row 1 to 50.

5. Format column D to wrap the text within each cell.

6. Type the data as shown in **Figure 7.2-A**.

7. Save the spreadsheet as **NBAHALL**.

8. Resize columns B and C so that all data is displayed.

9. Center the text in cell A1 vertically.

10. Carefully proofread your work for accuracy.

11. Be sure any changes have been saved.

12. Set the print area of the spreadsheet to include cells A1–D10.

13. Print preview and be sure that all cells containing data will be included in printing. Adjust the print area if necessary.

14. Print a copy of the spreadsheet if required by your instructor.

Figure 7.2-A

	A	B	C	D
1	NBA Hall of Fame			
2				
3	Player	Year Enshrined	Date of Birth	Biography Notes
4	Kareem Abdul-Jabbar	1995	4/16/47	From the time he stepped on the court as Lewis Alcindor at Power Memorial High School in his native New York City, to the years he owned college basketball at UCLA, to the time he retired as the NBA's all-time leader in nine statistical categories including the most points in NBA history, the 7-foot-2 superstar established himself as one of basketball's most talented and recognizable figures.
5	Nathaniel Archibald	1991	9/2/48	When Nate Archibald was selected in the second round of the 1970 NBA draft by the Cincinnati Royals, it was hoped the 6-foot-1 guard from the University of Texas–El Paso could handle the NBA game and stay in the league a few seasons.
6	Paul J. Arizin	1978	4/9/28	In high school he didn't try out for basketball until his senior year, and then he failed to make the team. Attending Villanova University without a scholarship, Arizin's hard work and perseverence paid off, earning him a place on the team as a sophomore.
7	Charles Barkley	2006	2/20/63	His larger-than-life personality made Barkley one of the game's greatest characters, while his hard-nosed style of play made him pound-for-pound and inch-for-inch one of the game's greatest rebounders.
8	Larry J. Bird	1998	12/7/56	Bird got his start in a small Indiana town, where he led Springs Valley High School to the state sectional championship. In 1979, Bird led Indiana State to the NCAA Championship Game.
9				
10	STUDENT NAME			

So You Think You Can Dance Season Winners

Editing Basics

Overview

Just like words in a word processing document, data in a spreadsheet can be cut, copied, and pasted to other places in your file. Shortcut keys like CTRL+C, CTRL+X, and CTRL+V are available in most spreadsheet applications. Using the keyboard can ensure that you are selecting and manipulating the exact data that you want, but your mouse can assist, too. Be aware of how your mouse pointer changes in a spreadsheet depending on what you are hovering over. For example, hovering over the column or row labels makes the mouse a resizing tool, whereas hovering over the edge of a selected cell turns the mouse into a drag-and-drop device.

In this lesson, you will create a spreadsheet that lists the winners of the popular television show *So You Think You Can Dance* and use shortcut keys to edit the worksheet.

New Skills / TEKS

Inserting and Deleting Rows • Selecting Cells • Using Cut • Using Copy • Using Paste

TEKS: 6.B.ii

Instructions

1. Create a new spreadsheet.

2. Use the default font and size of the spreadsheet software being used.

3. Type the data as shown in **Figure 7.3-A**. Resize all columns so that all data is displayed.

4. Save the spreadsheet as **SYTYCD**.

5. Copy and paste the following data to the following cells:

    a. Copy cell A3 to cells C13, C16, and C19.

    b. Copy cell A4 to cells C14 and C18.

    c. Copy cell A5 to cells C12 and C15.

    d. Copy cell A6 to cells C10 and C17.

    e. Copy cell A7 to cell C11.

6. Insert a new row between rows 13 and 14.

7. Cut and paste the data for Jeanine Mason into the new row after Joshua Allen. The season numbers should now be in order.

8. Delete rows 3–8. There should now be only one blank row between the title and the column headings.

9. Resize all columns so that all data is displayed.

10. Carefully proofread your work for accuracy.

11. Be sure any changes have been saved.

12. Print preview and be sure that all cells containing data will be included in printing. Adjust the print area if necessary.

13. Print a copy of the spreadsheet if required by your instructor.

Figure 7.3-A

	A	B	C	D	E	F	G	H
1	SYTYCD Season Winners							
2								
3	appearing							
4	dancing							
5	studying							
6	teaching							
7	winning							
8								
9	Winner's Name	Season	Now	Details				
10	Nick Lazzarini	1		teaching master classes in jazz and musical theatre				
11	Benji Schwimmer	2		1st place 5X at US Open Swing Dance Championship				
12	Sabra Johnson	3		spent a year with the Cedar Lake Contemporary Ballet				
13	Joshua Allen	4		appearing on television and in movies				
14	Russell Ferguson	6		performing in the dance crew Sidestreet				
15	Lauren Froderman	7		focusing on college				
16	Melanie Moore	8		starring as Peter Pan in "Finding Neverland"				
17	Chehon Wespi-Tschopp	9		operating a touring dance convention				
18	Amy Yakima	10		dancing with Shaping Sound Dance Company				
19	Jeanine Mason	5		starring in several television shows				
20								
21	STUDENT NAME							

Best-Selling Books

Editing Your Workbook

Overview

Viewing a worksheet in the most optimal way can save you time when working with data in a spreadsheet. When working with large amounts of data, you may want to be able to see column or row headings all the time as you move down and across the sheet. Freeze panes lock certain rows and columns and allow you to scroll through the content of your file while still seeing the frozen cells. This will ensure that you are entering or analyzing information that corresponds to the visible columns or rows.

In this lesson, you will create a spreadsheet that showcases a list of books that have sold over 100 million copies.

New Skills / TEKS

Inserting and Deleting Columns • Freezing Panes • Adding Worksheets • Renaming a Worksheet

TEKS: 6.B.ii

Instructions

1. Create a new spreadsheet.

2. Use the default font and size of the spreadsheet software being used.

3. Type the data as shown in **Figure 7.4-A**.

4. Resize all columns so that all data is displayed.

5. Save the spreadsheet as **BESTBOOKS**.

6. Copy and paste cell C4 into cells C5–C11.

7. Insert a new column to the left of column A.

8. Starting in cell A4, number each book 1–8.

9. Change the data in cell D7 to "French" and cell D10 to "Chinese."

10. Rename Sheet1 as **Book and Author**.

11. Freeze the panes in the first and second columns of the spreadsheet.

12. Resize all columns so that all data is displayed.

13. Select the entire worksheet and copy to a new sheet.

14. Rename Sheet2 as **Year Published**.

15. Delete columns C, D, and F in the **Year Published** sheet. Do not just clear the contents.

16. Carefully proofread your work for accuracy.

17. Be sure any changes have been saved.

18. Print preview both spreadsheets and be sure that all cells containing data will be included in printing. Adjust the print area if necessary.

19. Print a copy of the workbook if required by your instructor.

Figure 7.4-A

	A	B	C	D	E
1	Best-Selling Books				
2					
3	Title	Author	Language	Year	Sales
4	A Tale of Two Cities	Charles Dickens	English	1859	200 million
5	The Lord of the Rings	J.R.R. Tolkien		1954	150 million
6	The Hobbit	J.R.R. Tolkien		1937	140.6 million
7	The Little Prince	Antoine de Saint-Exupéry		1943	140 million
8	Harry Potter and the Philosopher's Stone	J.K. Rowling		1997	107 million
9	And Then There Were None	Agatha Christie		1939	100 million
10	Dream of the Red Chamber	Cao Xuequin		1754	100 million
11	She: A History of Adventure	H. Rider Haggard		1887	100 million
12					
13	STUDENT NAME				

Best-Selling Books 2

Retrieving and Proofing Your Worksheet

Overview

Spreadsheet data, like any document, should always be reviewed for spelling and grammatical mistakes. Although it is important to always proofread your work for errors, you can give yourself a head start with the built-in spelling and grammar check feature of the spreadsheet application you are using. It will find unintentional mistakes in your work and offer suggestions for how the error can be rectified. A built-in thesaurus can propose words to better describe what you are writing.

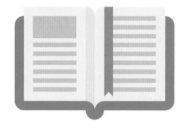

In this lesson, you will update a spreadsheet that was created in a previous lesson, spell check it, and use the thesaurus to find alternative words.

New Skills / TEKS

Revising, Renaming, and Saving an Existing Workbook • Using Spell Check and Thesaurus • Changing Page Orientation • Adjusting Page Scaling

TEKS: 6.B.ii

Instructions

1. Open the file **BESTBOOKS** previously created in **Lesson 7.4**.

2. Save the workbook as **BESTBOOKS2**.

3. In the sheet named Book and Author, type the new data as shown in columns G–J in **Figure 7.5-A**.

4. Resize all columns so that all data is displayed.

5. Use spell check to review the spelling of the text in your spreadsheet and correct any errors.

6. Select cell J4 and use the thesaurus to find an alternative word for the one provided.

7. Repeat step 6 and replace each word in cells J5–J11.

8. Carefully proofread your work for accuracy.

9. Be sure any changes have been saved.

10. Print preview and be sure that all cells containing data will be included in printing. Adjust the print area if necessary.

11. Change the page layout orientation to landscape and adjust the page scaling to fit to one page.

12. Print a copy of the spreadsheet if required by your instructor.

Figure 7.5-A

	G	H	I	J
1				
2				
3	Character	Character	Character	Reader's Opinion
4	Sydney Carton	Charles Darnay	Lucie Manette	Brilliant
5	Frodo Baggins	Samwise	Merry	Captivating
6	Bilbo Baggins	Gandalf	Thorin	Wonderful
7	The Rose	The Prince		Charming
8	Harry Potter	Ron Weasley	Hermione Granger	Enchanting
9	Anthony James Marston	Mrs. Ethel Rogers	Thomas Rogers	Exciting
10	Jia Baoyu	Lin Daiyu	Xue Boachai	Emotional
11	Horace Holly	Leo Vincey	Ayesha	Informative

Amazon

Using Headers and Footers

Overview

The many options available for printing a spreadsheet can really enhance the appearance of your work. Printing options include printing gridlines, row and column headings, as well as headers and footers. Including a header or footer in your spreadsheet is a great way to identify printed work without having to interfere with spreadsheet data. Your header and footer will appear on every printed page and can include any information you would like. You can customize what information will appear left aligned, center aligned, and right aligned in both the header and the footer. Using page numbers keeps pages organized when printing your work. Altering a spreadsheet's margins can make the printed copy more visually appealing, too.

In this lesson, you will create a spreadsheet that contains a custom header and footer with page numbers. The spreadsheet will contain names and prices of Amazon.com's top selling video games.

New Skills / TEKS

Inserting a Header • Inserting a Footer • Changing Page Margins • Printing Gridlines • Printing Row and Column Headings

TEKS: 6.B.ii

Instructions

1. Create a new spreadsheet.
2. Use the default font and size of the spreadsheet software being used.
3. Type the data as shown in **Figure 7.6-A**.
4. Resize all columns so that all data is displayed.
5. Save the spreadsheet as **AMAZON**.
6. Insert a page header that shows:

    Left Section: Your Name

    Center Section: Amazon

    Right Section: Current Date
7. Insert a page footer that shows the page number centered.

8. Adjust the page margins as follows:

Top:	2.5"
Bottom:	0.75"
Left:	2.5"
Right:	1.5"

9. Set the sheet to print gridlines and to show row and column headings.

10. Carefully proofread your work for accuracy.

11. Be sure any changes have been saved.

12. Print preview and be sure that all cells containing data will be included in printing. Adjust the print area if necessary.

13. Print a copy of the spreadsheet if required by your instructor.

Figure 7.6-A

	A	B	C
1	Amazon Top Selling Video Games		
2			
3	Game	Platform	List Price
4	Top Spin 4	Playstation 3	$69.25
5	Rock Band 2	Nintendo Wii	$48.99
6	Cabela's Big Game Hunter	Xbox 360	$74.99
7	Just Dance 2016	Wii U	$27.99
8	MLB Power Pros	Nintendo Wii	$38.99
9	Gran Turismo	Playstation 3	$11.10
10	FIFA Soccer 10	Xbox 360	$15.99
11	The Sims	PC	$24.61

Market Analysis

Formatting Data

Overview

Farm to Tables is a small, locally owned restaurant that is seeking funding to enlarge its dining area. One piece of its updated business plan is a market analysis that identifies potential new customers. The restaurant owner wants the data to be easy to read on paper and digitally. She wants to see font formatting used to help the reader find key facts and differentiate column and row headings from the actual data.

In this lesson, you will create and format a spreadsheet that contains market analysis information that will be included in a restaurant's updated business plan.

New Skills / TEKS

Changing Font • Changing Font Size • Applying Bold, Italics, and Underline • Aligning Text in Columns Horizontally

TEKS: 6.B.ii

Instructions

1. Create a new spreadsheet.
2. Use the default font and size of the spreadsheet software being used.
3. Type the data as shown in **Figure 7.7-A**.
4. Save the spreadsheet as **ANALYSIS**.
5. Change the font of the entire spreadsheet to Arial, 10 point.
6. Change the font size of cell A1 to 16 point and bold.

    HINT: Be sure you have typed the text using all caps.
7. Format cells A5–I5 to 12 point, bold, italic, and underlined.
8. Center align column D.
9. Right align columns E–I.
10. Format the width of columns D–I to 12.
11. Carefully proofread your work for accuracy.
12. Be sure any changes have been saved.
13. Print preview and be sure that all cells containing data will be included in printing. Adjust the print area if necessary.
14. Change the page layout orientation to landscape and adjust the page scaling to fit to one page.
15. Print a copy of the spreadsheet if required by your instructor.

Figure 7.7-A

	A	B	C	D	E	F	G	H	I
1	MARKET ANALYSIS								
2									
3									
4									
5	Potential Customers			% Growth	Year 1	Year 2	Year 3	Year 4	Year 5
6	Local workers			2%	4853	4950	5049	5150	5253
7	Local students			2%	2844	2901	2959	3018	3078
8	Seasonal tourists			3%	80558	82975	85464	88028	90669
9	Weekend shoppers			4%	4308	4480	4660	4846	5040
10	Area residents			2%	15000	15300	15606	15918	16236
11									
12	STUDENT NAME								

AT40

Formatting Cells and Centering a Page

Overview

The data in a spreadsheet cell can be formatted to have various horizontal alignments. Characters can be centered, right aligned, or left aligned to help keep information organized and easy to read.

In this lesson, you will practice how to align data in columns in a spreadsheet about the 20 best AT40 songs of all time. You will then format your spreadsheet so that it is centered both horizontally and vertically.

New Skills / TEKS

Formatting Cells as Text • Centering on a Page Horizontally and Vertically

TEKS: 6.B.ii

Instructions

1. Create a new spreadsheet.
2. Use the default font and size of the spreadsheet software being used.
3. Type the data as shown in **Figure 7.8-A**.
4. Resize all columns so that all data is displayed.
5. Save the spreadsheet as **AT40**.
6. Center align column B.
7. Format column C as text, and right align column D.
8. Change the font of the entire spreadsheet to Comic Sans MS, 10 point.
9. Format the height of row 1 to 70.
10. Change the font size of cell A1 to 36 point, and change the vertical alignment to center.
11. Underline and bold the column headings in row 3.
12. Change the page layout orientation to landscape and adjust the page scaling to fit to one page.
13. Format the spreadsheet to be centered both horizontally and vertically, and set the sheet to print gridlines.
14. Carefully proofread your work for accuracy and be sure any changes have been saved.
15. Print preview and be sure that all cells containing data will be included in printing. Adjust the print area if necessary.
16. Print a copy of the spreadsheet if required by your instructor.

Figure 7.8-A

	A	B	C	D
1	Top 20 Songs of All Time			
2				
3	Artist Name	Song Name	Year Released	Album
4	Radiohead	Creep	1992	Pablo Honey
5	Ben E. King	Stand By Me	1960	Stand By Me
6	Ray Charles	Georgia On My Mind	1960	Hit the Road Jack
7	Aretha Franklin	Respect	1967	Chain of Fools
8	The Archies	Sugar, Sugar	1969	Sugar, Sugar
9	The Monkees	I'm a Believer	1966	The Best of the Monkees
10	The Police	Every Breath You Take	1983	Synchronicity
11	Barbra Streisand	The Way We Were	1973	Memories
12	Outkast	Hey Ya!	2003	Speakerboxxx/The Love Below
13	Woody Guthrie	This Land is Your Land	1944	This Land is Your Land: The Asch Recordings, Vol. 1
14	Nirvana	Smells Like Teen Spirit	1991	Nevermind
15	Amy Winehouse	Rehab	2007	Back to Black
16	Elvis Presley	Heartbreak Hotel	1956	Let's Rock and Roll!
17	Stevie Wonder	Superstition	1972	The Definitive Collection
18	Righteous Brothers	You've Lost That Lovin' Feeling	1964	You've Lost That Lovin' Feeling
19	Beyonce	Crazy in Love	2003	Dangerously In Love
20	Bill Haley and His Comets	Rock Around the Clock	1954	Rock Around the Clock
21	The Impressions	People Get Ready	1965	I Have a Dream
22	Mariah Carey	Fantasy	1995	Daydream
23	Prince and the Revolutions	When Doves Cry	1984	Purple Rain
24				
25	STUDENT NAME			

TV Legend Interviews

Using Additional Number Formats

Overview

Spreadsheets assist a user in many ways, but applying formats to cells before data has been typed can save time. It also ensures that your data will be consistent in how it looks. Dates and times can be formatted in various ways, such as long and abbreviated. Time can show the time of day or a duration that includes hours, minutes, and seconds.

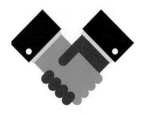

In this lesson, you will format cells to show the duration of several archived online interviews of celebrity hosts.

New Skills / TEKS

Formatting Cells as Duration • Using Merge and Center • Adding Borders

TEKS: 6.B.ii

Instructions

1. Create a new spreadsheet.

2. Use the default font and size of the spreadsheet software being used.

3. Format column D to display as h:mm:ss.

4. Type the data as shown in **Figure 7.9-A**.

5. Resize all columns so that all data is displayed.

6. Save the spreadsheet as **INTERVIEWS**.

7. Insert two new rows above row 1.

8. In cell A1, enter the title "Archive of American Television Interviews" and change the font size to 20 point.

9. Merge and center cell A1 across columns A–D.

10. Apply a thick bottom border to row 3.

11. Change the page layout orientation to landscape and adjust the page scaling to fit to one page.

12. Format the spreadsheet to be centered both horizontally and vertically.

13. Carefully proofread your work for accuracy.

14. Be sure any changes have been saved.

15. Print preview and be sure that all cells containing data will be included in printing. Adjust the print area if necessary.

16. Print a copy of the spreadsheet if required by your instructor.

Figure 7.9-A

	A	B	C
1	Legend First Name	Legend Last Name	Interview Highlight
2	Bob	Barker	On the origin and premise of the game show The Price is Right
3	Dick	Clark	On New Year's Rockin' Eve
4	Judge Judy	Sheindlin	On getting across the message that the justice system means business
5	Regis	Philbin	On Kelly Ripa becoming the co-host of Live with Regis and Kelly
6	Julia	Child	On the origins of her popular cooking show, The French Chef, on PBS
7	Tom	Bergeron	On his advice for aspiring hosts
8	Bill	Nye	On his advice for aspiring hosts
9	Al	Roker	On people blaming the weatherman for bad weather
10	Jeff	Probst	On his favorite tribal council segments
11	Bob	Costas	On how he became a television sportscaster
12			
13	STUDENT NAME		

	D
1	approximate length of interview
2	0:28:00
3	0:14:00
4	0:02:00
5	0:31:00
6	0:05:00
7	0:02:00
8	0:02:00
9	0:02:00
10	0:04:00
11	0:05:00
12	
13	

Excel Art

Formatting Cells

Overview

Formatting your spreadsheet with colors allows you to add some creativity to your work. You may also wish to highlight data with cell backgrounds and font colors. Like all good visual communication, a bold contrast of text and background colors is necessary when choosing what colors to add to your work. Individual cells can be formatted with colors as well as ranges of cells.

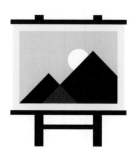

In this lesson, you will change the fill and font color of cells to create two pictures.

New Skills / TEKS

Applying Fill Color • Applying Font Color

TEKS: 6.B.ii

Instructions

1. Create a new spreadsheet.
2. Use the default font and size of the spreadsheet software being used.
3. Save the spreadsheet as **ART**.
4. Format the width of columns A–AD to 4.
5. Format the height of rows 1–15 to 24.
6. Refer to the finished smiley face and heart as shown in **Figure 7.10-A** as you create your own.

   NOTE: Be sure to include your name in cell A17.
7. To create the smiley face outline, fill the following cells with black:

F1–J1	A7–A10	N11–N12
D2–E2	O7–O10	G12–I12
K2–L2	C7–M7	C13
C3	C8–G8	M13
M3	I8–M8	D14–E14
B4–B5	D9–F9	K14–L14
N4–N5	J9–L9	F15–J15
A6–O6	B11–B12	

8. To create the smiley face inside color, fill the following cells with yellow:

F2–J2	H8	C11–M11
D3–L3	B9–C9	C12–F12
C4–M5	G9–I9	J12–M12
B7–B8	M9–N9	D13–L13
N7–N8	B10–N10	F14–J14

9. Type the text "COOL DUDE" in cell A6 and change the font color to white.

10. Change the font size of cell A6 to 18 point.

11. Merge cell A6 across columns A–O and center the text.

12. To create the heart, fill the following cells with pink:

R1–U1	P4–AD8	U13–Y13
Y1–AB1	Q9–AC9	V14–X14
Q2–V2	R10–AB10	W15
X2–AC2	S11–AA11	
Q3–AC3	T12–Z12	

13. Type the text "I LOVE YOU" in cell P6 and change the font color to white.

14. Change the font size of cell P6 to 24 point.

15. Merge cell P6 across columns P–AD and center the text.

16. Change the page layout orientation to landscape and adjust the page scaling to fit to one page.

17. Format the spreadsheet to be centered both horizontally and vertically.

18. Carefully proofread your work for accuracy.

19. Be sure any changes have been saved.

20. Print preview and be sure that all cells containing data will be included in printing. Adjust the print area if necessary.

21. Print a copy of the spreadsheet if required by your instructor.

Figure 7.10-A

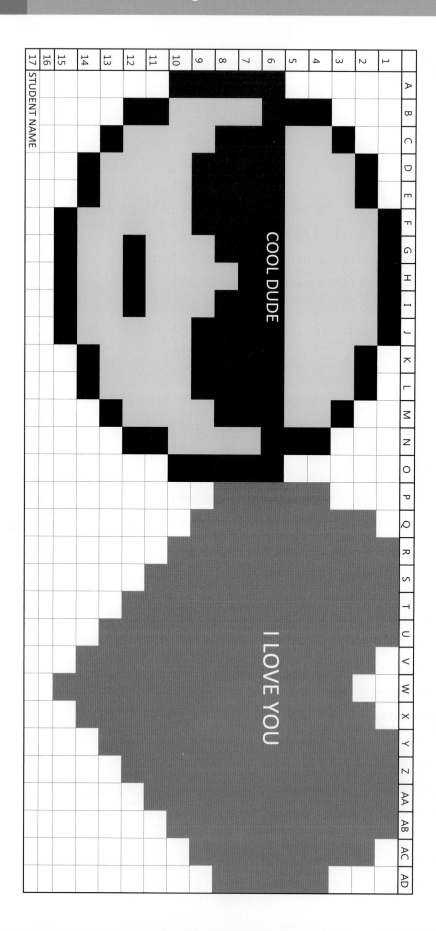

Forever 21

Formatting Numbers

Overview

The format of a cell can vary in many ways. Setting the format of a group of cells will make entering data easier and will change the way information is displayed and handled in a spreadsheet. Numbers are unique because they typically become part of formulas and calculations. When a number is entered with many decimal places, the cell takes on the value of that entire number. However, there may be times when not all decimal places are necessary to display. Numbers will be displayed as rounded up if the place value to the right of the number of designated decimal places to be displayed is five or higher.

In this lesson, you will format numbers with various decimal places after you have entered them for a list of items sold at the popular clothing store, Forever 21.

New Skills / TEKS

Formatting Cells as Numbers with Zero Decimals • Increasing/Decreasing Decimal Places

TEKS: 6.B.ii

Instructions

1. Create a new spreadsheet.
2. Use the default font and size of the spreadsheet software being used.
3. Type the data as shown in **Figure 7.11-A**.
4. Resize all columns so that all data is displayed.
5. Save the spreadsheet as **FOREVER**.
6. Change the font size of the title in cell A1 to 21 point.
7. Merge and center cell A1 across columns A–G.
8. Bold the column headings in row 3.
9. Apply a thick bottom border to cells A3–G3.
10. Format column B as Text.
11. Center align column D.
12. Copy cells E4–E26 to cells G4–G26.
13. Format columns E and F as Number with 0 decimal places.

14. Increase the decimal places in cells F4–F26 to 2.

15. Decrease the decimal places in cells G4–G26 to 1.

16. Format the spreadsheet to be centered both horizontally and vertically.

17. Set the sheet to print gridlines.

18. Change the page layout orientation to landscape and adjust the page scaling to fit to one page.

19. Carefully proofread your work for accuracy.

20. Be sure any changes have been saved.

21. Print preview and be sure that all cells containing data will be included in printing. Adjust the print area if necessary.

22. Print a copy of the spreadsheet if required by your instructor.

Figure 7.11-A

	A	B	C	D	E	F	G
1	Forever 21						
2							
3	Category	Item Number	Item Name	Style	Unit Cost	Suggested Selling Price	Gross Profit
4	Dresses	2000150074	A-line Mini Dress	Polyester	6.45	12.9	
5	Dresses	2000152247	Faux Suede Cami Romper	Polyester	14.95	29.9	
6	Dresses	2000187279	Criss Cross Front Dress	Rayon	12.45	24.9	
7	Men's Hoodies	2000154932	Zip Up Hoodie	Cotton	7.45	14.9	
8	Men's Hoodies	2000168633	Draw String Vest	Cotton	7.95	15.9	
9	Tops	2000150321	Dropped Dolphin Hem Shirt	Rayon	11.45	22.9	
10	Tops	2000182764	Contemporary Chiffon Twist Top	Chiffon	11.45	22.9	
11	Tops	2000182340	Tulip Back Tee	Cotton	8.95	17.9	
12	Tops	2000168820	Buttoned Striped Shirt	Cotton	9.95	19.9	
13	Tops	2000151093	Striped Panel Tee	Cotton	6.45	12.9	
14	Tops	2000162103	Longline Tee	Polyester	7.45	14.9	
15	Tees & Tanks	2000187095	Mineral Wash Tee	Cotton	7.45	14.9	
16	Tees & Tanks	2000167570	Knotted Hem Tee	Cotton	5.45	10.9	
17	Tees & Tanks	2000186989	Classic Striped Tee	Rayon	5.45	10.9	
18	Suits	2000101482	Classic 2 Button Blazer	Polyester	26.45	52.9	
19	Suits	2000181917	Satin Trim Blazer	Polyester	31.45	62.9	
20	Suits	2000163377	Creased Trousers	Polyester	14.95	29.9	
21	Sweaters	2000082489	Button Down Cardigan	Cotton	11.45	22.9	
22	Sweaters	2000165246	Vented Hem Sweater	Acrylic	13.95	27.9	
23	Sweaters	2000168488	Striped Sweater Top	Acrylic	11.45	22.9	
24	Sweaters	2000150158	Open Front Cardigan	Rayon	7.45	14.9	
25	Sweaters	2000157945	Mock Neck Sweater	Rayon	8.95	17.9	
26	Sweaters	2000174349	Ribbed Turtleneck	Wool	8.95	17.9	
27							
28	STUDENT NAME						

Accounts Payable—Nike Store

Formatting Currency and Percent

Overview

Values displayed as dollar amounts have two recognizable features. The numbers are formatted with two decimal places and contain a dollar sign ($) in front of the first digit. If the third decimal place is a five or higher, the displayed value will appear rounded up. However, any calculations with the cell will be done with the entered value regardless of how many decimal places are displayed.

Numbers with a percent format contain a percent symbol (%) to the right of the last decimal place. Like other number formats, such as currency, percentage format can have any number of decimal places displayed and will show as rounded up if the digit to the right of the last displayed decimal place is five or higher.

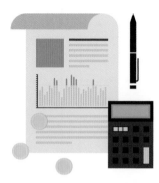

In this lesson, you will format numbers as currency and as percentages in a spreadsheet that lists the discount percent to be taken on invoices that are paid at a Nike Store.

New Skills / TEKS

Formatting Cells as Currency • Formatting Cells as Percentages

TEKS: 6.B.ii

Instructions

1. Create a new spreadsheet.
2. Use the default font and size of the spreadsheet software being used.
3. Type the data as shown in **Figure 7.12-A**.
4. Resize all columns so that all data is displayed.
5. Save the spreadsheet as **NIKE**.
6. Merge and center cell A1 across columns A–D.
7. Merge and center cell A2 across columns A–D.
8. Merge and center cell A3 across columns A–D.
9. Apply a bottom border to the merged cell A3.
10. Format column A as text.
11. Format cells C6–C20 as Currency displaying 2 decimal places.
12. Format cells D6–D20 as Percentage displaying 0 decimal places.

13. Center align column D.

14. Format the spreadsheet to be centered both horizontally and vertically.

15. Set the sheet to print gridlines.

16. Carefully proofread your work for accuracy.

17. Be sure any changes have been saved.

18. Print preview and be sure that all cells containing data will be included in printing. Adjust the print area if necessary.

19. Print a copy of the spreadsheet if required by your instructor.

Figure 7.12-A

	A	B	C	D
1	Nike Store			
2	Accounts Payable			
3	Summary for March			
4				
5	Invoice #	Vendor Name	Amount	Discount Percent
6	1144	American Cotton	345	0.04
7	1244	JM Designs	1145	0.03
8	1141	Graphic Unlimited	766	0.04
9	1245	Package Plus	1254	0.05
10	2648	JM Designs	883	0.02
11	2452	Graphic Unlimited	533	0.05
12	2869	Cleaning Services	933	0.02
13	1053	Far East Graphics	978	0.06
14	1272	International Footwear, Ltd.	720	0.05
15	1127	Package Plus	1537	0.06
16	1196	International Footwear, Ltd.	1092	0.03
17	2676	Graphic Unlimited	1506	0.01
18	2331	International Footwear, Ltd.	665	0.06
19	2135	Energy Plus	409	0.04
20	2466	Energy Plus	951	0.06
21				
22	STUDENT NAME			

Top 10 Most Expensive Flights

Applying Accounting Style

Overview

Numbers that show monetary value can be formatted two ways: as Currency or as Accounting. An Accounting format will display a dollar sign ($) as well as two decimal places as a default. Decimal places will be aligned and the $ will be aligned to the far left of the cell, making it easier to read. Negative numbers will display in parentheses, and zeros will appear as a dash. The Accounting format also includes the thousands-separator comma for very large amounts.

In this lesson, you will format numbers as Accounting in a spreadsheet that showcases the top 10 most expensive airline flights.

New Skills / TEKS

Formatting Cells as Accounting

TEKS: 6.B.ii

Instructions

1. Create a new spreadsheet.
2. Use the default font and size of the spreadsheet software being used.
3. Type the data as shown in **Figure 7.13-A**.
4. Resize all columns so that all data is displayed.
5. Save the spreadsheet as **FLIGHTS**.
6. Change the font size of the title in cell A1 to 20 point.
7. Merge and center cell A1 across columns A–E.
8. Bold the column headings in row 3.
9. Center align column A.
10. Right align cell E3.
11. Format the width of column E to 25.
12. Format cells E4–E13 as Accounting (if available) displaying 2 decimal places.
13. Center align column D.
14. Format the spreadsheet to be centered both horizontally and vertically.
15. Set the sheet to print gridlines.
16. Adjust the page scaling to fit to one page.

17. Carefully proofread your work for accuracy.

18. Be sure any changes have been saved.

19. Print preview and be sure that all cells containing data will be included in printing. Adjust the print area if necessary.

20. Print a copy of the spreadsheet if required by your instructor.

Figure 7.13-A

	A	B	C	D	E
1	Top 10 Most Expensive Flights				
2					
3	Rank	To	From	Airline	Price
4	10	Singapore	New York	Singapore Airlines	14000
5	9	Melbourne	Los Angeles	Quantas	14974
6	8	Tokyo	Los Angeles	Japan Airlines	16078
7	7	Singapore	New York	Virgin Atlantic	21000
8	6	Singapore	New York	Swiss Air	22265
9	5	New York	Hong Kong	Cathay Pacific	26572
10	4	Beijing	New York	Korean Air	27000
11	3	Abu Dhabi	San Francisco	Etihad Airways	28090
12	2	Dubai	Los Angeles	Emirates	30000
13	1	Hong Kong	New York	Lufthansa	43535
14					
15	STUDENT NAME				

Party Invitation List

Sorting Data

Overview

Sorting a list as you enter it in a spreadsheet can be very useful. Having your spreadsheet do it automatically is the more efficient way to go. When data is organized in columns with headings, your software can rearrange your list by sorting by any of the columns. Sorting either ascending or descending by various columns allows you to analyze data, understand your information, and find what you are looking for.

In this lesson, you will sort a list of party invitation addresses three ways so that you can easily analyze your data.

New Skills / TEKS

Sorting Data in Ascending Order • Sorting Data in Descending Order • Selecting Non-Adjacent Cells

TEKS: 6.B.ii

Instructions

1. Create a new spreadsheet.
2. Use the default font and size of the spreadsheet software being used.
3. Type the data **exactly** as shown in **Figure 7.14-A**.
4. Resize all columns so that all data is displayed.
5. Save the spreadsheet as **PARTY**.
6. Copy cells A3–G18 and paste into cells A21–G36 and again into cells A39–G54.
7. Change the font size of cells A1, A20, and A38 to 18 point.
8. Merge and center the cell A1 across columns A–G.
9. Merge and center the cell A20 across columns A–G.
10. Merge and center the cell A38 across columns A–G.
11. Bold the column headings in rows 3, 21, and 39.

     HINT: Use the control key to select these non-adjacent cells.
12. Sort cells A4–G18 by last name ascending–A to Z.
13. Sort cells A22–G36 by Zip code ascending–smallest to largest.
14. Sort cells A40–G54 by birth date descending–newest to oldest.
15. Type your name at the bottom of the spreadsheet below the data.
16. Format the spreadsheet to be centered both horizontally and vertically.

17. Set the sheet to print gridlines.

18. Carefully proofread your work for accuracy.

19. Be sure any changes have been saved.

20. Adjust the page scaling to fit to one page.

21. Print preview and be sure that all cells containing data will be included in printing. Adjust the print area if necessary.

22. Print a copy of the spreadsheet if required by your instructor.

Figure 7.14-A

	A	B	C	D	E	F	G
1	Party Invitation List by Last Name						
2							
3	Last Name	First Name	Street Address	City	State	Zip	Birth Date
4	Huff	Austin	80 Sycamore Street	Rolla	MO	65401	3/17/1999
5	Bush	Benjamin	91 Atlantic Avenue	Asheboro	NC	27205	10/11/1998
6	Colon	Deb	847 Monroe Drive	Cambridge	MA	20138	11/22/1995
7	Patton	Derek	22 Woodland Avenue	Jersey City	NJ	70302	11/5/1998
8	Cruz	Estelle	691 3rd Street West	Winchester	OH	43110	5/21/1996
9	Miller	Georgia	836 Cross Street	Conyers	GA	30012	11/17/1999
10	Harvey	Hugo	407 Pheasant Run	Marion	NC	28752	6/1/2000
11	Wood	Jeannette	91 Carriage Drive	Knoxville	TN	37918	3/26/1995
12	Mann	Kayla	47 Homestead Drive	Union	NJ	31061	6/17/1997
13	Owen	Leslie	6743 Garfield Avenue	Bel Air	MD	21014	12/21/1992
14	Mason	Lindsay	700 3rd Avenue	Middleton	NY	10952	9/22/1994
15	Rivera	Marcus	5920 Fieldstone Drive	Stone	GA	30083	8/4/1994
16	Walton	Melanie	1286 College Avenue	New York	NY	10002	6/8/1992
17	Patterson	Mike	450 Orange Street	Elkhart	IN	46514	5/27/1998
18	French	Pat	27 Cambridge Drive	Newington	CT	16111	12/2/1996
19							
20	Party Invitation List by Zip Code						
21							
22							
23							
24							
25							
26							
27							
28							
29							
30							
31							
32							
33							
34							
35							
36							
37							
38	Party Invitation List by Birthday						

You Say It's Your Birthday

Formatting Dates

Overview

Date formats in a spreadsheet come in various forms. Dates can be displayed as short dates, where only the number of the month, day, and year are shown. Dates can be formatted to include a spelled-out month. Long date formats include the day of the week. Even if you do not specify a particular date format, spreadsheets are smart enough to recognize a number typed as 2/3 as February 3rd. As a default, your spreadsheet will display 3-Feb, but you can format the cell to display months as numbers or words, days as numbers or words, and years as two digits or four digits.

In this lesson, you will create a list of birthdays with a long date format.

New Skills / TEKS

Formatting Cells as Dates

TEKS: 6.B.ii

Instructions

1. Create a new spreadsheet.
2. Use the default font and size of the spreadsheet software being used.
3. Type the data as shown in **Figure 7.15-A**.
4. Resize all columns so that all data is displayed.
5. Save the spreadsheet as **BIRTHDAY**.
6. Change the font size of the title in cell A1 to 20 point.
7. Merge and center cell A1 across columns A–E.
8. Bold and underline the column headings in row 3.
9. Format cells C4–C23 as a long date.
10. Delete the four rows with birthdays in the 1800s.
    NOTE: These dates may not have converted to a long date.
11. Sort the list by last name ascending (A–Z).
12. Format the spreadsheet to be centered both horizontally and vertically.
13. Set the sheet to print gridlines.
14. Carefully proofread your work for accuracy.

15. Be sure any changes have been saved.

16. Adjust the page scaling to fit to one page.

17. Print preview and be sure that all cells containing data will be included in printing. Adjust the print area if necessary.

18. Print a copy of the spreadsheet if required by your instructor.

Figure 7.15-A

	A	B	C	D	E
1	YOU SAY IT'S YOUR BIRTHDAY				
2					
3	First Name	Last Name	Birthday	Profession	Star Sign
4	Frederick	Douglass	2/14/1818	Abolitionist	Aquarius
5	Harriet	Beecher Stowe	6/14/1811	Abolitionist	Gemini
6	Harriet	Tubman	3/10/1813	Abolitionist	Aries
7	Adam	Sandler	9/9/1966	Actor	Virgo
8	Al	Pacino	4/25/1940	Actor	Taurus
9	Ashton	Kutcher	2/7/1978	Actor	Aquarius
10	Angelina	Jolie	6/4/1975	Actress	Gemini
11	Drew	Barrymore	2/22/1975	Actress	Pisces
12	Natalie	Portman	6/9/1981	Actress	Gemini
13	Charles	Schulz	11/26/1922	Cartoonist	Sagittarius
14	Matt	Groening	2/15/1954	Cartoonist	Aquarius
15	Adele	Adkins	5/5/1988	Singer	Taurus
16	Lady	Gaga	3/28/1986	Singer	Aries
17	Taylor	Swift	12/13/1989	Singer	Sagittarius
18	Ellen	DeGeneres	1/26/1958	Comedian	Aquarius
19	Jimmy	Fallon	9/19/1974	Comedian	Virgo
20	Jerry	Seinfeld	4/29/1954	Comedian	Taurus
21	Seth	Meyers	12/28/1973	Comedian	Sagittarius
22	Charlie	Chaplin	4/16/1889	Comedian	Aries
23	Larry	David	7/2/1947	Comedian	Cancer
24					
25	STUDENT NAME				

Major Holidays

Sequencing Made Easy

Overview

A unique feature available in spreadsheet software is called AutoFill. AutoFill is useful when a sequence needs to be completed in an adjacent range of cells. Simply start the sequence and your software will know what typically comes next. For example, AutoFill will complete the days of the week when used from a correctly typed day of the week. AutoFill can also be used to finish a sequence of numbers, months, or dates.

In this lesson, you will use AutoFill to complete a sequence of months and dates for a calendar of one-of-a-kind holidays.

New Skills / TEKS

Using AutoFill to Complete a Sequence

TEKS: 6.B.ii

Instructions

1. Create a new spreadsheet.

2. Use the default font and size of the spreadsheet software being used.

3. Type the data as shown in **Figure 7.16-A.**

4. Resize all columns so that all data is displayed.

5. Save the spreadsheet as **HOLIDAY**.

6. Change the font size of the title in cell B1 to 36 point.

7. Merge and center cell B1 across columns B–M.

8. Change the font size of cells A3–M34 to 14 point.

9. Format the height of rows 3–34 to 30.

10. Complete the sequence of dates in column A by selecting cells A4 and A5 and using AutoFill to drag down to cell A34.

11. Complete the sequence of months in row 3 by selecting cell B3 and using AutoFill to drag across to cell M3.

12. Bold the column headings in row 3.

13. Apply a double bottom border to row 3.

14. Format the spreadsheet to be centered both horizontally and vertically.

15. Set the sheet to print gridlines.

16. Change the page layout orientation to landscape and adjust the page scaling to fit to one page.

17. Carefully proofread your work for accuracy.

18. Be sure any changes have been saved.

19. Print preview and be sure that all cells containing data will be included in printing. Adjust the print area if necessary.

20. Print a copy of the spreadsheet if required by your instructor.

Figure 7.16-A

	A	B	C	D	E
1		Major Holidays			
2					
3	Date	January			
4	1	New Year's Day			April Fool's Day
5	2		Groundhog Day		
6		Festival of Sleep Day		National Anthem Day	
7			Thank a Mailman Day		School Librarian Day
8		National Bird Day			
9					
10			Send a Card to a Friend Day		Caramel Popcorn Day
11					
12					
13		Houseplant Appreciation Day			
14					
15			Abraham Lincoln's Birthday		
16		Stephen Foster Memorial Day			Scrabble Day
17		Dress Up Your Pet Day	Valentine's Day	National Pi Day	
18				Ides of March	
19					
20			Random Act of Kindness Day	Saint Patrick's Day	
21		Martin Luther King Day			
22					
23				International Earth Day	
24					
25			George Washington's Birthday		National Jelly Bean Day
26		National Handwriting Day			
27			National Tortilla Chip Day		
28				Waffle Day	
29					
30					Babe Ruth Day
31					
32		National Puzzle Day	Leap Day		
33					
34					
35	STUDENT NAME				

Figure 7.16-A (Continued)

	F	G	H	I
1				
2				
3				
4	May Day			
5				
6				
7	Star Wars Day	Hug Your Cat Day	Independence Day	U.S. Coast Guard Day
8	Cinco de Mayo			
9	National Nurses Day	National Yo-Yo Day		
10			Chocolate Day	
11		Best Friends Day		
12				Book Lovers Day
13	Clean Up Your Room Day			National S'mores Day
14			Cheer Up the Lonely Day	
15				
16				
17		Flag Day	Bastille Day	
18	National Chocolate Chip Day			
19				
20			Peach Ice Cream Day	
21		Go Fishing Day		
22				
23				
24				
25			Hammock Day	
26			National Hot Dog Day	
27			Amelia Earhart Day	
28	Tap Dance Day			
29		Forgiveness Day		National Dog Day
30				
31				
32				
33			International Day of Friendship	Toasted Marshmallow Day
34	National Macaroon Day	Mutts Day		
35				

Figure 7.16-A (Continued)

	J	K	L	M
1				
2				
3				
4		World Vegetarian Day		
5				
6		Techies Day	Sandwich Day	
7				
8	Cheese Pizza Day			
9				Mitten Tree Day
10				
11				
12	Teddy Bear Day	Fire Prevention Day		
13				
14	9/11 Remembrance		Veterans Day	
15	National Video Games Day			
16		International Skeptics Day		Violin Day
17				
18			Clean Your Refrigerator Day	
19	Mayflower Day			Ntl. Chocolate-Covered Anything Day
20			Take a Hike Day	
21	National Cheeseburger Day			Bake Cookies Day
22				
23				Go Caroling Day
24			World Hello Day	
25	Elephant Appreciation Day			
26				
27				
28				Christmas Day
29	Johnny Appleseed Day			
30				
31				
32				
33				
34		Halloween		New Year's Eve
35				

Presentation Rubric

Using Basic Calculations

Overview

The feature that really makes spreadsheet software different from a table in your word processing software is the powerful ability it has to work as a calculator. Basic math functions, such as addition or subtraction, are a breeze when data is used in formulas. When cell references are included in the formula, data in those referenced cells can change, and the formula will do the work of updating the math for you.

In this lesson, you will add cells with a formula, copy and paste that formula, and display your spreadsheet with formulas to see what is being calculated in a spreadsheet that focuses on a teacher's grading of student presentations.

New Skills / TEKS

Using Basic Formulas: Addition • Copying and Pasting Formulas • Displaying Formulas • Using Cell References

TEKS: 6.B.ii

Instructions

1. Create a new spreadsheet.

2. Use the default font and size of the spreadsheet software being used.

3. Type the data as shown in **Figure 7.17-A**.

4. Resize all columns so that all data is displayed.

5. Save the spreadsheet as **PRESENTATION**.

6. Change the font size of the title in cell A1 to 16 point.

7. Merge and center cell A1 across columns A–H.

8. Bold the column headings in row 2.

9. Use Autofill to complete the sequence of numbers in column A down to cell A22.

10. In cell H3, compute the Total Points for the first student by typing the formula =C3+D3+E3+F3+G3.

11. Copy and paste the formula in cell H3 to the remaining students by selecting cell H3 and using AutoFill to drag down to cell H22.

12. Display formulas in the spreadsheet to check for accuracy.

13. Format the spreadsheet to be centered both horizontally and vertically.

14. Set the sheet to print gridlines.

15. Change the page layout orientation to landscape and adjust the page scaling to fit to one page.

16. Carefully proofread your work for accuracy.

17. Be sure any changes have been saved.

18. Print preview and be sure that all cells containing data will be included in printing. Adjust the print area if necessary.

19. Print a copy of the spreadsheet if required by your instructor.

Figure 7.17-A

	A	B	C	D	E	F	G	H
1		Oral Presentation Grades						
2		Student Name	Voice Volume	Eye Contact	Presentation Length	Content Knowledge	Speech Structure	Total Points
3		1 Ruth	20	20	20	15	15	
4		2 Bradley	15	15	10	10	20	
5		Peggy	10	20	20	20	15	
6		Heather	20	20	20	20	20	
7		Randy	20	10	20	20	10	
8		Agnes	20	15	20	20	15	
9		Brandon	20	10	20	20	10	
10		Shaun	15	15	20	20	15	
11		Casey	10	10	20	20	20	
12		Allen	5	20	20	20	20	
13		Martin	15	15	20	10	20	
14		Olivia	20	15	10	10	20	
15		Tammy	20	20	10	10	20	
16		Joe	20	20	10	10	20	
17		Terri	20	20	15	10	20	
18		Mitchell	15	15	15	15	20	
19		Audrey	15	15	10	15	15	
20		Jessie	10	15	10	20	20	
21		Franklin	10	15	20	20	20	
22		Tyler	20	20	20	20	20	
23								
24		STUDENT NAME						

My Check Register

Adding Adjacent Cells

Overview

Any mathematical calculation you can do on a calculator, you can do with formulas in your spreadsheet. Including typed or selected cells in a formula along with mathematical operators such as + and – will produce a value. As an added bonus, your spreadsheet software comes equipped with predefined formulas known as functions. One of the most commonly used functions is the SUM function, which will add a range of adjacent cells. All functions and formulas can be copied and pasted to other cells and the row or column reference will be updated.

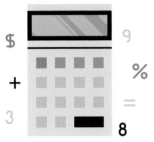

In this lesson, you will add cells with the SUM function and use a subtraction formula to complete the amounts in a checkbook register.

New Skills / TEKS

Using AutoSum • Using SUM • Using Basic Formulas: Subtraction

TEKS: 6.B.ii

Instructions

1. Create a new spreadsheet.
2. Use the default font and size of the spreadsheet software being used.
3. Type the data as shown in **Figure 7.18-A**.
4. Resize all columns so that all data is displayed.
5. Save the spreadsheet as **CHECKBOOK**.
6. Bold the column headings in row 1.
7. In cell F3, compute the balance after check #123 by typing the formula =F2-E3.
8. In cell F4, compute the balance after the deposit on 1/18/16 by typing the formula =F3+D4.
9. In cell F5, compute the balance after check #124 by typing the formula =F4+D5-E5.
10. Copy and paste the formula in cell F5 to the remaining transactions by selecting cell F5 and using AutoFill to drag down to cell F17.
11. In cell D18, compute the total of all deposits by typing the function =SUM(D2:D17).
12. In cell E18, compute the total of all withdrawals by using the AutoSum button and include cells E2–E17.
13. Display formulas in the spreadsheet to check for accuracy.
14. Format the spreadsheet to be centered both horizontally and vertically.

15. Set the sheet to print gridlines.

16. Change the page layout orientation to landscape and adjust the page scaling to fit to one page.

17. Carefully proofread your work for accuracy.

18. Be sure any changes have been saved.

19. Print preview and be sure that all cells containing data will be included in printing. Adjust the print area if necessary.

20. Print a copy of the spreadsheet if required by your instructor.

Figure 7.18-A

	A	B	C	D	E	F
1	Check Number	Date	Description	Deposit	Withdrawal	Balance
2		1/15/2016	Balance brought forward			547.96
3	123	1/15/2016	Auto Finance Solutions - car payment		189.64	
4	Deposit	1/18/2016	Deposit paycheck	864.33		
5	124	1/20/2016	National Electric - electric bill		33.29	
6	125	1/20/2016	USA Cable Providers - cable TV		75.05	
7	Deposit	2/5/2016	Deposit paycheck	864.33		
8	ATM	2/7/2016	ATM withdrawal of cash		100	
9	126	2/9/2016	Wireless Solutions - cell phone bill		57.63	
10	127	2/9/2016	A & M Management - rent		850	
11	Debit Card	2/16/2016	Clean Food Market - groceries		87.45	
12	128	2/20/2016	Statewide Insurance - car insurance		130.95	
13	Transfer	2/20/2016	Transfer to savings		150	
14	Deposit	2/24/2016	Deposit birthday gifts	200		
15	129	2/27/2016	Townfair Auto - gas for car		30	
16	Debit Card	2/28/2016	First Run Cinemas - movies with friends		32	
17	Debit Card	2/29/2016	My Apparel - clothes		55.95	
18			Total			
19						
20	STUDENT NAME					

Town Camp Summer Payroll

Using Multi-Math Formulas

Overview

Multi-math formulas are formulas that include more than one operation. When many employees are involved in the payroll register, spreadsheet software makes calculating payroll easy because formulas can be copied and pasted to adjoining rows.

Order of Operations: When writing formulas for spreadsheets, it's important to remember that there is a standard order of operations for calculations involving more than one arithmetic operation. Keep these three points in mind while you work:

1. Perform calculations within parentheses first.
2. Working from left to right, perform all multiplication and division in order.
3. Finally, working from left to right, perform all addition and subtraction in order.

In this lesson, you will complete a payroll register for a town summer camp and use multiplication and multi-math formulas to calculate deductions and net pay amounts.

New Skills / TEKS

Using Basic Formulas: Multiplication • Using Parentheses for Multi-Math Formulas

TEKS: 6.B.ii

Instructions

1. Create a new spreadsheet.
2. Use the default font and size of the spreadsheet software being used.
3. Type the data as shown in **Figure 7.19-A**.
4. Resize all columns so that all data is displayed.
5. Save the spreadsheet as **PAYROLL**.
6. Bold the column headings in row 1.
7. Locate the Federal Tax Rate in cell G2. Use the AutoFill feature to copy that rate in column G for all employees.
8. Locate the Social Security Tax Rate in cell I2. Use the AutoFill feature to copy that rate in column I for all employees.

9. Continue using the AutoFill feature to fill columns K, M, and O with the appropriate rates for all employees.

10. In cell F2, compute the Gross Pay for the first employee by typing the formula =D2*E2.

11. In cell H2, compute the Federal Tax for the first employee by typing the formula =F2*G2.

12. In cell J2, compute the Social Security Tax for the first employee by typing the formula =F2*I2.

13. In cell L2, compute the Medicare Tax for the first employee by typing the formula =F2*K2.

14. In cell N2, compute the State Tax for the first employee by typing the formula =F2*M2.

15. In cell P2, compute the Pension for the first employee by typing the formula =F2*O2.

16. In cell Q2, compute the Net Pay for the first employee by typing the multi-math formula =F2-(H2+J2+L2+N2+P2).

17. Copy and paste the formulas in cells F2, H2, J2, L2, N2, P2, and Q2 to the remaining employees using the AutoFill feature.

18. Format columns E, F, H, J, L, N, P, and Q as Currency displaying 2 decimal places.

19. Display formulas in the spreadsheet to check for accuracy.

20. Format the spreadsheet to be centered both horizontally and vertically.

21. Set the sheet to print gridlines.

22. Change the page layout orientation to landscape and adjust the page scaling to fit to one page.

23. Carefully proofread your work for accuracy.

24. Be sure any changes have been saved.

25. Print preview and be sure that all cells containing data will be included in printing. Adjust the print area if necessary.

26. Print a copy of the spreadsheet if required by your instructor.

Figure 7.19-A

	A	B	C	D	E	F	G	H	I
1	Employee Number	Last Name	First Name	Hours Worked	Hourly Rate	Gross Pay	Federal Tax Rate	Federal Tax	Social Security Tax Rate
2	34628	Dean	Sherry	28	12.5		15%		6.2%
3	34784	Bennett	Guy	18	13.5				
4	34949	Blair	Kelley	26	10.5				
5	34910	Hodges	Earl	27	12				
6	34756	Kennedy	Doug	33	15				
7	35917	Bowers	Terry	18	12.5				
8	34975	Mack	Will	22	10.5				
9	34764	Evans	Nora	22	10.5				
10	35261	Green	Hope	16	11.25				
11	35200	Summers	Tricia	26	12.25				
12	34877	Hanson	Dexter	21	10.5				
13	35603	Pag	Cesar	18	11.25				
14	34869	Miles	Isabel	39	11.25				
15	34953	Swanson	Brad	15	15.75				
16	35848	Boyd	Stacy	15	15				
17	35385	Nichols	Meredith	39	12				
18	35291	Mathis	Becky	35	12.25				
19	35233	Garner	Kristina	18	10				
20	35632	Carter	Ron	18	11.5				
21	35986	Reed	June	39	11.5				
22									
23	STUDENT NAME								

Figure 7.19-A (Continued)

	J	K	L	M	N	O	P	Q
	Social Security Tax	Medicare Tax Rate	Medicare Tax	State Tax Rate	State Tax	Pension Rate	Pension	Net Pay
1		1.45%		4%		3%		
2								
3								
4								
5								
6								
7								
8								
9								
10								
11								
12								
13								
14								
15								
16								
17								
18								
19								
20								
21								
22								
23								

Event Budget

Practicing Cell References

Overview

Companies often host events for a variety of reasons. Whether planning a dinner, a reception, or some kind of ceremony, there will be expenses. Without a budget to work with, expenses for any kind of event can quickly get out of control.

In this lesson, you will create a budget spreadsheet that lists the projected income and expenses for an Alumni Homecoming Party hosted by Knowledge College. In the course of creating the spreadsheet, you will add formulas to determine the estimated profit and to manage expenses.

New Skills / TEKS

There are no new skills being introduced in this reinforcement lesson.

TEKS: 6.B.ii

Instructions

1. Create a new spreadsheet.

2. Change the font of the entire spreadsheet to Arial, 10 point.

3. Type the data as shown in **Figure 7.20-A**.

4. Save the spreadsheet as **BUDGET**.

5. Change the font size of cell A1 to 16 point and bold.

6. Change the font size of cell A2 to 14 point and bold.

7. Format rows 5, 7, 9, 10, 16, 18, 24, 26, 30, 32, 36, 38, 41, 43, 46, 48, and 49 to bold and italic.

8. Format the width of column A to 32.

9. Format the width of columns B–D to 18.

10. Center align column B and format as Number displaying 0 decimal places.

11. Right align columns C and D and format as Currency displaying 2 decimal places.

12. In cell D6, compute the Flat Rate Production Fee by typing the formula =B6*C6.

13. Copy the formula in cell D6 and paste it in cells D11–D15, D19–D23, D27–D29, D33–D35, D39–D40, and D44–D45 to compute the totals for the remaining items in the budget.

14. In cell D7, compute the Total Income by typing the formula =D6.

15. In cell D16, compute the total for the Site Costs by typing the formula =SUM(D11:D15).

16. Enter formulas in cells D24, D30, D36, D41, and D46 to compute the totals for the remaining expense categories as follows:

    a. In cell D24, type =SUM(D19:D23).

    b. In cell D30, type =SUM(D27:D29).

    c. In cell D36, type =SUM(D33:D35).

    d. In cell D41, type =SUM(D39:D40).

    e. In cell D46, type =SUM(D44:D45).

17. In cell D48, compute the Total Expenses by typing the formula =D16+D24+D30+D36+D41+D46.

18. Enter a formula to compute the Estimated Profit in cell D49 by subtracting the Total Expenses in cell D48 from the Total Income in cell D7. In cell D49, type =D7-D48.

19. Display formulas in the spreadsheet to check for accuracy.

20. Carefully proofread your work for accuracy.

21. Be sure any changes have been saved.

22. Adjust the page scaling to fit to one page.

23. Print preview and be sure that all cells containing data will be included in printing. Adjust the print area if necessary.

24. Print a copy of the spreadsheet if required by your instructor.

Figure 7.20-A

	A	B	C	D
1	KNOWLEDGE COLLEGE			
2	Budget for Alumni Homecoming Party			
3				
4				
5	INCOME	QUANTITY	RATE	TOTAL
6	Flat Rate Production Fee	1	50000	
7	TOTAL INCOME			
8				
9	EXPENSES	QUANTITY	RATE	TOTAL
10	SITE			
11	Room and hall fee	1	1200	
12	Production staff	150	15	
13	Equipment	1	350	
14	Tables	25	7	
15	Chairs	250	5	
16	TOTAL SITE COSTS			
17				
18	DECORATIONS			
19	Floral centerpieces	25	35	
20	Candle sets	25	5	
21	Lighting	1	320	
22	Balloon package	1	60	
23	Paper supplies	1	150	
24	TOTAL DECORATIONS			
25				
26	PUBLICITY			
27	Graphics work	1	1500	
28	Photocopying/printing	1	850	
29	Postage	1	280	
30	TOTAL PUBLICITY			
31				
32	REFRESHMENTS			
33	Food and drinks	250	10	
34	Linen tablecloths	35	8	
35	Staff and gratuities	40	100	
36	TOTAL REFRESHMENTS			
37				
38	PROGRAM			
39	Performers	2	8000	
40	Speakers	1	3000	
41	TOTAL PROGRAM			
42				
43	PRIZES			
44	Ribbons/plaques/trophies	5	125	
45	Gifts	250	15	
46	TOTAL PRIZES			
47				
48	TOTAL EXPENSES			
49	ESTIMATED PROFIT			
50				
51	STUDENT NAME			

Basic Baseball Stats

Calculating Statistics

Overview

Spreadsheets can help you organize data and make calculations. However, an important spreadsheet software feature is called What If Analysis. By using cell references in formulas, data can be changed at any time and formulas will recalculate the results automatically. Baseball fans know the importance of statistics. Using a spreadsheet to calculate some basic baseball stats will make the job of updating information on your favorite player a walk in the park.

In this lesson, you will compute six baseball statistics using division formulas in your spreadsheet.

New Skills / TEKS

Using Basic Formulas: Division

TEKS: 6.B.ii

Instructions

1. Create a new spreadsheet.

2. Use the default font and size of the spreadsheet software being used.

3. Type the data as shown in **Figure 7.21-A**.

4. Resize all columns so that all data is displayed.

5. Save the spreadsheet as **STATS**.

6. Format the width of columns A–J to 20. Format columns A–J to wrap text within each cell.

7. Format the height of rows 2, 5, 8, 11, 14, and 17 to 100.

8. Bold the column headings in rows 1, 4, 7, 10, 13, and 16.

9. In cell G2, compute the Batting Average by typing the formula =F2/E2.

10. In cell G5, compute the Earned Run Average by typing the formula =(E5*9)/F5.

11. In cell G8, compute the W-L Percentage by typing the formula =E8/F8.

12. In cell G11, compute the Slugging Percentage by typing the formula =E11/F11.

13. In cell J14, compute the On-Base Percentage by typing the formula =(F14+G14+H14)/(E14+G14+H14+I14).

14. In cell H17, compute the Fielding Average by typing the formula =(E17+F17)/(E17+F17+G17).

15. Decrease the decimal places for cells G2, G5, G8, G11, J14, and H17 to 2 decimal places.

16. Display formulas in the spreadsheet to check for accuracy.

17. Format the spreadsheet to be centered both horizontally and vertically.

18. Set the sheet to print gridlines.

19. Change the page layout orientation to landscape and adjust the page scaling to fit to one page.

20. Carefully proofread your work for accuracy.

21. Be sure any changes have been saved.

22. Print preview and be sure that all cells containing data will be included in printing. Adjust the print area if necessary.

23. Print a copy of the spreadsheet if required by your instructor.

Figure 7.21-A

	A	B	C	D	E
1	Statistic Name	Statistic Abbreviation	Description	Example	At Bats
2	Batting Average	AVG	Divide the number of base hits by the total number of at bats.	Tony Gwynn has 600 at bats and 206 hits. What is his AVG?	600
3					
4	Statistic Name	Statistic Abbreviation	Description	Example	Runs
5	Earned Run Average	ERA	Multiply the total number of earned runs by nine, and divide the results by the total innings pitched.	Randy Johnson has allowed 67 runs in 220 innings. What is his ERA?	67
6					
7	Statistic Name	Statistic Abbreviation	Description	Example	Wins
8	W-L Percentage		Divide the number of games won by the total number of decisions.	Pedro Martinez has a 16-3 record. What is his W-L Percentage?	16
9					
10	Statistic Name	Statistic Abbreviation	Description	Example	Total Bases
11	Slugging Percentage	SLG	Divide the total number of base hits by the total number of times at bat.	Sammy Sosa has 282 total bases and 440 at bats. What is his SLG?	282
12					
13	Statistic Name	Statistic Abbreviation	Description	Example	At Bats
14	On-Base Percentage	OBP	Divide the total number of hits plus bases on balls plus hits by pitch BY at bats plus bases on balls plus hits by pitch plus Sacrifice Flies	In Derek Jeter's 434 at-bats, he has 152 hits, 59 walks, has been hit by 9 pitches, and he's hit 6 sacrifice flies. What is his OBP?	434
15					
16	Statistic Name	Statistic Abbreviation	Description	Example	Putouts
17	Fielding Average		Divide the total number of putouts and assists by the total number of putouts, assists, and errors.	Edgardo Alfonzo has 218 putouts and 290 assists, while committing only 2 errors. What is his fielding average?	218
18					
19	STUDENT NAME				

Figure 7.21-A (Continued)

	F	G	H	I	J
1	# of Hits	AVG			
2	206				
3					
4	Innings	ERA			
5	220				
6					
7	Total Games	W-L Percentage			
8	19				
9					
10	At Bats	SLG			
11	440				
12					
13	Hits	Walks	Pitches	Sacrifices	OBP
14	152	59	9	6	
15					
16	Assists	Errors	Fielding Average		
17	290	2			
18					
19					

Accounts Payable

Commonly Used Formulas

Overview

Sparkle and Shine is an office cleaning service that is experiencing an increase in business. This means the company will be making more purchases from its preferred suppliers. Sparkle and Shine has negotiated purchase discounts from its top suppliers. The company needs a new format for its accounts payable spreadsheet that will factor in the new purchase discounts.

In this lesson, you will create and format an accounts payable spreadsheet that Sparkle and Shine could use to determine how much it owes its suppliers.

New Skills / TEKS

Using Average, Maximum, and Minimum

TEKS: 6.B.ii

Instructions

1. Create a new spreadsheet.
2. Change the font of the entire spreadsheet to Arial, 10 point.
3. Type the data as shown in **Figure 7.22-A**.
4. Save the spreadsheet as **PAYABLE**.
5. Change the font size of cell A1 to 16 point and bold.
6. Change the font size of cell A2 to 14 point and bold.
7. Format rows 5 and 6 to bold.
8. Format the width of column A to 30 and left align.
9. Format the width of column B to 15 and right align.
10. Format column B as Currency displaying 2 decimal places.
11. Format the width of column C to 15 and center align.
12. Format cells C8–C27 as Percentage displaying 0 decimal places.
13. Format the width of columns D–G to 15 and right align.
14. Format cells D8–G27 as Currency displaying 2 decimal places.
15. Bold rows 29–32.
16. Format cells D29–G32 as Currency displaying 2 decimal places.
17. In cell D8, compute the Purchase Discount by typing the formula =B8*C8.

18. In cell E8, compute the Subtotal by typing the formula =B8-D8.

19. In cell F8, compute the Sales Tax of 8% by typing the formula =E8*0.08.

20. In cell G8, compute the Amount Owed by typing the formula =E8+F8.

21. Use the AutoFill feature to copy the formulas in cells D8–G8 down for the remaining companies.

22. In cell B29, compute the Total for column B by typing the formula =SUM(B8:B27).

23. In cell B30, compute the Average for column B by typing the formula =AVERAGE(B8:B27).

24. In cell B31, compute the Maximum for column B by typing the formula =MAX(B8:B27).

25. In cell B32, compute the Minimum for column B by typing the formula =MIN(B8:B27).

26. Copy the formulas in cells B29–B32 and paste them in cells D29–D32, E29–E32, F29–F32, and G29–G32.

27. Display formulas in the spreadsheet to check for accuracy.

28. Carefully proofread your work for accuracy.

29. Be sure any changes have been saved.

30. Adjust the page scaling to fit to one page.

31. Print preview and be sure that all cells containing data will be included in printing. Adjust the print area if necessary.

32. Print a copy of the spreadsheet if required by your instructor.

Figure 7.22-A

	A	B	C	D	E	F	G
1	Sparkle and Shine						
2	Accounts Payable						
3							
4							
5		AMOUNT	%	PURCHASE			AMOUNT
6	COMPANY	OWED	DISCOUNT	DISCOUNT	SUBTOTAL	SALES TAX	OWED
7							
8	Jones Janitorial Supply	445	0.03				
9	ACME Uniforms	875	0.04				
10	Home Depot	625	0.05				
11	Lowe's	845	0.03				
12	Walmart	753	0.02				
13	Ace Hardware	542	0.06				
14	Scotts	684	0.03				
15	Bluebird Hardware	375	0.05				
16	Gemplers	157	0.04				
17	Target	460	0.03				
18	Lesco	587	0.04				
19	Extremely Green Cleaners	575	0.05				
20	Rayfield Hardware	250	0.05				
21	Neeps	982	0.04				
22	Global Supply	1740	0.04				
23	Jack's Small Engines	687	0.05				
24	Commercial Machines	575	0.04				
25	Greene's Janitorial	442	0.05				
26	Sears	542	0.04				
27	U-Clean Janitorial Equipment	214	0.04				
28							
29	TOTALS						
30	AVERAGE						
31	MAXIMUM						
32	MINIMUM						
33							
34	STUDENT NAME						

Skittles

Formatting Fractions

Overview

Decimals can be represented as percentages and also as fractions. For example, the number 0.25 can be expressed as 25% or 1/4. Formatting numbers in your spreadsheet as fractions produces a perfectly reduced fraction when numbers are entered or calculated as decimal values. When typing fractions, always format the cells as fractions so that your numbers are not converted to dates. For example, typing 3/4 in an unformatted cell will result in 4-Mar.

In this lesson, you will compute the fraction of a particular color of Skittles candy based on all of the Skittles you have given to six friends.

New Skills / TEKS

Formatting Cells as Fractions

TEKS: 6.B.ii

Instructions

1. Create a new spreadsheet.
2. Use the default font and size of the spreadsheet software being used.
3. Type the data as shown in **Figure 7.23-A**.
4. Resize all columns so that all data is displayed.
5. Save the spreadsheet as **SKITTLES**.
6. Change the font size of the title in cell A1 to 20 point.
7. Merge and center cell A1 across columns A–I.
8. Bold and center align the column headings in row 3.
9. Apply a purple fill to cell B3.
10. Apply a blue fill to cell C3.
11. Apply a green fill to cell D3.
12. Apply a yellow fill to cell E3.
13. Apply an orange fill to cell F3.
14. Apply a red fill to cell G3.
15. In cell H4, compute the total of the first friend's Skittles by typing the formula =SUM(B4:G4).
16. In cell I4, compute the Fraction of Purple Skittles for the first friend by typing the formula =B4/H4.

17. Format column I as a Fraction.

18. Select cells H4–I4 and copy and paste the formulas down to the remaining friends using the AutoFill feature.

19. In cell B10, compute the Total of Purple Skittles by typing the formula =SUM(B4:B9).

20. Copy and paste the formula in cell B10 across to the remaining colors using the AutoFill feature.

21. Display formulas in the spreadsheet to check for accuracy.

22. Format the spreadsheet to be centered both horizontally and vertically.

23. Set the sheet to print gridlines.

24. Change the page layout orientation to landscape and adjust the page scaling to fit to one page.

25. Carefully proofread your work for accuracy.

26. Be sure any changes have been saved.

27. Print preview and be sure that all cells containing data will be included in printing. Adjust the print area if necessary.

28. Print a copy of the spreadsheet if required by your instructor.

Figure 7.23-A

	A	B	C	D	E	F	G	H	I
1	Skittles for My Friends								
2									
3		Purple	Blue	Green	Yellow	Orange	Red	Total	Fraction of Purple
4	Friend #1	10	2	5	8	3	2		
5	Friend #2	8	8	2	8	6	2		
6	Friend #3	7	5	5	9	10	6		
7	Friend #4	7	5	10	10	8	9		
8	Friend #5	7	4	6	10	7	7		
9	Friend #6	4	3	5	8	5	8		
10	Totals								
11									
12	STUDENT NAME								

Sales Projection

Working with Absolute Cell Reference

Overview

Sparkle and Shine, an office cleaning service, has experienced a 15 percent increase in sales this past year as a result of an aggressive marketing campaign. It was so successful that they plan to run it again in January. They are even considering franchising Sparkle and Shine now that they have proven the business is profitable. Management wants a sales projection for the coming year that they can show to potential franchisors.

In this lesson, you will use the year-end sales figures and percentages of projected growth to calculate a sales projection for Sparkle and Shine.

New Skills / TEKS

Using Absolute Cell References

TEKS: 6.B.ii

Instructions

1. Create a new spreadsheet.

2. Change the font of the entire spreadsheet to Arial, 10 point.

3. Type the data as shown in **Figure 7.24-A**. Resize all columns so that data is displayed properly.

4. Save the spreadsheet as **PROJECTION**.

5. Format cell A1 to 16 point and bold.

6. Format rows 3, 6, and 7 to bold.

7. Format the width of column A to 29.

8. Format the width of columns B–E to 18 and right align.

9. Format cells B8–D16 as Currency displaying 2 decimal places.

10. In cell B16, compute the total Sales This Year by typing the formula =SUM(B8:B14).

11. In cell C8, compute the Projected 15% Growth by typing the formula =15%*B8.

12. Use the AutoFill feature to copy the formula down column C to C14.

13. In cell D8, compute the Sales Next Year by typing the formula =B8+C8.

14. Use the AutoFill feature to copy the formula down column D to D14.

15. Using absolute cell reference, in cell E8, compute the % of Sales by typing the formula =B8/$B$16.

16. Use the AutoFill feature to copy the formula down column E to E14.

17. Use the AutoFill feature to copy the formula from cell B16 across to cells C16–E16.

18. Format column E as Percentage displaying 2 decimal places.

19. Display formulas in the spreadsheet to check for accuracy.

20. Set the sheet to print gridlines.

21. Carefully proofread your work for accuracy.

22. Be sure any changes have been saved.

23. Adjust the page scaling to fit to one page.

24. Print preview and be sure that all cells containing data will be included in printing. Adjust the print area if necessary.

25. Print a copy of the spreadsheet if required by your instructor.

Figure 7.24-A

	A	B	C	D	E
1	Sparkle and Shine				
2					
3	Annual Sales Forecast				
4					
5					
6		SALES	PROJECTED	SALES	% OF
7	SERVICES	THIS YEAR	15% GROWTH	NEXT YEAR	SALES
8	Daily basic cleaning	29808.8			
9	Weekly basic cleaning	21000.24			
10	Semi-monthly cleaning	5280.56			
11	Semi-annual deep cleaning	12150.78			
12	Window cleaning	5400.62			
13	Move-in/move-out cleaning	23700.52			
14	Carpet cleaning	27000.45			
15					
16	TOTALS				
17					
18	STUDENT NAME				

Forever 21 Part 2

Determining the Number of Items

Overview

Although your spreadsheet software has numbered rows, it is often difficult to determine how many items your worksheet contains. The COUNT function is a reliable way to count the number of items in a range of cells that contain data. It is even more difficult to discern just how many items satisfy a certain criteria. For instance, suppose you have surveyed 10 people about their favorite ice cream and you have entered the choices in a spreadsheet. Now you want to know how many people chose vanilla. Using the COUNTIF function for the range of responses would automatically tally up the results of the chosen criterion—vanilla.

In this lesson, you will use the COUNTIF function to tally the specific types of items in the inventory spreadsheet you created in a previous lesson for Forever 21.

New Skills / TEKS

Using the COUNTIF Function

TEKS: 6.B.ii

Instructions

1. Open the file **FOREVER** previously created in **Lesson 7.11**.

2. Save the spreadsheet as **FOREVER2**.

3. Click on cell A28 and move it to cell A38.

4. Type the new data as shown in **Figure 7.25-A**.

5. Resize all columns so that all data is displayed.

6. Bold row 29.

7. Right align cells A29–A36.

8. Center align cells B30–B36 and cells D30–D36.

9. Format cells B30–B36 and D30–D36 as Numbers displaying 0 decimal places.

10. In cell B30, compute the number of Dresses in the list by typing the formula =COUNTIF(A4:A26, "Dresses").

11. In cell B31, compute the number of Men's Hoodies in the list by typing the formula =COUNTIF(A4:A26, "Men's Hoodies").

12. In cell B32, compute the number of Tops in the list by typing the formula =COUNTIF(A4:A26, "Tops").

13. In cell B33, compute the number of Tees & Tanks in the list by typing the formula =COUNTIF(A4:A26, "Tees & Tanks").

14. In cell B34, compute the number of Suits in the list by typing the formula =COUNTIF(A4:A26, "Suits").

15. In cell B35, compute the number of Sweaters in the list by typing the formula =COUNTIF(A4:A26, "Sweaters").

16. In cell B36, use AutoSum to compute the total number of items in cells B30–B35.

17. In cell D30, compute the number of items that are Cotton in the list by typing the formula =COUNTIF(D4:D26, "Cotton").

18. In cell D31, compute the number of items that are Acrylic in the list by typing the formula =COUNTIF(D4:D26, "Acrylic").

19. In cell D32, compute the number of items that are Rayon in the list by typing the formula =COUNTIF(D4:D26, "Rayon").

20. In cell D33, compute the number of items that are Polyester in the list by typing the formula =COUNTIF(D4:D26, "Polyester").

21. In cell D34, compute the number of items that are Wool in the list by typing the formula =COUNTIF(D4:D26, "Wool").

22. In cell D35, compute the number of items that are Chiffon in the list by typing the formula =COUNTIF(D4:D26, "Chiffon").

23. In cell D36, use AutoSum to compute the total number of items in cells D30–D35.

24. Apply a bottom border to cells B35 and D35.

25. Apply a double bottom border to cells B36 and D36.

26. Display formulas in the spreadsheet to check for accuracy.

27. Carefully proofread your work for accuracy.

28. Be sure any changes have been saved.

29. Print preview and be sure that all cells containing data will be included in printing. Adjust the print area if necessary.

30. Print a copy of the spreadsheet if required by your instructor.

Figure 7.25-A

	A	B	C	D
29	Category Quantities		Style Quantities	
30	Number of Dresses		Number of items that are Cotton	
31	Number of Men's Hoodies		Number of items that are Acrylic	
32	Number of Tops		Number of items that are Rayon	
33	Number of Tees & Tanks		Number of items that are Polyester	
34	Number of Suits		Number of items that are Wool	
35	Number of Sweaters		Number of items that are Chiffon	
36	Total Items			
37				
38	STUDENT NAME			

The Ultimate Pay Raise

Working with Conditions

Overview

It is difficult to make consistent decisions. Any time you can automate a process that is based on an agreed-upon condition, you are saving yourself time and ensuring consistent results. The IF function in your spreadsheet software is made to decide for you. Based on an entered criterion and result, the function will determine what is entered in a cell. For example, in an effort to even out employee salaries, Gravity, Inc. announced a pay raise for all employees based on the current employee salaries. Employees who currently earn under $50K will receive a $5K pay raise, and those who earn above $50K will receive a $4K pay raise.

In this lesson, you will use the IF function and an addition formula to calculate the new salary for 25 employees.

New Skills / TEKS

Using Conditions in Formulas

TEKS: 6.B.ii

Instructions

1. Create a new spreadsheet.

2. Use the default font and size of the spreadsheet software being used.

3. Type the data as shown in **Figure 7.26-A**.

4. Resize all columns so that all data is displayed.

5. Save the spreadsheet as **RAISE**.

6. Change the font size of the title in cell A1 to 12 point.

7. Merge and center cell A1 across columns A–E.

8. Bold the column headings in row 3.

9. In cell D4, compute the Pay Raise for the first employee by typing the conditional formula =IF(C4<50000,5000,4000).

10. In cell E4, compute the New Salary for the first employee by typing the formula =C4+D4.

11. Select cells D4–E4 and copy and paste the formulas down to the remaining employees.

12. Format cells C4–E28 as Accounting (if available) displaying two decimal places.

13. Display formulas in the spreadsheet to check for accuracy.

14. Format the spreadsheet to be centered both horizontally and vertically.

15. Set the sheet to print gridlines.

16. Change the page layout orientation to landscape and adjust the page scaling to fit to one page.

17. Carefully proofread your work for accuracy.

18. Be sure any changes have been saved.

19. Print preview and be sure that all cells containing data will be included in printing. Adjust the print area if necessary.

20. Print a copy of the spreadsheet if required by your instructor.

Figure 7.26-A

	A	B	C	D	E
1	Gravity, Inc. Pay Scale Raises				
2					
3	EMPLOYEE LAST NAME	EMPLOYEE FIRST NAME	Current Salary	Pay Raise	New Salary
4	Powers	Jeremiah	73650		
5	Harmon	Donald	74713		
6	Mack	Greg	47968		
7	Young	Angel	68140		
8	Boyd	Dana	91584		
9	Wood	Eric	53703		
10	Freeman	Patricia	40324		
11	Gibbs	Kara	84462		
12	Pitman	James	99127		
13	Curtis	Lilly	58335		
14	Lawson	Natalie	91464		
15	Gordon	David	92777		
16	Wallace	Michelle	57567		
17	Copeland	Doreen	95507		
18	Jacobs	Will	53074		
19	Watson	Stephanie	42327		
20	Casey	Tracy	49408		
21	Cain	Brandon	83546		
22	Richards	Kerry	62615		
23	Fuller	Kelsey	91438		
24	Webster	Sasha	79991		
25	Smith	Sarah	56509		
26	Anderson	Michael	71109		
27	Barber	Daniel	55994		
28	Perry	Kyra	74557		
29					
30	STUDENT NAME				

Dream House Mortgage

Determining Loan Payments

Overview

Mortgage rates over the years have seen many lows and highs. The price of a home in America has also been wide ranging.

Wouldn't it be interesting to compare what the monthly mortgage payment on the average home prices throughout the years would be with both the lowest and highest interest rates? What would our great-great-grandparents have thought of these high prices and low rates? The PMT function will do the job of calculating the monthly payment based on a loan amount, interest rate, and 30 years of monthly payments.

In this lesson, you will use the PMT function to find the monthly mortgage payment of the average American mortgage from 1971 through 2010.

New Skills / TEKS

Using the Payment (PMT) Function

TEKS: 6.B.ii

Instructions

1. Create a new spreadsheet.
2. Use the default font and size of the spreadsheet software being used.
3. Type the data as shown in **Figure 7.27-A**.
4. Resize all columns so that all data is displayed.
5. Save the spreadsheet as **MORTGAGE**.
6. Change the font size of the title in cell A1 to 18 point.
7. Merge and center cell A1 across columns A–I.
8. Bold the column headings in row 2.
9. Format cells B3–D42 as Accounting (if available) displaying two decimal places.
10. Select cells A3–A4 and use AutoFill to complete the sequence of years through 2010.
11. Copy and paste cell E3 into cells E4–E42.
12. Copy and paste cell F3 into cells F4–F42.
13. In cell G3, compute the Monthly Payment at 4% by typing the formula =PMT(F3/12,E3,D3,1).
14. Select cell G3 and copy and paste the formula into the remaining years using the AutoFill feature.
15. Copy and paste cell H3 down through cell H42.

16. In cell I3, compute the Monthly Payment at 18% by typing the formula =PMT(H3/12,E3,D3,1).

17. Select cell I3 and copy and paste the formula down to the remaining years using the AutoFill feature.

18. Format columns G and I to Currency displaying 2 decimal places.

19. Display formulas in the spreadsheet to check for accuracy.

20. Format the spreadsheet to be centered both horizontally and vertically.

21. Set the sheet to print gridlines.

22. Change the page layout orientation to landscape and adjust the page scaling to fit to one page.

23. Carefully proofread your work for accuracy.

24. Be sure any changes have been saved.

25. Print preview and be sure that all cells containing data will be included in printing. Adjust the print area if necessary.

26. Print a copy of the spreadsheet if required by your instructor.

Figure 7.27-A

	A	B	C	D	E	F
1	Mortgage Payments in America					
2		Sale Price	Down Payment	Loan Amount	Number of Payments	Interest Rate
3	1971	$ 25,200.00	$ 5,040.00	$ 20,160.00	360	4%
4	1972	$ 27,600.00	$ 5,520.00	$ 22,080.00		
5		$ 32,500.00	$ 6,500.00	$ 26,000.00		
6		$ 35,900.00	$ 7,180.00	$ 28,720.00		
7		$ 39,300.00	$ 7,860.00	$ 31,440.00		
8		$ 44,200.00	$ 8,840.00	$ 35,360.00		
9		$ 48,800.00	$ 9,760.00	$ 39,040.00		
10		$ 55,700.00	$ 11,140.00	$ 44,560.00		
11		$ 62,900.00	$ 12,580.00	$ 50,320.00		
12		$ 64,600.00	$ 12,920.00	$ 51,680.00		
13		$ 68,900.00	$ 13,780.00	$ 55,120.00		
14		$ 69,300.00	$ 13,860.00	$ 55,440.00		
15		$ 75,300.00	$ 15,060.00	$ 60,240.00		
16		$ 79,900.00	$ 15,980.00	$ 63,920.00		
17		$ 84,300.00	$ 16,860.00	$ 67,440.00		
18		$ 92,000.00	$ 18,400.00	$ 73,600.00		
19		$ 104,500.00	$ 20,900.00	$ 83,600.00		
20		$ 112,500.00	$ 22,500.00	$ 90,000.00		
21		$ 120,000.00	$ 24,000.00	$ 96,000.00		
22		$ 122,900.00	$ 24,580.00	$ 98,320.00		
23		$ 120,000.00	$ 24,000.00	$ 96,000.00		
24		$ 121,500.00	$ 24,300.00	$ 97,200.00		
25		$ 126,500.00	$ 25,300.00	$ 101,200.00		
26		$ 130,000.00	$ 26,000.00	$ 104,000.00		
27		$ 133,900.00	$ 26,780.00	$ 107,120.00		
28		$ 140,000.00	$ 28,000.00	$ 112,000.00		
29		$ 146,000.00	$ 29,200.00	$ 116,800.00		
30		$ 152,500.00	$ 30,500.00	$ 122,000.00		
31		$ 161,000.00	$ 32,200.00	$ 128,800.00		
32		$ 169,000.00	$ 33,800.00	$ 135,200.00		
33		$ 175,200.00	$ 35,040.00	$ 140,160.00		
34		$ 187,600.00	$ 37,520.00	$ 150,080.00		
35		$ 195,000.00	$ 39,000.00	$ 156,000.00		
36		$ 221,000.00	$ 44,200.00	$ 176,800.00		
37		$ 240,900.00	$ 48,180.00	$ 192,720.00		
38		$ 246,500.00	$ 49,300.00	$ 197,200.00		
39		$ 247,900.00	$ 49,580.00	$ 198,320.00		
40		$ 232,100.00	$ 46,420.00	$ 185,680.00		
41		$ 216,700.00	$ 43,340.00	$ 173,360.00		
42		$ 221,800.00	$ 44,360.00	$ 177,440.00		
43						
44	STUDENT NAME					

Figure 7.27-A (Continued)

	G	H	I
1			
2	Monthly Payment at 4%	Interest Rate	Monthly Payment at 18%
3		18%	
4			
5			
6			
7			
8			
9			
10			
11			
12			
13			
14			
15			
16			
17			
18			
19			
20			
21			
22			
23			
24			
25			
26			
27			
28			
29			
30			
31			
32			
33			
34			
35			
36			
37			
38			
39			
40			
41			
42			
43			
44			

College Savings

Determining the Future Value of Savings

Overview

Saving for college has never been so important. The rising cost of college has forced families to become serious about investing money early on to pay for their child's college education. However, it's never too late to start investing for a goal. Experts recommend making consistent payments to your investment up until your expected college graduation date. The FV function in your spreadsheet software can help you see just how much that monthly investment will yield. Decisions can then be made as to how much your payment each month should be based on what the future value of your investment will turn out to be.

In this lesson, you will use the FV function to compute the future value of possible consistent monthly payments to an investment that is predicted to yield 6%.

New Skills / TEKS

Using the Future Value (FV) Function

TEKS: 6.B.ii

Instructions

1. Create a new spreadsheet.
2. Use the default font and size of the spreadsheet software being used.
3. Type the data as shown in **Figure 7.28-A**.
4. Resize all columns so that all data is displayed.
5. Save the spreadsheet as **COLLEGE**.
6. Change the font size of the title in cell A1 to 28 point.
7. Merge and center cell A1 across columns A–L.
8. Bold row 3.
9. Format the width of column A to 14 and columns C–L to 12.
10. Apply wrap text to cell A3.
11. Format cell B3 as Percentage displaying 0 decimal places and change the vertical alignment to center.
12. Change the font size of cell C3 to 18 point and change the vertical alignment to center.
13. Merge and center cell C3 across columns C–L.
14. Center align cells B4–B30.

15. Bold and underline cell B4.

16. Format cells B5–L30 as Currency displaying 2 decimal places.

17. Bold and center align cells C4–L4.

18. Apply a thick bottom border to cells C4–L4.

19. Shade cells C3–L4 with 15% gray.

20. In cell C5, compute the Future Value of the first possible monthly payment by typing the formula =FV($B$3/12,C$4*12,-$B5).

21. Select cell C5 and copy and paste the formula down into the remaining months using the AutoFill feature.

22. Select cells C5–C30 and copy and paste the formulas across to the remaining years until college graduation using the AutoFill feature.

23. Display formulas in the spreadsheet to check for accuracy.

24. Format the spreadsheet to be centered both horizontally and vertically.

25. Set the sheet to print gridlines.

26. Change the page layout orientation to landscape and adjust the page scaling to fit to one page.

27. Carefully proofread your work for accuracy.

28. Be sure any changes have been saved.

29. Print preview and be sure that all cells containing data will be included in printing. Adjust the print area if necessary.

30. Print a copy of the spreadsheet if required by your instructor.

Figure 7.28-A

	A	B	C	D	E	F	G	H	I	J	K	L
1	How Much Will You Save for College?											
2												
3	Expected Annual Rate of Return from Investment		0.06									
4												
5		Possible Constant Savings per Month	Years Until College Graduation									
			1	2	3	4	5	6	7	8	9	10
6		10										
7		20										
8		50										
9		75										
10		100										
11		150										
12		175										
13		200										
14		225										
15		250										
16		275										
17		300										
18		325										
19		350										
20		375										
21		400										
22		425										
23		450										
24		475										
25		500										
26		525										
27		550										
28		575										
29		600										
30		625										
31		650										
32	STUDENT NAME											

Town Camp Summer Payroll 2

Calculating Payroll Deductions

Overview

The ROUND function doesn't just increase or decrease the decimal place; ROUND actually changes the value of the number. Changing the decimal place does not do this as it only changes what appears or shows in the cell. ROUND can be useful if your spreadsheet has many calculations that reference rounded cells. Additional formulas and functions will incorporate the rounded value, whereas a cell with increased or decreased decimals would still have a value that includes all decimal places.

In this lesson, you will use the ROUND function to expand on a previous lesson and calculate payroll deductions that are rounded to a specified number of decimal places.

New Skills / TEKS

Using the ROUND Function • Rotating Cell Orientation

TEKS: 6.B.ii

Instructions

1. Open the file **PAYROLL** previously created in **Lesson 7.19**.

2. Save the spreadsheet as **PAYROLL2**.

3. Insert additional columns as shown in **Figure 7.29-A**. Type the column headings for the new columns as shown.

4. Right align row 1 and set the rotation of the column headings to 60 degrees.

5. Resize all columns so that all data is displayed.

6. In cell I2, compute the rounded Federal Tax for the first employee by typing the formula =ROUND((F2*G2),0).

7. In cell L2, compute the rounded Social Security Tax for the first employee by typing the formula =ROUND((F2*J2),0).

8. In cell O2, compute the rounded Medicare Tax for the first employee by typing the formula =ROUND((F2*M2),0).

9. In cell R2, compute the rounded State Tax for the first employee by typing the formula =ROUND((F2*P2),0).

10. In cell U2, compute the rounded Pension for the first employee by typing the formula =ROUND((F2*S2),0).

11. In cell W2, compute the Net Pay with Rounded Deductions for the first employee by typing the formula =F2-(I2+L2+O2+R2+U2).

12. Use AutoFill to copy the formulas in cells I2, L2, O2, R2, U2, and W2 down to the remaining employees.

13. Select columns I, L, O, R, U, and W and apply a yellow fill.

14. Display formulas in the spreadsheet to check for accuracy.

15. Carefully proofread your work for accuracy.

16. Be sure any changes have been saved.

17. Print preview and be sure that all cells containing data will be included in printing. Adjust the print area if necessary.

18. Print a copy of the spreadsheet if required by your instructor.

Figure 7.29-A

	A	B	C	D	E	F	G	H
1	Employee Number	Last Name	First Name	Hours Worked	Hourly Rate	Gross Pay	Federal Tax Rate	Federal Tax
2	34628	Dean	Sherry	28	$12.50	$350.00	15%	$52.50
3	34784	Bennett	Guy	18	$13.50	$243.00	15%	$36.45
4	34949	Blair	Kelley	26	$10.50	$273.00	15%	$40.95
5	34910	Hodges	Earl	27	$12.00	$324.00	15%	$48.60
6	34756	Kennedy	Doug	33	$15.00	$495.00	15%	$74.25
7	35917	Bowers	Terry	18	$12.50	$225.00	15%	$33.75
8	34975	Mack	Will	22	$10.50	$231.00	15%	$34.65
9	34764	Evans	Nora	22	$10.50	$231.00	15%	$34.65
10	35261	Green	Hope	16	$11.25	$180.00	15%	$27.00
11	35200	Summers	Tricia	26	$12.25	$318.50	15%	$47.78
12	34877	Hanson	Dexter	21	$10.50	$220.50	15%	$33.08
13	35603	Pag	Cesar	18	$11.25	$202.50	15%	$30.38
14	34869	Miles	Isabel	39	$11.25	$438.75	15%	$65.81
15	34953	Swanson	Brad	15	$15.75	$236.25	15%	$35.44
16	35848	Boyd	Stacy	15	$15.00	$225.00	15%	$33.75
17	35385	Nichols	Meredith	39	$12.00	$468.00	15%	$70.20
18	35291	Mathis	Becky	35	$12.25	$428.75	15%	$64.31
19	35233	Garner	Kristina	18	$10.00	$180.00	15%	$27.00
20	35632	Carter	Ron	18	$11.50	$207.00	15%	$31.05
21	35986	Reed	June	39	$11.50	$448.50	15%	$67.28
22								
23	STUDENT NAME							

	I	J	K	L
1	Rounded Federal Tax	Social Security Tax Rate	Social Security Tax	Rounded Social Security Tax
2		6.2%	$21.70	
3		6.2%	$15.07	
4		6.2%	$16.93	
5		6.2%	$20.09	
6		6.2%	$30.69	
7		6.2%	$13.95	
8		6.2%	$14.32	
9		6.2%	$14.32	
10		6.2%	$11.16	
11		6.2%	$19.75	
12		6.2%	$13.67	
13		6.2%	$12.56	
14		6.2%	$27.20	
15		6.2%	$14.65	
16		6.2%	$13.95	
17		6.2%	$29.02	
18		6.2%	$26.58	
19		6.2%	$11.16	
20		6.2%	$12.83	
21		6.2%	$27.81	
22				
23				

Figure 7.29-A (Continued)

	M	N	O	P	Q	R
1	Medicare Tax Rate	Medicare Tax	Rounded Medicare Tax	State Tax Rate	State Tax	Rounded State Tax
2	1.45%	$5.08		4%	$14.00	
3	1.45%	$3.52		4%	$9.72	
4	1.45%	$3.96		4%	$10.92	
5	1.45%	$4.70		4%	$12.96	
6	1.45%	$7.18		4%	$19.80	
7	1.45%	$3.26		4%	$9.00	
8	1.45%	$3.35		4%	$9.24	
9	1.45%	$3.35		4%	$9.24	
10	1.45%	$2.61		4%	$7.20	
11	1.45%	$4.62		4%	$12.74	
12	1.45%	$3.20		4%	$8.82	
13	1.45%	$2.94		4%	$8.10	
14	1.45%	$6.36		4%	$17.55	
15	1.45%	$3.43		4%	$9.45	
16	1.45%	$3.26		4%	$9.00	
17	1.45%	$6.79		4%	$18.72	
18	1.45%	$6.22		4%	$17.15	
19	1.45%	$2.61		4%	$7.20	
20	1.45%	$3.00		4%	$8.28	
21	1.45%	$6.50		4%	$17.94	
22						
23						

	S	T	U	V	W
1	Pension Rate	Pension	Rounded Pension	Net Pay	Net Pay With Rounded Deductions
2	3%	$10.50		$246.23	
3	3%	$7.29		$170.95	
4	3%	$8.19		$192.06	
5	3%	$9.72		$227.93	
6	3%	$14.85		$348.23	
7	3%	$6.75		$158.29	
8	3%	$6.93		$162.51	
9	3%	$6.93		$162.51	
10	3%	$5.40		$126.63	
11	3%	$9.56		$224.06	
12	3%	$6.62		$155.12	
13	3%	$6.08		$142.46	
14	3%	$13.16		$308.66	
15	3%	$7.09		$166.20	
16	3%	$6.75		$158.29	
17	3%	$14.04		$329.24	
18	3%	$12.86		$301.63	
19	3%	$5.40		$126.63	
20	3%	$6.21		$145.62	
21	3%	$13.46		$315.52	
22					
23					

Dinner Menu

Working with Illustrations

Overview

There are many ways to enhance the appearance of a spreadsheet. Changing fonts, shading cells, and applying borders all add to the overall look of your spreadsheet. A simple spreadsheet can be improved with the addition of an image. Look for clear images from your software's clip art collection or from your own collection of saved images.

In this lesson, you will format a dinner menu for a week and enhance the look of the spreadsheet with the addition of a clip art image.

New Skills / TEKS

Inserting a Clip Art Image

TEKS: 6.B.ii

Instructions

1. Create a new spreadsheet.
2. Use the default font and size of the spreadsheet software being used.
3. Type the data as shown in **Figure 7.30-A**.
4. Resize all columns so that all data is displayed.
5. Save the spreadsheet as **DINNER**.
6. Below the data, insert a clip art image depicting a family having dinner. Be sure it does not cover any text. Resize the clip art so that it is in proportion with the spreadsheet data.
7. Change the font size of the title in cell A1 to 18 point, then merge and center cell A1 across columns A–F.
8. Right align column A.
9. Center align row 2 and columns B–F.
10. Bold row 2 and column A.
11. Format the spreadsheet to be centered both horizontally and vertically.
12. Change the page layout orientation to landscape and adjust the page scaling to fit to one page.
13. Carefully proofread your work for accuracy.
14. Be sure any changes have been saved.
15. Print preview and be sure that all cells containing data will be included in printing. Adjust the print area if necessary.
16. Print a copy of the spreadsheet if required by your instructor.

Figure 7.30-A

	A	B	C	D	E	F
1	Weekly Dinner Menu					
2		Monday	Tuesday	Wednesday	Thursday	Friday
3	Appetizer	Veggies and Dip	Nachos and Salsa	Garlic Bread	Spinach Dip and Pita Chips	Stuffed Mushrooms
4	Main Course	Poached Salmon	Chicken Enchiladas	Spaghetti and Meatballs	Pulled Pork	Pesto Pizza
5	Side Dish	Brown Rice	Green Salad	Caesar Salad	Corn Bread	Arugula Salad
6	Dessert	Raspberry Sorbet	Vanilla Custard	Chocolate Cake	Cinnamon Rolls	Ice Cream Sundaes
7	Beverage	Sparkling Water	Lemonade	Pomegranate Juice	Apple Cider	Root Beer
8						
9						
10						
11						
12						
13						
14						
15						
16						
17						
18						
19						
20						
21						
22						
23						
24						
25						
26	STUDENT NAME					

Paying the Bills

Annotating a Worksheet

Overview

Paying your bills every month is a necessity. Using a spreadsheet to calculate your checkbook balance ensures that you are less likely to make mathematical errors. Inserting comments to cells in the spreadsheet is a great way to save important payment details, such as check numbers, dates, and confirmation numbers.

It is useful to update existing spreadsheets with new data, because the existing spreadsheets can contain formulas, functions, and formats that you prefer. If you have inserted comments, it may be necessary to delete them, since they are probably specific for the cells to which they are attached.

In this lesson, you will insert and delete comments as you update a personal check register spreadsheet that tracks payments, deposits, balances, and check numbers used.

New Skills / TEKS

Inserting and Removing Comments or Notes for Cells

TEKS: 6.B.ii

Instructions

1. Create a new spreadsheet.
2. Use the default font and size of the spreadsheet software being used.
3. Type the data as shown in **Figure 7.31-A**.
4. Resize all columns so that all data is displayed.
5. Save the spreadsheet as **BILLS**.
6. Bold row 1 and column A.
7. Format columns B–D as Accounting (if available) displaying 0 decimal places.
8. Apply a bottom border to cells B13–D13.
9. In cell B14, compute the Total Expenses for the first month by typing the formula =SUM(B2:B13).
10. Select cell B14 and copy the formula across for the remaining months using the AutoFill feature.
11. In cell B18, reference the Total Expenses for the first month by typing the formula =B14.
12. Select cell B18 and copy the formula across for the remaining months using the AutoFill feature.
13. In cell B19, compute the Balance Forward for the first month by typing the formula =B16+B17-B18.
14. Select cell B19 and copy the formula across for the remaining months using the AutoFill feature.

15. In cell C16, reference the Balance Forward for the second month's Bank Balance by typing the formula =B19.

16. In cell D16, reference the Balance Forward for the third month's Bank Balance by typing the formula =C19.

17. In cell B2, insert a comment that reads, "Paid with debit card."

18. In cell B3, insert a comment that reads, "Paid CK #256."

19. Using **Table 7.31** below, continue to insert comments for each expense and month.

Table 7.31

Expense	January	February	March
Groceries	Paid with debit card	Paid with debit card	Paid with debit card
Home Mortgage	Paid CK #256	Paid CK #264	Paid CK #272
Gas to Heat Home	Paid CK #257	Paid CK #265	Paid CK #273
Car Insurance	Paid CK #258	Paid CK #266	Paid CK #274
Cell Phone	Paid CK #259	Paid CK #267	Paid CK #275
Cable	Paid CK #260	Paid CK #268	Paid CK #276
Car Payment	Paid CK #261	Paid CK #269	Paid CK #277
Electric	Paid CK #262	Paid CK #270	Paid CK #278
Water			Paid CK #279
Property Insurance			Paid CK #280
Life Insurance	Paid CK #263	Paid CK #271	Paid CK #281

20. Format the spreadsheet to be centered both horizontally and vertically.

21. Set the sheet to print gridlines.

22. Change the page layout orientation to landscape and adjust the page scaling to fit to one page.

23. Save the **BILLS** spreadsheet.

24. Print a copy of the spreadsheet (with comments) if required by your instructor, then close the spreadsheet.

25. Open the **BILLS** spreadsheet previously created and save it as **BILLS2**.

26. Insert three new columns and in cell E1, type "April." In cell F1, type "May." In cell G1, type "June."

27. Apply a bottom border to cells E13–G13.

28. Copy and paste cells B3–D3 into cells E3–G3.

29. Copy and paste cells B8–D8 into cells E8–G8.

30. Copy and paste cells B10–D13 into cells E10–G13.

31. Select cells E3–G13 and delete the comments.

32. Select cell D14 and copy the formula across to the remaining months using the AutoFill feature.

33. Select cell D16 and copy the formula across to the remaining months using the AutoFill feature.

34. Resize all columns so that all data is displayed.

    NOTE: The #s indicate that the cell is too narrow for the cell contents.

35. Copy and paste the data in cell D17 into cells E17–G17.

36. Select cell D18 and copy the formula across to the remaining months using the AutoFill feature.

37. Select cell D19 and copy the formula across to the remaining months using the AutoFill feature.

38. Display formulas in the spreadsheet to check for accuracy.

39. Carefully proofread your work for accuracy.

40. Be sure any changes have been saved.

41. Print preview and be sure that all cells containing data will be included in printing. Adjust the print area if necessary.

42. Print a copy of the spreadsheet if required by your instructor.

Figure 7.31-A

	A	B	C	D
1	Expense	January	February	March
2	Groceries	483.01	455.45	387.61
3	Home Mortgage	925.78	925.78	925.78
4	Gas to Heat Home	141.32	48.93	35.88
5	Car Insurance	121.65	121.65	121.65
6	Cell Phone	82.95	78.54	82.78
7	Cable	180.05	188.65	175.24
8	Car Payment	325.23	325.23	325.23
9	Electric	125.67	114.89	109.65
10	Water	0	0	49.9
11	Property Insurance	0	0	902.78
12	Life Insurance	23.5	23.5	23.5
13	Transfers to Savings	200	200	200
14	Total Expense			
15				
16	Bank Balance	2583.92		
17	Deposits	2707.98	2707.98	2707.98
18	Expenses			
19	Balance Forward			
20				
21	STUDENT NAME			

Take a Ride

Adding Text Elements

Overview

Spreadsheets are clearly a tool for numeric data, but even the most complex formulas and functions can be enhanced by graphics that improve the look of the file. An interesting design element available in spreadsheet software is WordArt. WordArt is a decorative way to display text using any font. Fill colors, outline colors, and shadows can be applied to the text. WordArt can be transformed into a variety of shapes, such as arches or waves.

In this lesson, you will insert and format WordArt into a spreadsheet that lists the top cars teens want.

New Skills / TEKS

Inserting WordArt

TEKS: 6.B.ii

Instructions

1. Create a new spreadsheet.
2. Use the default font and size of the spreadsheet software being used.
3. Type the data in rows 4 through 16 as shown in **Figure 7.32-A**.
4. Resize column A to 20 and columns B and C to 15.
5. Save the spreadsheet as **RIDE**.
6. Insert a WordArt image similar to the one shown in **Figure 7.32-A**. Edit the WordArt text to read "Top Cars Teens Want" and change the font size to 28.
7. Select the font of your choice and place the WordArt image so it is centered above the data entered in columns A–C.

    HINT: You may need to make row 3 larger so that the WordArt does not interfere with any data.
8. Bold row 4.
9. Format column C as Accounting (if available) displaying 2 decimal places.
10. Format the spreadsheet to be centered both horizontally and vertically.
11. Adjust the page scaling to fit to one page.
12. Carefully proofread your work for accuracy.
13. Be sure any changes have been saved.

14. Print preview and be sure that all cells containing data will be included in printing. Adjust the print area if necessary.

15. Print a copy of the spreadsheet if required by your instructor.

Figure 7.32-A

	A	B	C
1			
2	Top Cars Teens Want		
3			
4	Make	Model	MSRP
5	Nissan	Altima	19900
6	Ford	F-150	21565
7	Ford	Focus	15520
8	Toyota	Prius	22000
9	Toyota	Camry	19395
10	Toyota	Corolla	15350
11	Volkswagen	Beetle	18290
12	Honda	Accord	20905
13	Honda	Civic	15305
14	Ford	Mustang	20995
15			
16	STUDENT NAME		

Binge Watch List

Adding Shapes

Overview

Just as you might in a presentation or document, spreadsheets can also be enhanced with shapes. Basic shapes such as lines, rectangles, and ovals can be resized and positioned anywhere on a spreadsheet. You can keep shapes symmetrical by holding down the shift key as you draw them with your mouse. For example, to achieve a perfectly horizontal line, hold down the Shift key as you draw the line across columns so that the line will be straight.

In this lesson, you will insert a line shape into a spreadsheet that lists the best television shows to binge watch.

New Skills / TEKS

Inserting Shapes

TEKS: 6.B.ii

Instructions

1. Create a new spreadsheet.

2. Use the default font and size of the spreadsheet software being used.

3. Type the data as shown in **Figure 7.33-A**.

4. Save the spreadsheet as **BINGE**.

5. Change the font size of the title in cell A1 to 18 point.

6. Merge and center the title across columns A–G.

7. Change the font size of the column headings in row 3 to 16 point.

8. Resize all columns so that all data is displayed.

9. Insert a new row above row 4.

10. Format the height of this new row to 35.

11. Center align column A.

12. Insert a horizontal line between rows 3 and 5. Change the line weight to 3 points and the color to black. Resize the line so that it stretches across columns A–G. Hold the Shift key down as you resize so that the line will be straight.

13. Format the spreadsheet to be centered both horizontally and vertically.

14. Set the sheet to print gridlines.

15. Change the page layout orientation to landscape and adjust the page scaling to fit to one page.

16. Carefully proofread your work for accuracy.

17. Be sure any changes have been saved.

18. Print preview and be sure that all cells containing data will be included in printing. Adjust the print area if necessary.

19. Print a copy of the spreadsheet if required by your instructor.

Figure 7.33-A

	A	B	C	D	E	F	G
1	Best TV Shows to Binge Watch						
2							
3	Rank	Show Name	Year Premiered	Number of Episodes	Number of Seasons	Creator	Network
4	1	Breaking Bad	2008	54	5	Vince Gilligan	AMC
5	2	Dexter	2006	80	7	James Manos, Jr.	Showtime
6	3	Game of Thrones	2011	34	3	David Benioff & D. B. Weiss	HBO
7	4	The Walking Dead	2010	35	3	Frank Darabont	AMC
8	5	House of Cards	2013	13	1	Beau Willimon	Netflix
9	6	Sherlock	2010	8	3	Steven Moffat, Mark Gatiss	BBC
10	7	Lost	2004	121	6	J.J. Abrams, Jeffrey Lieber, Damon Lindelof	ABC
11	8	House	2004	177	8	David Shore	FOX
12	9	Firefly	2002	14	1	Joss Whedon	FOX
13	10	Parks and Recreation	2009	28	4	Greg Daniels	NBC
14	11	Friends	1994	236	10	David Crane, Marta Kauffman	NBC
15	12	The X-Files	1993	202	9	Chris Carter	FOX
16	13	Scrubs	2001	181	9	Bill Lawrence	ABC
17	14	Doctor Who	1963	798	26	Sydney Newman, C. E. Webber, Donald Wilson	BBC
18	15	The Sopranos	1999	86	6	David Chase	HBO
19							
20	STUDENT NAME						

Shoes, Shoes, Shoes!

Using Multiple Worksheets

Overview

Think of your spreadsheet file as a three-ring binder. Your binder may have many pages that are sectioned off with tabbed separators. Each tabbed separator sheet may contain a name for that section, and in the section there could be multiple pages. A spreadsheet works in a similar way. Along the bottom of your screen, you will find tabs with default names such as Sheet1 and Sheet2. You can rename the sheets with a name that makes sense based on the data on the sheet. Cells on multiple worksheets can be referenced in other sheets. You can reference the contents of a cell, or in the case of values, incorporate the cell reference in a formula.

In this lesson, you will create a spreadsheet with multiple sheets and format formulas with referenced cells from the file's multiple sheets.

New Skills / TEKS

Referencing Cells from Other Worksheets • Printing Multiple Worksheets

TEKS: 6.B.ii

Instructions

1. Create a new spreadsheet.
2. Use the default font and size of the spreadsheet software being used.
3. Rename Sheet1 as **DETAIL**.
4. Rename Sheet2 as **SUMMARY**.
5. Save the spreadsheet as **SHOES**.
6. Make the following changes to the **DETAIL** sheet:
   a. Type the data as shown in **Figure 7.34-A - DETAIL**.
      HINT: Be sure you are using the correct figure.
   b. Resize all columns so that all data is displayed.
   c. Change the font size of the title in cell A1 to 18 point.
   d. Merge and center cell A1 across columns A–F.
   e. Bold the column headings in row 3.
   f. Apply a thick bottom border to cells B24, E6, and F6.
   g. In cell B25, compute the Total Store Sales for 1994–2014 by typing the formula =SUM(B4:B24).

h. In cell E7, compute the Total Annual Sales for the three stores by typing the formula =SUM(E4:E6).

i. Select cell E7 and copy the formula across to the Total Number of Stores in cell F7 using the AutoFill feature.

j. Format columns B and E as Currency displaying 2 decimal places.

k. Format column F as Number displaying 0 decimal places and a comma separator.

l. Be sure any changes have been saved.

7. Make the following changes to the **SUMMARY** sheet:

a. Type the data as shown in **Figure 7.34-B - SUMMARY**.

   HINT: Be sure you are using the correct figure.

b. Resize all columns so that all data is displayed.

c. Change the font size of the title in cell A1 to 16 point.

d. Merge and center cell A1 across columns A–C.

e. Bold the row headings in cells A3, A5, A7, A9, and A13.

f. Underline row 9.

g. Right align cells B9 and C9.

h. Apply a thick bottom border to cells B12 and C12.

i. In cell B3, reference the Total Store Sales for 1994–2014 by typing the formula =DETAIL!B25.

j. In cell B5, reference the Total Annual Sales of the Top 3 Retailers by typing the formula =DETAIL!E7.

k. In cell B7, reference the Total Number of Stores of the Top 3 Retailers by typing the formula =DETAIL!F7.

l. In cell A10, reference the Name of the first store by typing the formula =DETAIL!D4.

m. Copy and paste the formula in cell A10 into cells A11–A12.

n. In cell B10, compute the % of Total Sales for the first store by typing the formula =DETAIL!E4/DETAIL!$E$7.

   HINT: Using an absolute cell reference in this formula allows you to copy the cell with AutoFill.

o. In cell C10, compute the % of Total Stores for the first store by typing the formula =DETAIL!F4/DETAIL!$F$7.

   HINT: Using an absolute cell reference in this formula allows you to copy the cell with AutoFill.

p. Select cells B10 and C10 and copy the formulas down to the remaining stores using the AutoFill feature.

q. In cell B13, compute the Total % of Total Sales using the AutoSum feature.

r. In cell C13, compute the Total % of Total Stores using the AutoSum feature.

s. Format cells B3 and B5 as Currency displaying 2 decimal places.

t. Format cell B7 as Number displaying 0 decimal places and a comma separator.

u. Format cells B10–C13 as Percentage displaying 0 decimal places.

v. Be sure any changes have been saved.

8. Make the following changes to both the **DETAIL** and **SUMMARY** worksheets:

   a. Display formulas in the spreadsheet to check for accuracy.

   b. Format the spreadsheet to be centered both horizontally and vertically.

   c. Set the sheet to print gridlines.

   d. Change the page layout orientation to landscape and adjust the page scaling to fit to one page.

   e. Carefully proofread your work for accuracy.

   f. Be sure any changes have been saved.

   g. Print preview and be sure that all cells containing data will be included in printing. Adjust the print area if necessary.

   h. Print a copy of the workbook if required by your instructor.

Figure 7.34-B - SUMMARY

	A	B	C
1	Shoe Industry Statistics - Summary		
2			
3	Total Store Sales 1994-2014		
4			
5	Annual Sales of the Top 3 Shoe Retailers		
6			
7	Number of Stores for the Top 3 Shoe Retailers		
8			
9	Percent Distributions of Top 3 Shoe Retailers	% of Total Sales	% of Total Stores
10			
11			
12			
13	Total		
14			
15	STUDENT NAME		

Figure 7.34-A - DETAIL

	A	B	C	D	E	F
1	Shoe Industry Statistics - Detail					
2						
3	Year	Store Sales (in Billions)	Store Name		Annual Sales (in Billions)	Number of Stores
4	2014	31.32	Payless ShoeSource		3.8	4470
5	2013	29.55	Foot Locker		5.25	4000
6	2012	28.21	The Brown Shoe Company		3.01	1600
7	2011	24.99	Total			
8	2010	26.68				
9	2009	26.83				
10	2008	26.70				
11	2007	25.28				
12	2006	23.69				
13	2005	23.19				
14	2004	23.22				
15	2003	22.90				
16	2002	22.89				
17	2001	22.70				
18	2000	22.25				
19	1999	21.46				
20	1998	21.25				
21	1997	20.35				
22	1996	19.92				
23	1995	19.04				
24	1994	18.63				
25	Total					
26						
27	STUDENT NAME					

Most Popular Features

Creating a Pie Chart

Overview

A pie chart is a type of graph in which a circle is divided into sections that each represent a portion of the whole. The size of each slice is proportional to the quantity it represents. Pie charts can be used to display statistics, determine the popularity of products, and more. Pie charts are very widely used in business and mass media, and can be used to show percentages of a whole and represent percentages at a set point in time. However, they do not show changes over time.

The management of Tutoring That Works! is preparing for an annual planning session. They want to consider the promoted features of their program and their value to customers. To identify which of these features are most popular and how they are relative to one another, they want to see this information displayed visually in a pie chart.

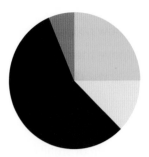

In this lesson, you will create a spreadsheet that lists the most popular features provided by Tutoring That Works! You will then use the spreadsheet data to create a pie chart. You will enhance the pie chart by changing colors and fonts.

New Skills / TEKS

Inserting a Pie Chart • Formatting a Pie Chart

TEKS: 6.B.ii, 11.C.i

Instructions

1. Create a new spreadsheet.

2. Change the font of the entire spreadsheet to Arial, 10 point.

3. Type the data as shown in **Figure 7.35-A**.

4. Save the spreadsheet as **FEATURES**.

5. Change the font size of cell A1 to 16 point.

6. Format cells A1–B3 to bold.

7. Format the width of column A to 26.

8. Format the width of column B to 20.

9. Create a pie chart using the data in cells A4–B9.

10. Format the style of the chart as follows:

    a. Enter the chart title as "Most Popular Tutoring That Works! Features" above the chart.

    b. Display the legend to the right of the pie chart.

    c. Show no data labels.

    d. Move the chart to a new sheet and name the sheet **Pie Chart**.

11. Format the Chart Area with a background fill color of light orange.

12. Format the colors of each piece of the pie chart as follows:

    a. Choose your location: light blue

    b. Private or small group: orange

    c. Flexible scheduling: blue

    d. Credentialed tutors: green

    e. Catch up quickly: red

    f. Best material retention: yellow

13. Format the chart's legend background to olive green and change the font size to 16.

14. Format the chart's title to blue, and change the font size to 24 point and bold.

15. Adjust the page scaling to fit to one page for both the spreadsheet and pie chart.

16. Carefully proofread your work for accuracy.

17. Be sure any changes have been saved.

18. Print preview and be sure that all cells containing data will be included in the printing. Adjust the print area if necessary.

19. Print a copy of the workbook and pie chart if required by your instructor.

Figure 7.35-A

	A	B
1	Tutoring That Works!	
2		
3	SERVICES	TOP SIX
4	Choose your location	32
5	Private or small group	12
6	Flexible scheduling	8
7	Credentialed tutors	18
8	Catch up quickly	25
9	Best material retention	5
10		
11	STUDENT NAME	

Sales History

Creating a Line Graph

Overview

A line graph is one of the most frequently used graph types, and is typically used to show trends over a period of time. Line graphs display information as a series of data points called "markers," which are connected by straight line segments. Line graphs are often used to visualize a trend in data over periods of time; therefore, the line is often drawn chronologically.

An annual report is being prepared for Tutoring That Works! This company has been in business for five years, and the report will include highlights of the company's history of steady growth in sales revenue. Management wants this information to be presented in a visually appealing way and have requested a colorful line graph that will tell the story.

In this lesson, you will create a spreadsheet that shows the sales history of Tutoring That Works! You will use the spreadsheet data to create a colorful line graph.

New Skills / TEKS

Creating a Line Graph • Formatting a Line Graph • Using the Fill Effects Feature in a Graph

TEKS: 6.B.ii, 11.C.ii

Instructions

1. Create a new spreadsheet.
2. Change the font of the entire spreadsheet to Arial, 10 point.
3. Type the data as shown in **Figure 7.36-A**.
4. Save the spreadsheet as **HISTORY**.
5. Change the font size of cell A1 to 16 point and bold.
6. Bold the column headings in row 3.
7. Format the width of column A to 10 and right align cells A4–A8.
8. Format the width of column B to 36.
9. Format column C as Currency displaying 0 decimal places.
10. Format the width of column C to 22.
11. Create a line graph using the data in cells A3–A8 and C3–C8 simultaneously. To do this, select cells A3–A8, and then hold down <CTRL> and select cells C3–C8.

12. Select Line with Data Labels for the graph sub-type (if available).

13. Format the graph as follows:

    a. Enter the graph title as "Tutoring That Works! Sales History," the title for the vertical axis as "ANNUAL GROSS SALES," and the title for the horizontal axis as "YEARS IN BUSINESS."

    b. Rotate the Primary Vertical Axis title if necessary.

    c. Display the legend to the right of the graph.

    d. Format the Vertical (Value) Axis as Currency displaying $ and 0 decimal places.

    e. Move the graph to a new sheet and name the sheet **Line Graph**.

14. Format the style and colors of the line graph as follows:

    a. Change the background color of the graph using the Fill Effects feature. Choose a Gradient effect with two colors. Set Color 1 to blue and Color 2 to light pink with horizontal shading style.

    b. Change the background color of the Plot Area to peach.

    c. Change the font size of the graph title to 20 point and bold.

15. Adjust the page scaling to fit to one page.

16. Carefully proofread your work for accuracy.

17. Be sure any changes have been saved.

18. Print preview and be sure that all cells containing data will be included in the printing. Adjust the print area if necessary.

19. Print a copy of the spreadsheet and line graph if required by your instructor.

Figure 7.36-A

	A	B	C
1	Tutoring That Works! Sales History		
2			
3	Years	Milestones	Annual Gross Sales
4	1	Startup - in-home tutoring only	358201
5	2	Started hiring credentialed teachers	500498
6	3	Expanded tutoring schedule	764321
7	4	Added tutoring center	950768
8	5	Expanded to 2 tutoring centers	1349683
9			
10	STUDENT NAME		

Sales Forecast

Creating a Column Chart

Overview

A column chart is another useful way to display data. Column charts display vertical bars going across the chart, with the *y*-axis being displayed on the left side of the chart. Column charts are used for comparing a single category of information, such as profit analysis, sales projections, and expenditures.

An account executive at Sparkle and Shine has been using the data presented in the Sales Projection spreadsheet during meetings where the discussion is focused on making accurate predictions about future revenue for the company. She is discovering that some attendees have an easier time understanding the forecasts she's making when they can see a graphic representation of the data, such as a chart or graph.

In this lesson, you will use the Sales Projection spreadsheet created in a previous lesson to create a column chart that displays Sparkle and Shine's percentage of sales.

New Skills / TEKS

Creating a Column Chart • Formatting a Column Chart • Aligning Text in a Chart

TEKS: 6.B.ii, 11.C.i

Instructions

1. Open the file **PROJECTION** previously created in **Lesson 7.24**.

2. Save the spreadsheet as **FORECAST**.

3. Create a column chart using the data in cells A8–A14 and E8–E14.

4. For the chart sub-type, select Clustered Column (if available).

5. Format the chart as follows:

   a. Enter the chart title as "Services as Percentages of Sales," the title for the vertical axis as "PERCENTAGES," and the title for the horizontal axis as "SERVICES."

   b. Rotate the Primary Vertical Axis title if necessary.

   c. Display the legend to the right of the chart.

   d. Rename 'Series 1' as 'Sales.'

   e. Show no data labels.

   f. Move the chart to a new sheet and name the sheet **Column Chart**.

6. Format the style of the chart as follows:

    a. Change the font size of the services to 9 point.

    b. Change the font size of the chart title to 16 point and bold.

    c. Change the text direction of the services to display on an angle.

7. Change the page layout orientation to landscape, and adjust the page scaling to fit to one page.

8. Carefully proofread your work for accuracy.

9. Be sure any changes have been saved.

10. Print preview and be sure that all cells containing data will be included in the printing. Adjust the print area if necessary.

11. Print a copy of the spreadsheet and column chart if required by your instructor.

Fast-Food Nutrition

Creating a Bar Chart

Overview

Bar charts are similar to column charts because they also compare data; however, column charts have limited space on the *y*-axis. Bar charts should be used when the *y*-axis data labels are long, which makes reading the *x*- and *y*-axis labels easier. Labels of each category are shown on the vertical axis and values of each category are shown on the horizontal axis. Like all charts, bar charts can be included on the same worksheet as your data or on their own sheet.

In this lesson, you will create a spreadsheet and bar chart to compare the sodium in popular fast-food items.

New Skills / TEKS

Inserting a Bar Chart • Formatting a Bar Chart

TEKS: 6.B.ii, 11.C.i

Instructions

1. Create a new spreadsheet.
2. Use the default font and size of the spreadsheet software being used.
3. Type the data as shown in **Figure 7.38-A**.
4. Resize all columns so that all data is displayed.
5. Save the spreadsheet as **FASTFOOD**.
6. Change the font size of the title in cell A1 to 26 point, then merge and center it across columns A–F.
7. Bold the column headings in row 3.
8. Format column B as Number displaying 0 decimal places.
9. Create a bar chart that compares the sodium content for each item as follows:
   a. Select the non-adjacent cells A4–A13 and F4–F13, and select a bar chart as your chart type.
   b. Enter the chart title as "Sodium" in 24 point.
   c. Format the chart to show no data labels or legend.
   d. Move the chart to a new sheet and name the sheet **Sodium Chart**.
   e. Format the fill color of the bars to green.
10. Format the spreadsheet to be centered both horizontally and vertically.
11. Change the page layout orientation to landscape and adjust the page scaling to fit to one page.
12. Carefully proofread your work for accuracy, and be sure any changes have been saved.
13. Print preview and be sure that all cells containing data will be included in printing. Adjust the print area if necessary. Print a copy of the workbook and bar chart if required by your instructor.

Figure 7.38-A

	A	B	C	D	E	F
1	Fast-Food Nutrition					
2						
3	Item	Calories	Protein (g)	Total Fat (g)	Total Carbs (g)	Sodium (mg)
4	4-piece Chicken McNuggets	190	9	12	12	360
5	Grilled Chicken Sandwich	360	33	6	43	960
6	Premium Buttermilk Crispy Chicken Deluxe Sandwich	580	29	24	62	900
7	Grilled Chicken Bacon Clubhouse Sandwich	610	45	26	50	1750
8	McChicken	370	14	17	40	650
9	McWrap Chicken and Bacon, Buttermilk Crispy	690	36	34	58	1450
10	Bacon Ranch Salad with Buttermilk Crispy Chicken	490	34	29	26	1000
11	Ranch Snack Wrap	380	16	21	33	760
12	McWrap Chicken and Bacon, Grilled	500	19	41	41	1570
13	Premium Southwest Salad with Grilled Chicken	380	33	11	26	920
14						
15	STUDENT NAME					

Exercise Habits

Creating an Exploded Pie Chart

Overview

Pie charts create a visual comparison of data. Each slice of the pie can be formatted with colors, and data labels can be inserted to clarify what percent each slice is. Exploded pie charts can add a second level of emphasis to a chart. Typically used to highlight the smallest or largest slice of data, exploded pie charts can draw attention to individual parts of your pie chart. Simply moving the selected slice away from the entire pie chart turns a standard chart into an attention-grabbing illustration of the most important piece of data.

In this lesson, you will create a spreadsheet and exploded pie chart to compare America's favorite types of exercise.

New Skills / TEKS

Inserting an Exploded Pie Chart • Formatting an Exploded Pie Chart

TEKS: 6.B.ii, 11.C.i

Instructions

1. Create a new spreadsheet.

2. Use the default font and size of the spreadsheet software being used.

3. Type the data as shown in **Figure 7.39-A**.

4. Resize all columns so that all data is displayed.

5. Save the spreadsheet as **EXERCISE**.

6. Change the font size of the title in cell A1 to 12 point and bold.

7. Change the font size of the subtitle in cell A2 to 12 point.

8. Merge and center the title and subtitle across columns A–B.

9. In cell B13, compute the total number of people surveyed about the Types of Exercise by typing the formula =SUM(B5:B12).

10. In cell B27, compute the total number of People Surveyed about the types of fitness classes by typing the formula =SUM(B18:B26).

11. Create an exploded pie chart that compares the types of exercise as follows:

    a. Select cells A5–B12.

    b. Select a pie chart as your chart type.

    c. Enter the chart title as "Types of Exercise" in 32 point.

    d.   Show percentage data labels on the pie chart.

    e.   Display the legend to the right in 16 point.

    f.   Move the chart to a new sheet and name the sheet **Types of Exercise Chart**.

    g.   Select the largest piece of the pie chart (walking, 29%), and drag the piece out (explode it) to add emphasis.

12.   Create an exploded pie chart that compares the types of fitness classes as follows:

    a.   Select cells A18–B26.

    b.   Select a pie chart as your chart type.

    c.   Enter the chart title as "Types of Fitness Classes" in 32 point.

    d.   Show percentage data labels on the pie chart.

    e.   Display the legend to the right in 16 point.

    f.   Move the chart to a new sheet and name the sheet **Types of Classes Chart**.

    g.   Select the smallest piece of the pie chart (boot camp, 3%), and drag the piece out (explode it) to add emphasis.

13.   Format the spreadsheets to be centered both horizontally and vertically.

14.   Change the page layout orientation to landscape.

15.   Carefully proofread your work for accuracy.

16.   Be sure any changes have been saved.

17.   Print preview and be sure that all cells containing data will be included in printing. Adjust the print area if necessary.

18.   Print a copy of the spreadsheet and charts if required by your instructor.

Figure 7.39-A

	A	B
1	Americans' Favorite Types of Exercise	
2	Survey of 100 People	
3		
4	Types of Exercise	
5	walking	29
6	running outdoors	11
7	bike riding	8
8	running on a treadmill	4
9	lifting weights	7
10	swimming	15
11	attending a fitness class	12
12	other	14
13	Total	
14		
15		
16		
17	Types of Fitness Classes	
18	aerobics	14
19	barre	20
20	boot camp	3
21	kickboxing	5
22	pilates	8
23	spinning	6
24	step	4
25	zumba	29
26	yoga	21
27	Total	
28		
29	STUDENT NAME	

Customer Traffic Pattern Analysis

Creating, Editing, Collaborating, and Sharing

Overview

The ability to collaborate and share using online spreadsheet software, such as Google Sheets, offers a variety of advantages for users. Several people can contribute to the spreadsheet content by editing cells, adding graphics and charts, etc. all at the same time. This is ideal for group projects as the workload can then be distributed evenly. In addition, comments can be shared on the spreadsheet to allow for fast and convenient communication.

In this lesson, you will collaborate and share with a partner to create a customer traffic pattern analysis spreadsheet and bar chart.

Farm to Tables has collected customer traffic data on a daily basis for two weeks. The owner, Ophelia McDonald, would like to organize the data as a spreadsheet and bar chart so she can adequately schedule employees during the busiest times of the day and week.

New Skills / TEKS

Creating, Editing, and Sharing an Online Spreadsheet • Collaborating Using Online Spreadsheet Software

TEKS: 6.B.ii, 11.D.i, 11.D.ii, 11.D.iii

Instructions

IMPORTANT NOTE BEFORE YOU BEGIN: To complete this lesson, you must be assigned a partner with whom you will collaborate. Once partners have been assigned, determine who will take on the role of Student A and who will take on the role of Student B. As you complete this lesson, refer to **Figures 7.40-A** and **7.40-B** for visual guidance.

STUDENT A

1. Using Google Sheets, or a similar online spreadsheet application, create a new spreadsheet.
2. Rename or save the spreadsheet as **CUSTOMERTRAFFIC**.
3. Share the spreadsheet with Student B and assign the "Can Edit" permission.
4. Rename Sheet1 as **Week 1 Data**.
5. Type the data as shown in the sheet **Week 1 Data** using **Figure 7.40-A**.

   HINT: Use AutoFill to complete the list of days in column A.
6. Bold the column headings in row 1.
7. Center align columns B–D.
8. In cell B10, compute the Average number of customers by typing the formula =AVERAGE(B2:B8)
9. Select cell B10 and use AutoFill to copy the formula across to cells C10–D10.

10. Using the data in cells A1–D8, create a bar chart and customize it as follows:

    a. Enter the chart title as "Week 1 Customer Traffic Chart" in 16 point, the title for the left vertical axis as "Day of the Week" in 10 point, and the title for the horizontal axis as "Number of Customers" in 10 point.

    b. Display the legend to the right of the chart in 10 point.

11. Move the chart to a new sheet, and name the sheet **Week 1 Chart**.

12. Download and save the Farm to Tables logo from the Logos folder on the BIM Companion Website: **www.MyCompanionSite.com**.

13. Insert the Farm to Tables logo in the **Week 1 Chart** sheet.

14. Resize the logo and place it below the legend.

STUDENT B

1. Retrieve and open the **CUSTOMERTRAFFIC** spreadsheet from your "Shared with me" drive (if applicable).

2. Add a new sheet to the spreadsheet.

3. Rename the new sheet as **Week 2 Data**.

4. Type the data as shown in the sheet **Week 2 Data** using **Figure 7.40-B**.

    HINT: Use AutoFill to complete the list of days in column A.

5. Bold the column headings in row 1.

6. Center align columns B–D.

7. In cell B10, compute the Average number of customers by typing the formula =AVERAGE(B2:B8)

8. Select cell B10 and use AutoFill to copy the formula across to cells C10–D10.

9. Using the data in cells A1–D8, create a bar chart and customize it as follows:

    a. Enter the chart title as "Week 2 Customer Traffic Chart" in 16 point, the title for the left vertical axis as "Day of the Week" in 10 point, and the title for the horizontal axis as "Number of Customers" in 10 point.

    b. Display the legend to the right of the chart in 10 point.

10. Move the chart to a new sheet, and name the sheet **Week 2 Chart**.

11. Download and save the Farm to Tables logo from the Logos folder on the BIM Companion Website: **www.MyCompanionSite.com**.

12. Insert the Farm to Tables logo in the **Week 2 Chart** sheet.

13. Resize the logo and place it below the legend.

STUDENTS A AND B

1. Carefully proofread your work for accuracy.

2. Use the Comment feature to collaborate and inform each other that you have completed your portion of the lesson.

3. Print preview all of the sheets and be sure that all of the data will be included in printing. Adjust the print area if necessary.

4. Use the Comment feature to communicate and decide which of you will share the spreadsheets and charts with your instructor.

5. Share or print a copy of the spreadsheets and bar charts if required by your instructor.

Figure 7.40-A

	A	B	C	D
1	WEEK 1 DATA	10 AM - 12 PM	12 PM - 2 PM	2 PM - 4 PM
2	Monday	22	31	30
3	Tuesday	26	35	31
4	Wednesday	25	39	39
5	Thursday	34	46	41
6	Friday	45	60	58
7	Saturday	60	71	64
8	Sunday	55	67	65
9				
10	Average			
11				
12	STUDENT A NAME			

Figure 7.40-B

	A	B	C	D
1	WEEK 2 DATA	10 AM - 12 PM	12 PM - 2 PM	2 PM - 4 PM
2	Monday	29	33	33
3	Tuesday	35	34	30
4	Wednesday	31	41	37
5	Thursday	36	49	35
6	Friday	49	66	60
7	Saturday	68	71	70
8	Sunday	61	67	65
9				
10	Average			
11				
12	STUDENT B NAME			

Competitive Pricing Comparisons

Using Online Charts and Graphs

Overview

When selling a product or service, it's important for a company to track how its prices compare to those of its competitors. If prices are too high, customers will buy from another company. If prices are too low, the company may not earn enough to stay in business.

Farm to Tables specializes in serving locally grown food. One challenge the owner constantly faces is that serving locally grown food is almost always more expensive than using food shipped in from elsewhere. The restaurant needs to charge enough to cover costs but still be economical enough that students, a large percentage of their customer base, can afford to eat there. The owner wants to use a spreadsheet she can access online and share with key staff so everyone is aware of how their pricing compares to other local restaurants. She also wants the spreadsheet to include links to her competitors' menus.

In this lesson, you will create and share a spreadsheet that includes pricing information for entrees and vegetables on Farm to Tables' menu that also appear on the menus of three competing restaurants.

New Skills / TEKS

Creating a Bar Chart in an Online Spreadsheet

TEKS: 6.B.ii, 11.D.i, 11.D.ii, 11.D.iii

Instructions

1. Create a new online spreadsheet.
2. Type the data as shown in **Figure 7.41-A**.
3. Rename the spreadsheet **PRICINGCOMPARISONS**.
4. Change the font of the entire spreadsheet to Arial, 10 point.
5. Change the font size of row 1 to 11 point, bold, and center aligned.
6. Resize all columns so that all data is displayed.
7. Format cells B2–H6 as Currency displaying 2 decimal places.
8. In cell F2, compute the total Maximum Price by typing the formula =MAX(B2:E2).
9. Select cell F2 and copy the formula down to cells F3 to F6 using the AutoFill feature.
10. In cell G2, compute the Minimum Price by typing in the formula =MIN(B2:E2).

11. Select cell G2 and copy the formula down to cells G3 to G6 using the AutoFill feature.

12. In cell H2, compute the Average Price by typing in the formula =AVERAGE(B2:E2).

13. Select cell H2 and copy the formula down to cells H3 to H6 using the AutoFill feature.

14. Select cells A1–E6 and insert a chart that compares the pricing information for Farm to Tables and three of their competitors' menu items.

15. Select the Clustered Bar Chart option.

16. Format the chart as follows:

    a. Enter the chart title as "Competitive Pricing Comparisons" in 18 point, and insert it above the chart.

    b. Display the legend to the right of the chart in 10 point.

    c. Save the chart in the existing sheet.

17. Change the page layout orientation to landscape and adjust the page scaling to fit to one page.

18. Carefully proofread your work for accuracy.

19. Be sure any changes have been saved.

20. Print preview and be sure that all the cells containing data and the bar chart will be included in printing. Adjust the print area if necessary.

21. Share or print a copy of the spreadsheet if required by your instructor, or email your instructor to let them know the file is ready for review.

Figure 7.41-A

	A	B	C	D	E	F	G	H
1	Item	Farm to Market	Carrie's Café	Dad's Home Cooking	Smith's Inn	Maximum Price	Minimum Price	Average Price
2	Mixed Green Salad	6.25	5	5.5	6.75			
3	Vegetable Side Dishes	3.5	3.75	1.4	3.5			
4	Grilled Chicken	15.99	9.99	7.99	14.99			
5	Macaroni and Cheese	13.49	8.5	7.99	11.5			
6	Steamed Veggie Platter	14.5	9.99	8.99	13.5			
7								
8	STUDENT NAME							

Comparing Enrollment

Creating an Infographic

Overview

An infographic is a combination of text and images that create a representation of information, and it is designed to make the data understandable at a glance. People use infographics to easily communicate a message, to simplify the appearance of large amounts of data, to see data patterns, and to monitor changes in variables over time. Infographics can be found in everyday life, such as in advertisements, subway maps, weather charts, and more.

Hamilton High School would like to compare enrollment numbers in six popular courses: English, Math, Science, Social Studies, Physical Education, and CTE. They have asked you to create an infographic displaying this data for them to review.

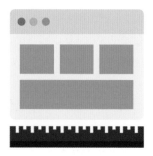

In this lesson, you will create and format an infographic that displays enrollment information for Hamilton High School.

New Skills / TEKS

Creating an Infographic • Formatting an Infographic

TEKS: 6.B.ii, 11.C.iii

Instructions

1. Create a new spreadsheet.
2. Use the default font and size of the spreadsheet software being used.
3. Type the data as shown in **Figure 7.42-A**.
4. Save the spreadsheet as **ENROLLMENT**.
5. Create a column chart using the data in cells A4–B9.

    NOTE: The column chart will be the foundation of your infographic.

6. Format the chart as follows:

    a. Enter the chart title as "Hamilton High School Enrollment," the title for the vertical axis as "NUMBER OF STUDENTS," and the title for the horizontal axis as "CLASSES."

    b. Move the chart to a new sheet and name the sheet **Infographic**.

7. Format the style of the chart as follows:

    a. Change the font of the chart title to Arial, 16 point, and bold.

    b. Change the font of the vertical and horizontal axis titles to Arial, 14 point.

    c. Resize the chart so that it is easily readable.

8. Select the column that represents the number of students enrolled in English class and insert an image that best illustrates this subject, such as a book.

9. Change the Format Data Point Fill option to "Stack and Scale with" 500 units/picture.

   HINT: This means that every picture that appears in this column will represent 500 students.

10. Repeat steps 8 and 9 for the remaining columns.

    HINT: Fill "Math" with an image of a calculator, "Science" with an image of a microscope, "Social Studies" with an image of a globe, etc.

11. Format the spreadsheet to be centered both horizontally and vertically.

12. Change the page layout orientation to landscape and adjust the page scaling to fit to one page.

13. Carefully proofread your work for accuracy.

14. Be sure any changes have been saved.

15. Print preview and be sure that all cells containing data will be included in the printing. Adjust the print area if necessary.

16. Print a copy of the infographic if required by your instructor.

Figure 7.42-A

	A	B
1	Hamilton High School Enrollment	
2		
3	Classes	Number of Students
4	English	1431
5	Math	1359
6	Science	1103
7	Social Studies	1027
8	Physical Education	780
9	CTE	922
10		
11	STUDENT NAME	

Unit 8
Presentations

TEKS

12.A.i, 12.A.ii, 12.A.iii, 12.B.i, 12.C.i, 12.C.ii

What is Presentation Software?

Presentation software is primarily used to help support a speech or present information to an audience in the form of a slide show. By using a combination of text, images, charts, transitions, animations, video, and sound, many businesses use presentation software to make a meeting, training session, or new product launch come to life. Presentation software essentially helps the speaker with visual access to their ideas, and helps the audience with visual illustrations and information which complements the speaker. This type of software is designed to be easy-to-use and learn, and can be used by individuals or businesses to create practically any type of presentation for many different audiences.

Why Learn Presentations?

Businesses, teachers, and students can use presentation software to display information in exciting and engaging ways. Presentations can be used as visual aids for a variety of personal and business uses. It was not too long ago that business meetings were made up of handouts, flip charts, posters, and hard-to-read overhead transparencies. Today, presentation software allows users to easily modify or reorder slides with the click of a button. Presenters have the advantage of maintaining eye contact with their audience by simply advancing their slides automatically, and can organize presentations in a way that allows handouts to be eliminated.

Using online presentation software, such as Google Slides, allows users to work with other people in a collaborative manner. This is especially useful in business settings where teamwork is an important factor. Team members or business associates can collaborate on and contribute to a presentation by sharing a presentation or by using the "Comment" feature. Additionally, presentations can be easily shared with people who missed a speaker's original talk by uploading the presentation to a website or server.

Types of Presentation Software

Many types of presentation software have three major functions: a feature that allows text to be inserted, edited, and formatted, a way to insert and resize graphics and shapes, and a slide show arrangement to display the presentation. However, there are some considerations to make when choosing a type of presentation software. For example, if you need to create a complex slide show with several charts and graphs and want to make the presentation stand out with several backgrounds, animations, and transitions, a great software option would be Microsoft PowerPoint. However, if your presentation requires you to share it and collaborate with other presenters, Google Slides may be a better fit.

To determine which software would be better to use, begin by evaluating the context and purpose of your presentation, as well as the audience. What is the key idea you need to address in your presentation? How many people will be there? What does your audience know about the subject? Is there any background information you need to give them to help them understand your main point?

Once you have determined the appropriate software to use for your presentation, it is also important to consider what other technology is needed to deliver an effective presentation. If you have a large audience or need to provide additional information, it may be useful to provide handouts or use a laser pointer to highlight important parts of your presentation. You can also provide additional information in a follow up email, or upload your presentation to a server or website so people can view your presentation after your speech or lecture. It is important to remember that the main objective of your presentation is to communicate an idea or persuade the audience, and you need to know what delivery tools are needed to effectively reach that goal.

The Most Popular Presentation Software

 Microsoft PowerPoint is a widely used slide show presentation program designed by Microsoft. PowerPoint is a component of the Microsoft Office Suite, but can be used as a stand-alone product. Microsoft PowerPoint was launched in 1990, and is available on both Windows and Macintosh operating systems.

 Keynote is a presentation software that was developed by Apple, Inc. It is part of the iWork productivity suite, and runs on Apple's OS X and iOS operating systems. The first version of Keynote was released in 2003. Keynote supports QuickTime videos in slide shows, and is offered for free to anyone with an iOS device.

 Google Slides is a free web-based presentation application in which slide shows can be created, edited, and stored online. Files can be accessed from any computer with an Internet connection and a web browser. Google Slides was released to the public in 2007, and is integrated with Google Drive.

Guidelines for Using Fonts, Graphics, and Special Effects

There are many decisions you must make when developing your presentation slides. For example, you must decide which fonts to use, what type of graphics to use, and which font effects will work best and why. Some guidelines to help you use fonts and graphics effectively in your presentations are below.

Font Categories

There are three basic categories of fonts: Serif, Sans-Serif, and Script, as described in **Figure 8.0**.

Figure 8.0

Serif Fonts	Sans-Serif Fonts	Script Fonts
A **serif** font is one that has serifs (or tails) at the end of each letter. The most common serif fonts are Times Roman, Bookman, Century, and Garamond. Serif fonts are harder to read when projected, so it is recommended to only use these fonts for a title where the text size will be larger.	A **sans-serif** font does not have the serifs (or tails) and is the easiest font category to read. Arial, Calibri, Helvetica, and Verdana are a few of the most popular sans-serif fonts. This type of font is best used for either title or body text because it allows the audience to focus their attention on the speaker rather than struggle to read the slide.	A **script** font is one that looks very similar to handwriting and is often very difficult to read. Some script fonts are Brush Script, Freestyle Script, and Papyrus. This font category should be avoided in presentations since the audience may be forced to spend too much time reading the words rather than focusing on the speaker's message.
Serif Examples Times Roman ABC abc Garamond ABC abc	**Sans-Serif Examples** Arial ABC abc Calibri ABC abc	**Script Examples** *Brush Script* *ABC abc* *Freestyle Script* *ABC abc*

Font Sizes

Determining the appropriate font size to use truly depends on both the size of the screen and the room. As a general rule, the font size must be large enough so that the entire audience can read the text on the slide. Since you may not know the exact size of the room where you are presenting, a guideline to follow that will almost always work well is that the title font should be between 36 and 44 point, and the body font should be between 24 and 32 point.

Font Effects

To add extra emphasis to text and distinguish it from other text on the slide, you can use font effects, such as bold, underline, and shadow. Some general guidelines to follow when applying font effects to the text on your slides are below.

Applying **bold** to text makes the lines of the font thicker. Using bold doesn't always project well, so use sparingly and with caution.

The use of applying **underline** to text has changed because of the Internet age. Today, most people assume that an underlined word means that the word is hyperlinked to a website rather than the intended use of placing extra emphasis on the word.

Using **italic** should be avoided and used sparingly in presentations because this slanted effect is difficult to read.

Applying a **shadow** effect places a gray shadow of each letter behind and slightly below the letter. You should consider avoiding using the shadow effect because it can be difficult to actually see the shadow, therefore it loses its intended effect.

Today, using **all caps** is seen as shouting at a person and would not be viewed favorably. You should use all capital letters sparingly.

WordArt is an effect where text can be modified through shadows, outlines, gradients, and 3D effects. When used appropriately, WordArt can enhance the overall appearance of a slide; however, it should not be overused as it can be distracting and difficult to read.

Graphics

Besides text, the most common element on a slide is a graphic. It is important that the graphics that you select increase the impact of your message rather than detract from it. Some points to follow as you plan the selection of graphics to use in your presentation are below.

- Use graphics that support and reinforce the key point or message of the slide.
- Use graphics that are unique and add visual variety to the slide.
- Avoid using the images that you have seen a thousand times such as "the handshake," "the globe," and "the target."
- Pay attention to the colors of the photographs you select and make sure they contrast well with the background of the slide.
- Make sure the graphics on your slide are large enough to be viewed by your audience.
- When resizing a graphic, be sure not to distort it.
- Crop areas of your image that you don't want to appear on your slide.

Special Effects

After you have decided which fonts and graphics you will use in your presentation, you can determine what types of special effects to incorporate. Some special effects include transitions, sound effects, videos, and animations, to name a few. Used appropriately, these can enhance the message of your presentation for audiences. However, use caution when choosing special effects, as too many effects can distract your audiences from the most important part of your slide show: the main message. Some general strategies to follow when applying special effects to your presentation are below.

1. Limit the number of transitions used in a presentation to one to two.

2. The audience should listen to the presenter rather than read the slide. Therefore, it can be more effective to use animation and have bulleted points appear one at a time.

3. Avoid flashy images and noisy animation effects unless they relate directly to the slide.

4. Overuse of special effects, such as animation and sounds, may make your presentation look unprofessional and could negatively impact your credibility.

5. Avoid the use of flashy transitions, such as text fly-ins. These features may seem impressive at first, but can be distracting.

6. After adding special effects to your slides, be sure to preview your presentation prior to showing it to your audience.

7. Remember, the goal is to have your audience focus on your message, not on showy special effects.

Delivering Effective Presentations

Preparing for a presentation is just as important as the delivery itself. It is the prep work done ahead of time that will undoubtedly relieve you of stress when it's time to take the stage. Use the following guidelines when creating an effective presentation.

1. Create your presentation in a logical progression.

    a. Introduction: Introduce yourself and tell your audience what you are going to present.

    b. Body: Use clear, concise content about the topic you are presenting.

    c. Summary: Summarize what you have presented to your audience.

2. Always consider your audience when creating a presentation; research the knowledge base of your audience and tailor your presentation to it.

3. Consider how the presentation will be delivered.

    a. Will it be printed? If so, select a light colored background and dark text for readability.

    b. Will it run automatically in a loop? If so, keep the content of the slides short to ensure the viewer has enough time to read each slide.

    c. Will it be delivered via the Internet? If so, use high quality audio.

    d. Will it be a standalone presentation? If so, include navigation tools for the viewer.

4. Apply a consistent theme to all slides. Use the same fonts and colors, and repeat elements such as bullets and backgrounds throughout the presentation.

5. Limit bullet points to no more than five points per slide.

6. Limit the number of fonts to two per slide.

7. Use contrasting colors for text emphasis.

8. Avoid the use of pastel colors, which can be hard to read.

9. Use charts, tables, and pictures to illustrate key points.

10. Use consistent sound, transitions, and animations so they do not distract the audience from the content.

11. Be clear about the message of the slides and know your time limit. If your presentation goes on for too long, you will lose the interest of your audience.

12. Avoid using slang, incorrect grammar, or abbreviations that your audience may not understand.

13. Dress appropriately, speak clearly, and make eye contact with your audience.

Hardware Requirements for Presentation Applications

In this unit, you will create a series of presentations that require the use of presentation software. As with all software applications, there are certain hardware requirements necessary to complete this task.

Hardware refers to the physical elements of a computer, so in this textbook's case, in order for you to use presentation software, you will need some type of computer to run the software, such as a desktop computer, tablet, or mobile phone. Input devices that you will need include a mouse and a keyboard, or audio input and output if you are using sound in your presentation. If you are going to print any of your presentations, you will need a printer. If the presentation software requires access to the Internet, such as Google Slides, then a router and Internet connection are required.

A LOOK AHEAD TO YOUR FINAL ASSESSMENT

Pitch It!™

As a final assessment (Unit 10), you will be divided into teams and "pitch" a new product idea to your instructor. This assessment will give you exciting, first-hand knowledge of how presentations can be used as a tool for creating and organizing information. Pay close attention to the skills you will be learning in this unit, as you will draw on them again in the "Pitch It!" final assessment.

Unit 8 Review

1. Visit **www.MyCompanionSite.com**.
2. Download and complete the **Unit 8 Review** worksheet.
3. Submit your completed worksheet to your instructor.

Employee Welcome

Creating Your First Presentation

Overview

It takes time for new employees to fully integrate into a company. Assume the following scenario: You have been asked by your employer, Knowledge College, to create a presentation that all new employees will watch during their first day. The purpose of the presentation is to help new employees become familiar with tasks they need to accomplish during their first week of employment.

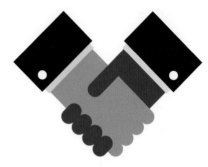

In this lesson, you will create and save a presentation that Knowledge College can show to new employees.

New Skills

Creating a Blank Presentation • Saving a Presentation • Changing Font and Font Size • Inserting New Slides • Viewing a Slide Show • Closing a Presentation • Printing a Presentation • Using Bulleted Lists • Removing Bullets

Instructions

1. Using presentation software, create a new presentation.

2. Save the presentation as **WELCOME**.

3. Read through the instructions prior to inserting your slides.

4. Insert five new slides using a slide layout that is appropriate to the instructions and content provided for each slide in **Figure 8.1-A**.

SLIDE 1:

5. In separate text boxes, type the text as shown.

6. Change the font in text box 1 to Cambria, the font size to 96 point, and center align.

7. Change the font size in text box 2 to 60 point and center align.

SLIDE 2:

8. In separate text boxes, type the text as shown.

9. Change the font in text box 1 to Cambria, the font size to 48 point, and center align.

10. Format the list in text box 2 using standard bullets and change the font size to 36 point.

SLIDE 3:

11. In separate text boxes, type the text as shown.

12. Change the font in text box 1 to Cambria, the font size to 60 point, and center align.

13. Change the font size in text box 2 to 36 point.

SLIDE 4:

14. In separate text boxes, type the text as shown.

15. Change the font in text box 1 to Cambria, the font size to 60 point, and center align.

16. Change the font size in text box 2 to 28 point. Format only the list of **documents** using standard bullets. Remove the bullet on the first line if necessary.

SLIDE 5:

17. In separate text boxes, type the text as shown.

18. Change the font in text box 1 to Cambria, the font size to 60 point, and center align.

19. Change the font size in text box 2 to 28 point. Format only the list of **topics covered** using standard bullets. Remove the bullet on the first line if necessary.

SLIDE 6:

20. Type the text as shown.

21. Change the font in text box 1 to Cambria, the font size to 72 point, and center align.

ALL SLIDES:

22. Format the size, style, and placement of the text and elements (if applicable) so that this presentation projects a professional appearance.

23. Carefully proofread your work for accuracy.

24. Be sure that all changes have been saved.

25. View your presentation as a slide show.

26. Print a copy of the presentation if required by your instructor.

27. Save and close your presentation.

28. If required, present this presentation to your instructor and/or your class.

Figure 8.1-A

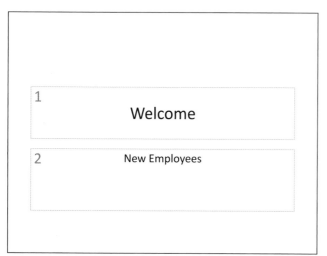

Slide 1

1
Your First Day at Knowledge College

2 Welcome

Initial Paperwork

HR Orientation Meeting

Slide 2

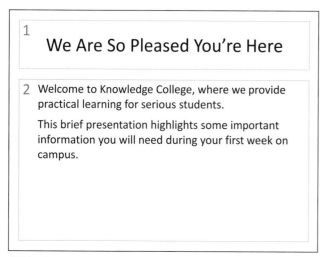

Slide 3

1
Initial Paperwork

2 These documents must be completed and returned to HR by the end of your first week:

Acceptable Use Policy

Emergency Contact Information

Initial Payroll Documents

Faculty/Staff Directory Information

The department secretary will have a packet waiting for you.

Slide 4

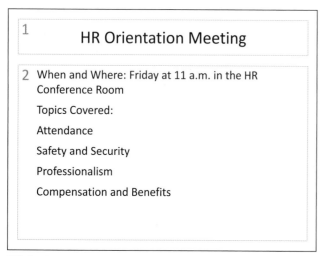

Slide 5

1
Next Steps...

Slide 6

Employee Welcome 2

Formatting Text Basics

Overview

In Lesson 8.1, you created a presentation to help new employees at Knowledge College familiarize themselves with tasks they need to accomplish during their first week of employment. Before the presentation is made available to new hires, the director of Human Resources has asked you to make formatting changes to enhance the style and appearance of the text that appears on the slides.

In this lesson, you will revise an existing presentation by making basic formatting changes.

New Skills

Opening an Existing Presentation • Revising an Existing Presentation • Using Save As • Changing Font Color • Applying Bold, Italic, Underline, and Text Shadow

Instructions

1. Open the **WELCOME** presentation you previously created in Lesson 8.1.
2. Save the file as **WELCOME2**.
3. Make the following changes to the slides in the presentation.

SLIDE 1:
4. Change the font size in text box 1 to 138 point.
5. Change the text in text box 1 to bold and italics.
6. Apply text shadow of your choice in text box 1 (if available).
7. Change the font color in text box 1 to blue.

SLIDES 2-4:
8. Apply text shadow in text box 1 (if available) and change the font color to blue.

SLIDE 5:
9. Apply text shadow in text box 1 (if available) and change the font color to blue.
10. Apply bold and underline to **When and Where** in text box 2.
11. Apply bold and underline to **Topics Covered** in text box 2.

SLIDE 6:

12. Apply text shadow in text box 1 (if available) and change the font color to blue.

ALL SLIDES:

13. Format the size, style, and placement of the text and elements (if applicable) so that this presentation projects a professional appearance.

14. Carefully proofread your work for accuracy.

15. Be sure that all changes have been saved.

16. View your presentation as a slide show.

17. Print a copy of the presentation if required by your instructor.

18. If required, present this presentation to your instructor and/or your class.

Choosing a College Major

Formatting Paragraphs

Overview

In order to get students thinking about their future, your Career Readiness instructor has just given a new assignment to every student in class. Your assignment is to prepare a presentation on the topic, "Choosing a College Major."

In this lesson, you will practice using bullets and numbering to enhance the overall appearance of the presentation.

New Skills

Using Numbered Lists • Increasing List Levels • Changing Line Spacing • Aligning Text

Instructions

1. Create a new blank presentation.
2. Save the file as **MAJOR**.
3. Read through the instructions prior to inserting your slides.
4. Insert five new slides using a slide layout that is appropriate to the instructions and content provided for each slide in **Figure 8.3-A**.

SLIDE 1:

5. In separate text boxes, type the text as shown.
6. Change the font in text box 1 to Cambria, the font size to 72 point, bold, and center align.
7. Apply text shadow in text box 2 (if available), change the font size to 48 point, and center align.

SLIDE 2:

8. In separate text boxes, type the text as shown.
9. Change the font in text box 1 to Cambria, the font size to 54 point, bold, and center align.
10. Use standard bullets for the list in text box 2.
11. Change the font size of the bulleted list in text box 2 to 48 point.
12. Change the bulleted list in text box 2 to a numbered list.

SLIDE 3:

13. In separate text boxes, type the text as shown.
14. Change the font in text box 1 to Cambria, the font size to 66 point, bold, and center align.
15. Use standard bullets for the list in text box 2, and change the font size to 44 point.

SLIDE 4:

16. In separate text boxes, type the text as shown.

17. Change the font in text box 1 to Cambria, the font size to 66 point, bold, and center align.

18. Use standard bullets for the list in text box 2, and change the font size to 40 point.

19. Increase the indent level one time to the text in the third and fourth bullets.

    NOTE: The font size will automatically decrease in size.

SLIDE 5:

20. In separate text boxes, type the text as shown.

21. Change the font in text box 1 to Cambria, the font size to 54 point, bold, and center align.

22. Use standard bullets for only the **lists** in text boxes 2 and 3, and change the font size of both lists to 28 point.

23. For the heading **List the Pros** in text box 2, change the font size to 40 point, the font color to green, underline, and bold. Remove the bullet next to this heading if necessary.

24. For the heading **List the Cons** in text box 3, change the font size to 40 point, the font color to red, underline, and bold. Remove the bullet next to this heading if necessary.

SLIDE 6:

25. In separate text boxes, type the text as shown.

26. Change the font in text box 1 to Cambria, the font size to 40 point, italics, and center align.

27. Change the line spacing of text box 1 to 1.5.

28. Change the font in text box 2 to 36 point, then right align.

ALL SLIDES:

29. Format the size, style, and placement of the text and elements (if applicable) so that this presentation projects a professional appearance.

30. Carefully proofread your work for accuracy.

31. Be sure that all changes have been saved.

32. View your presentation as a slide show.

33. Print a copy of the presentation if required by your instructor.

34. If required, present this presentation to your instructor and/or your class.

Figure 8.3-A

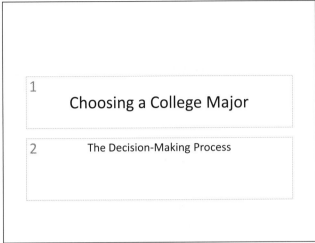

Slide 1

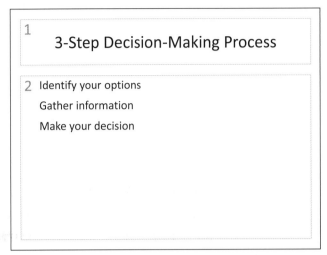

Slide 2

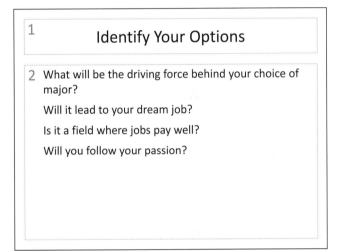

Slide 3

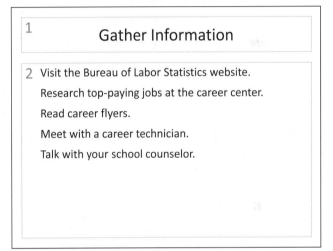

Slide 4

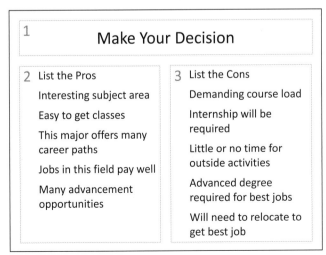

Slide 5

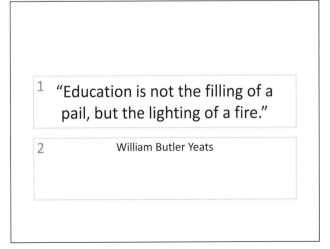

Slide 6

Geometric Shapes

Using Basic Shapes

Overview

The principal at a nearby elementary school has asked the geometry teacher at your school to see if any of her students would volunteer to create a presentation that the fourth grade teachers could use to help students learn eight basic geometric shapes. You like the idea of helping younger students, and offer to help by creating the requested presentation.

In this lesson, you will practice working with text and shapes to prepare a presentation.

New Skills

Inserting Basic Shapes • Resizing Shapes • Inserting a Text Box • Deleting a Slide • Aligning Text within a Text Box

Instructions

1. Create a new blank presentation.

2. Save the file as **SHAPES**.

3. Read through the instructions prior to inserting your slides.

4. Insert five new slides using a slide layout that is appropriate to the instructions and content provided for each slide in **Figure 8.4-A**.

SLIDE 1:

5. Insert a triangle, a square, and a circle across the top of the slide as shown in **Figure 8.4-A**.

6. Type the text as shown in text box 1.

7. Change the font size in text box 1 to 72 point, change the font color to red, and center align.

8. In a new text box, type "For Fourth Grade Students," change the font size to 60 point, and center align.

9. Resize each shape to make them larger.

SLIDE 2:

10. In separate text boxes, type the text as shown.

11. Change the font size in text box 1 to 66 point, change the font color to red, and center align.

12. Insert a rectangle and position as shown.

   HINT: Use the resizing handles to make the square into a rectangle.

13. Insert a square and position as shown.

14. Resize the shapes to make them larger.

15. Change the font size in text boxes 2 and 3 to 40 point and center align. Center the text boxes below the corresponding shapes.

SLIDE 3:

16. In separate text boxes, type the text as shown.

17. Change the font size in text box 1 to 66 point, change the font color to red, and center align.

18. Insert a circle and position as shown.

19. Insert a trapezoid and position as shown.

20. Resize the shapes to make them larger.

21. Change the font size in text boxes 2 and 3 to 40 point and center align. Center the text boxes below the corresponding shapes.

SLIDE 4:

22. In separate text boxes, type the text as shown.

23. Change the font size in text box 1 to 66 point, change the font color to red, and center align.

24. Insert a triangle and position as shown.

25. Insert a hexagon and position as shown.

26. Resize the shapes to make them larger.

27. Change the font size in text boxes 2 and 3 to 40 point and center align. Center the text boxes below the corresponding shapes.

SLIDE 5:

28. In separate text boxes, type the text as shown.

29. Change the font size in text box 1 to 66 point, change the font color to red, and center align.

30. Insert a pentagon and position as shown.

31. Insert a parallelogram and position as shown.

32. Resize the shapes to make them larger.

33. Change the font size in text boxes 2 and 3 to 40 point and center align. Center the text boxes below the corresponding shapes.

SLIDE 6:

34. Delete Slide 6.

ALL SLIDES:

35. Format the size, style, and placement of the text and elements (if applicable) so that this presentation projects a professional appearance.

36. Carefully proofread your work for accuracy.

37. Be sure that all changes have been saved.

38. View your presentation as a slide show.

39. Print a copy of the presentation if required by your instructor.

40. If required, present this presentation to your instructor and/or your class.

Figure 8.4-A

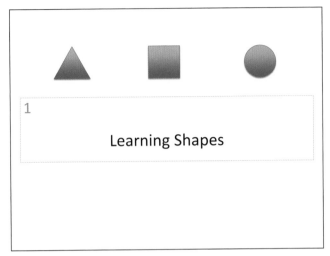

Slide 1

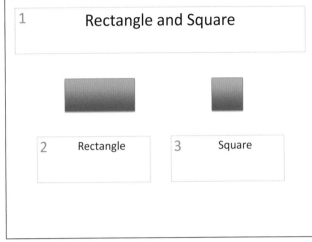

Slide 2

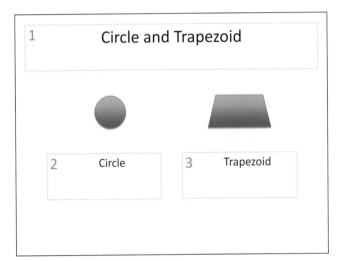

Slide 3

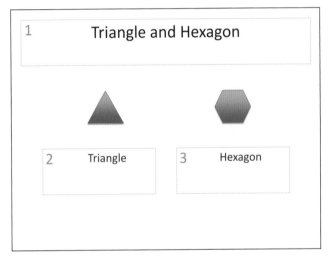

Slide 4

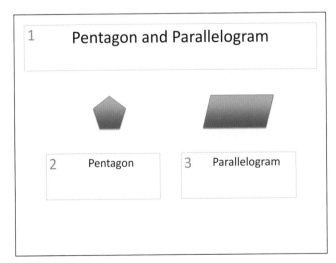

Slide 5

Slide 6

Geometric Shapes 2

Formatting Basic Shapes

Overview

In Lesson 8.4, you used basic shapes to create a presentation about Geometric Shapes for fourth grade students. In this lesson, you will use shape enhancement tools to make the presentation more visually appealing for your audience.

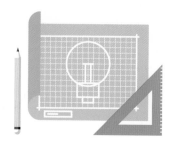

In this lesson, you will apply fill color, outline color, and Shape Effects in order to enhance an existing presentation.

New Skills

Changing Shape Fill • Changing Shape Outline • Adding Text to a Shape • Using Shape Effects • Using Quick Styles

Instructions

1. Open the **SHAPES** presentation you previously created in Lesson 8.4.
2. Save the file as **SHAPES2.**
3. Make the following changes to the slides in the presentation.

SLIDE 1:

4. Change the fill color of the triangle to yellow.
5. Type the text "Triangle" in the triangle shape and change the font size to 16 point and bold. Change the font color to black.

   NOTE: If necessary, resize the shapes so that the text fits appropriately.

6. Change the fill color of the square to a texture of your choice (if available).
7. Type the text "Square" in the square shape and change the font size to 16 point and bold. Change the font color to black.
8. Change the fill color of the circle to a gradient of your choice (if available).
9. Type the text "Circle" in the circle shape and change the font size to 16 point and bold. Change the font color to black.

SLIDE 2:

10. Change the fill color of the rectangle to orange, and the outline color to purple with a 4½ point border.
11. Apply the same formatting changes that you made to the rectangle to the square.

SLIDE 3:

12. Change the fill color of the circle to a gradient of your choice (if available).

13. Change the outline color of the circle to red with a 6 point border.

14. Apply the same formatting changes that you made to the circle to the trapezoid.

SLIDE 4:

15. Change the fill color of the triangle to yellow.

16. Change the Shape Effects of the triangle to a shadow option of your choice (if available).

17. Apply the same formatting changes that you made to the triangle to the hexagon.

SLIDE 5:

18. Use Quick Styles (if available) to change the pentagon color to a fill color of your choice.

19. Use Quick Styles (if available) to change the parallelogram color to a fill color of your choice.

ALL SLIDES:

20. Format the size, style, and placement of the text and elements (if applicable) so that this presentation projects a professional appearance.

21. Carefully proofread your work for accuracy.

22. Be sure that all changes have been saved.

23. View your presentation as a slide show.

24. Print a copy of the presentation if required by your instructor.

25. If required, present this presentation to your instructor and/or your class.

Building a House

Arranging and Enhancing Shapes and Objects

Overview

The fourth grade students at the nearby elementary school have enjoyed learning from the shape presentation you designed. The principal has requested that you create another presentation using objects and shapes the students can rearrange to build something, such as a house.

In this lesson, you will practice arranging objects and shapes to create a presentation on how to use various shapes to build a house.

New Skills

Changing Shape Height • Changing Shape Width • Aligning Objects • Arranging Objects • Grouping Objects • Rotating Objects • Using Copy and Paste

Instructions

1. Create a new blank presentation.
2. Save the file as **HOUSE**.
3. Read through the instructions prior to inserting your slides.
4. Insert **one** new slide using a slide layout that is appropriate to the instructions and content provided for each slide in **Figure 8.6-A**.

SLIDE 1:

5. In separate text boxes, type the text as shown.
6. Change the font size in text box 1 to 72 point and center align.
7. Change the font size in text box 2 to 48 point and center align.

SLIDE 2:

8. Insert a square, change the fill color to red, and change the outline to black with a 2¼ point border.
9. Change the height of the square to 3" and the width to 3.5" and position as shown in **Figure 8.6-A**.
10. Insert a triangle, change the fill color to green, and change the outline to black with a 2¼ point border.
11. Change the height of the triangle to 2.5" and the width to 4.5" and position as shown.
12. Insert a square, change the fill color to brown, and change the outline to black with a 2¼ point border.
13. Change the height of the square to 1.2" and the width to 0.7" and position as shown.
14. Insert a square, change the fill color to red, and change the outline to black with a 1 point border.

15. Change the height of the square to 1" and the width to 0.5" and position as shown.

16. Insert a square, change the fill color to white, and change the outline to black with a 1 point border.

17. Change the height of the square to 0.7" and the width to 0.7" and position as shown.

18. Use copy and paste to duplicate the white square and position as shown.

19. Insert a black 0.8" vertical line and rotate it 30 degrees and position as shown.

20. Duplicate the vertical line, flip it vertically, and position as shown.

21. Duplicate Slide 2.

SLIDE 3

22. Arrange the shapes so that they appear similar to the house shown on Slide 3.

23. Use guidelines to help you align the shapes.

    HINT: Position the chimney behind the roof.

24. Group all elements on the slide and position as shown.

ALL SLIDES:

25. Format the size, style, and placement of the text and elements so that this presentation projects a professional appearance.

26. Carefully proofread your work for accuracy.

27. Be sure that all changes have been saved.

28. View your presentation as a slide show.

29. Print a copy of the presentation if required by your instructor.

30. If required, present this presentation to your instructor and/or your class.

Figure 8.6-A

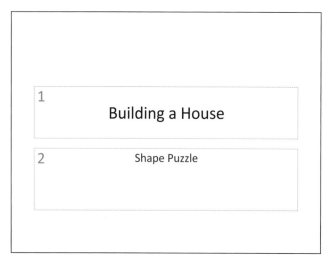

Slide 1

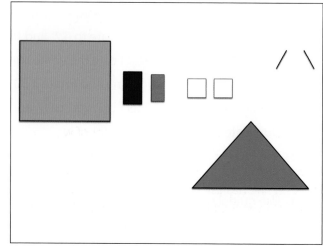

Slide 2

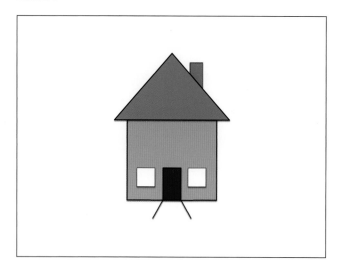

Slide 3

Touring Washington, D.C.

Working with and Enhancing Images

Overview

Your school is planning a field trip to Washington, D.C. Fundraising to cover costs for the trip requires a lot of work. This year, the teacher who is coordinating the trip has decided to include a presentation in the funding pitch she makes to local service groups. She has asked you to create a presentation that will highlight the field trip's agenda using pictures and picture styles.

In this lesson, you will practice using pictures to increase the effectiveness of a slide presentation.

New Skills

Inserting Pictures • Cropping a Picture • Aligning Pictures • Using Picture Styles • Applying Picture Borders • Applying Picture Effects • Applying an Image as a Background

Instructions

1. Create a new blank presentation.
2. Save the file as **TOURING**.
3. Read through the instructions prior to inserting your slides.
4. Insert five new slides using a slide layout that is appropriate to the instructions and content provided for each slide in **Figure 8.7-A**.

SLIDE 1:
5. In separate text boxes, type the text as shown.
6. Change the font size of the quote in text box 1 to 60 point, change the text "Danny Kaye" to 40 point, and center align.
7. Change the font size in text box 2 to 44 point and center align.

SLIDE 2:
8. In separate text boxes, type the text as shown.
9. Change the font size in text box 1 to 44 point, and the font size in text box 2 to 36 point.
10. Center align the text in both text boxes, then resize and position text box 2 as shown in **Figure 8.7-A**.
11. Insert three images of a zoo, farm, and park.

12. Crop and resize each image to a height of approximately 3".

13. Align the images in the middle of the slide and distribute horizontally (if available).

SLIDE 3:

14. In separate text boxes, type the text as shown.

15. Change the font size in text box 1 to 48 point, change the font color to red, bold, and center align.

16. Change the font size in text box 2 to 28 point and format only the list of **activities** using standard bullets.

    HINT: Remove the bullet on the first line if necessary.

17. Insert an image that best illustrates the contents of the slide.

SLIDE 4:

18. In separate text boxes, type the text as shown.

19. Change the font size in text box 1 to 48 point, change the font color to red, bold, and center align.

20. Change the font size in text box 2 to 28 point and format only the list of **activities** using standard bullets.

    HINT: Remove the bullet on the first line if necessary.

21. Insert an image that best illustrates the contents of the slide.

SLIDE 5:

22. In separate text boxes, type the text as shown.

23. Change the font size in text box 1 to 48 point, change the font color to red, bold, and center align.

24. Change the font size in text box 2 to 28 point and format only the list of **activities** using standard bullets.

    HINT: Remove the bullet on the first line if necessary.

25. Insert an image that best illustrates the contents of the slide.

SLIDE 6:

26. In separate text boxes, type the text as shown.

27. Change the font size in text box 1 to 48 point, change the font color to red, bold, and center align.

28. Change the font size in text box 2 to 28 point and format only the list of **historic sites** using standard bullets.

    HINT: Remove the bullet on the first line if necessary.

29. Insert an image that best illustrates the contents of the slide.

30. Review Slides 3 through 6 and resize the images (if necessary) to make them all approximately the same size and proportion.

ALL SLIDES:

31. Format the size, style, and placement of the text and elements (if applicable) so that this presentation projects a professional appearance.

32. Carefully proofread your work for accuracy.

33. Be sure that all changes have been saved.

34. View your presentation as a slide show.

35. Print a copy of the presentation if required by your instructor, then close the presentation.

36. Open the presentation **TOURING** previously created and save the file as **TOURING2**.

37. Make the following changes to the slides in the presentation.

SLIDE 1:

38. Insert an image as a background. Select an image that best depicts the theme of the presentation.

39. Adjust the placement of the text boxes, the colors of the font, and/or the fill color of the text boxes accordingly so that the slide is readable and projects a professional image.

SLIDE 2:

40. Group the images on the slide, and apply picture effects of your choice (if available).

41. Add a picture border of your choice and change the border weight to 1 point.

SLIDES 3–6:

42. Apply picture styles to each image (if available).

ALL SLIDES:

43. Format the size, style, and placement of the text and elements (if applicable) so that this presentation projects a professional appearance.

44. Carefully proofread your work for accuracy.

45. Be sure that all changes have been saved.

46. View your presentation as a slide show.

47. Print a copy of the presentation if required by your instructor.

48. If required, present this presentation to your instructor and/or your class.

Figure 8.7-A

Slide 1

1 "To travel is to take a journey into yourself."
Danny Kaye

2 Our Trip to Washington, D.C.

Slide 1

Slide 2

1 We often think of field trips as day trips to zoos, farms, or parks.

2 But we are planning an intensive 5-day tour of our nation's capital.

Slide 2

Slide 3

1 Legislative Branch

2 Monday's Agenda:

Meet one of our state's senators

Interview our U.S. representative

Tour the Capitol

Slide 3

Slide 4

1 Judicial Branch

2 Tuesday's Agenda:

Meet with a Supreme Court Justice's clerk

Talk with an attorney about the federal judicial system

Tour the Supreme Court Building

Slide 4

Slide 5

1 Executive Branch

2 Wednesday's Agenda:

Meet with a Vice Presidential Aide

Interview a staff member about the work of the Cabinet

Tour the White House

Slide 5

Slide 6

1 Memorials/Historic Sites

2 Thursday's Agenda:

Jefferson Memorial

Washington Monument

Lincoln Memorial

Vietnam Veterans Memorial

National World War II Memorial

Slide 6

The Impact of Scents

Using Tables and More Slide Elements

Overview

Did you know that when a house is for sale, real estate agents often suggest that the homeowner burn a scented candle or bake bread just before a prospective buyer comes to look at the house? There's a powerful reason for that. How a home smells can make or break a sale. It's also possible that scents around us impact how we are feeling. This presentation describes how several different scents make us feel.

In this lesson, you will create a presentation about the impact that scents have on people. Along with shapes and objects, you will practice using footers, tables, and WordArt.

New Skills

Using Footers • Changing Slide Layout • Using WordArt • Inserting and Formatting a Table • Inserting a Hyperlink • Changing Background Color

Instructions

1. Create a new blank presentation.
2. Save the file as **SCENTS**.
3. Read through the instructions prior to inserting your slides.
4. Insert two new slides using a slide layout that is appropriate to the instructions and content provided for each slide in **Figure 8.8-A**.

SLIDE 1:

5. In the footer of the slide, insert the date (left aligned), your name (center aligned), and the slide number (right aligned) and apply to all slides as shown in **Figure 8.8-A**.
6. Change the slide layout to Title Only (if available).
7. In text box 1, type the text as shown.
8. Change the font size in text box 1 to 72 point and center align.
9. Insert a WordArt style of your choice and type the text "SCENTS."
10. Resize the WordArt so it is the largest element on the slide and projects a professional appearance.

11. Change the colors of each letter in the WordArt text as follows:

S to Red	E to Purple	T to Orange
C to Brown	N to Yellow	S to Green

12. Change the background of the slide to a color of your choice and apply it to all slides.

SLIDE 2:

13. Change the slide layout to Title Only (if available).

14. Type the text as shown.

15. Change the font size of the text to 40 point and center align.

16. Hyperlink the word "scents" to an online definition of the word.

17. Insert four to five images that best illustrate the contents of the slide.

18. Resize each image so that they are the same size (approximately).

SLIDE 3:

19. Change the slide layout to Title Only (if available).

20. Type the text as shown.

21. Change the font size of the text to 72 point and center align.

22. Insert a table with two columns and seven rows and position as shown in **Figure 8.8-A**.

23. Type the text in the table as shown in **Figure 8.8-A**, and change the font size to 28 point. Adjust the column widths as shown.

24. Change the cells in the top row of the table to black, and the font color to white.

25. Continue to change each row color as follows:

Apple: red	Lavender: purple	Orange: orange
Cinnamon: light brown	Lemon: yellow	Rose: pink

26. Change the font color of the text in the red, light brown, and purple rows to white. Change the font color of the text in the yellow, orange, and pink rows to black.

ALL SLIDES:

27. Format the size, style, and placement of the text and elements (if applicable) so that this presentation projects a professional appearance.

28. Carefully proofread your work for accuracy.

29. Be sure that all changes have been saved.

30. View your presentation as a slide show.

31. Print a copy of the presentation if required by your instructor.

32. If required, present this presentation to your instructor and/or your class.

Figure 8.8-A

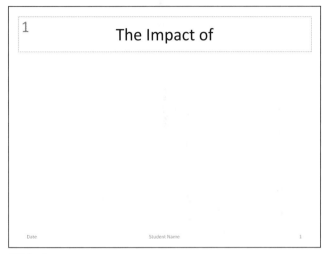

Slide 1

Slide 2

Slide 3

Individual Sports

Using a Template

Overview

There are many pre-designed templates and themes available in presentation software. These themes and templates allow you to choose from a collection of slide layouts that have pre-selected theme colors, fonts, and effects. Templates go even further by including sample slides that show how you might add content for a professional-looking presentation.

New Skills

Using Templates • Using Video in a Slide • Reordering Slides

In this lesson, you will use a presentation software template to create a photo album using images of your choice that are related to the topic.

Instructions

1. Create a new presentation and select Classic Photo Album (if available) from the Templates options.

2. Save the file as **INDIVIDUAL**.

3. Read through the instructions prior to inserting your slides.

SLIDES 1-2:

4. Replace the sample text with the text as shown in **Figure 8.9-A**.

5. Replace the sample image with an image of your choice. Select an image that best illustrates the contents and theme of the slide.

SLIDE 3:

6. Replace the sample text with the text as shown in **Figure 8.9-A**.

7. Replace the three sample images with images of your choice. Select images that best illustrate the contents and theme of the slide.

SLIDE 4:

8. Replace the sample text with the text as shown in **Figure 8.9-A**.

9. Replace the sample image with an image of your choice. Select an image that best illustrates the contents and theme of the slide.

SLIDE 5:

10. Replace the sample text with the text as shown in **Figure 8.9-A**.

11. Replace the three sample images with images of your choice. Select images that best illustrate the contents and theme of the slide.

SLIDE 6:

12. Replace the three sample images with images of your choice. Select images that best illustrate the contents and theme of this presentation.

SLIDE 7:

13. Delete the sample image.

14. Insert an online video file of your choice. Select a video that enhances the contents and theme of this presentation.

15. Move Slide 7 after Slide 3.

ALL SLIDES:

16. Format the size, style, and placement of the text and elements (if applicable) so that this presentation projects a professional appearance.

17. Carefully proofread your work for accuracy.

18. Be sure that all changes have been saved.

19. View your presentation as a slide show.

20. Print a copy of the presentation if required by your instructor.

21. If required, present this presentation to your instructor and/or your class.

Figure 8.9-A

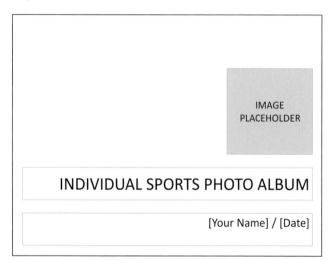

Slide 1

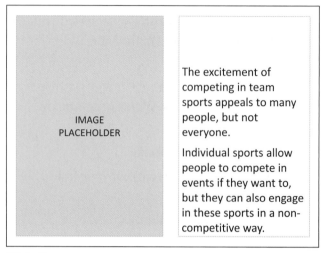

Slide 2

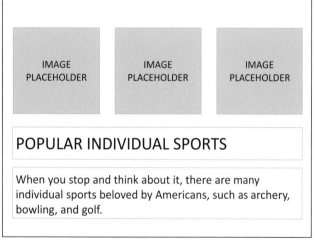

Slide 3

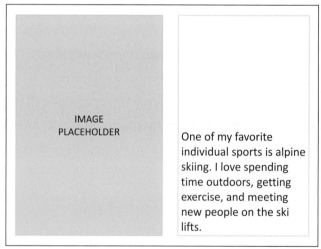

Slide 4

Figure 8.9-A (Continued)

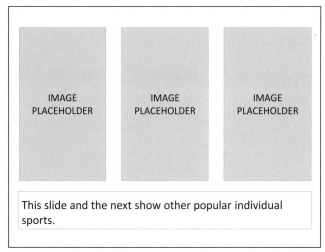

This slide and the next show other popular individual sports.

Slide 5

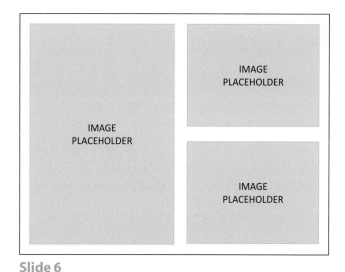

Slide 6

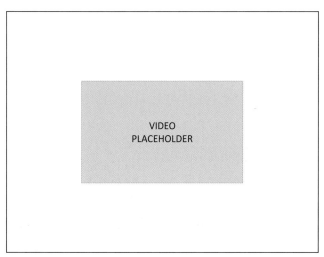

Slide 7

Team Sports

Using Slide Themes

Overview

In Lesson 8.9, you used a pre-designed template to create a presentation about individual sports. In this lesson, you will use a pre-designed theme to create a presentation about team sports.

New Skills

Applying a Slide Theme • Changing a Slide Theme

In this lesson, you will practice using themes to enhance your presentation.

Instructions

1. Create a new blank presentation.
2. Read through the instructions prior to choosing your theme.
3. From the Themes menu, apply a theme of your choice, and save the file as **TEAM**.

    NOTE: As all themes do not look alike, your presentation may vary from **Figure 8.10-A**. It is recommended that you select a theme that best fits the contents of this presentation.

4. Choose six new slides using a slide layout that is appropriate to the instructions and content provided for each slide in **Figure 8.10-A**.

SLIDE 1:

5. In separate text boxes, type the text as shown in **Figure 8.10-A**. Arrange the text boxes as shown.

SLIDES 2-7:

6. In separate text boxes, type the text as shown.
7. Insert images of your choice. Select images that best illustrate the contents of each slide and position appropriately.
8. Resize the images as needed.

ALL SLIDES:

9. Change the color scheme of the theme to one of your choice.
10. Format the size, style, and placement of the text and elements (if applicable) so that this presentation projects a professional appearance.
11. Carefully proofread your work for accuracy.

12. Be sure that all changes have been saved.

13. View your presentation as a slide show.

14. Print a copy of the presentation if required by your instructor.

15. If required, present this presentation to your instructor and/or your class.

Figure 8.10-A

Slide 1

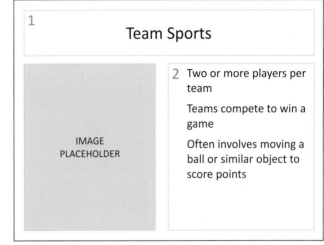

Slide 2

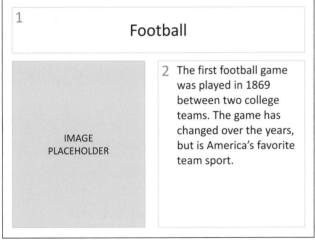

Slide 3

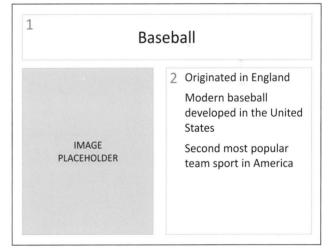

Slide 4

Figure 8.10-A (Continued)

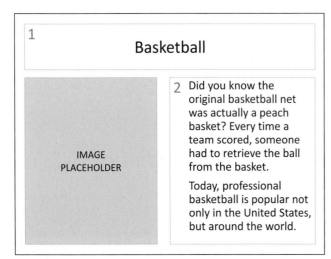

Slide 5

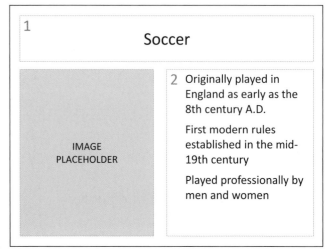

Slide 6

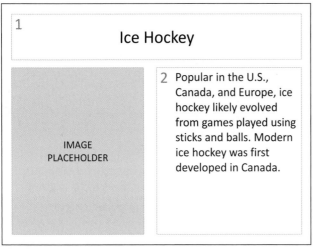

Slide 7

Individual Sports 2

Applying Transitions

Overview

You have been running slide shows using your presentation program's default method, which displays each slide one at a time with no special effects between each slide. Most presentation software includes a feature called Transitions, which allows you to control the visual effect when a slide show changes from one slide to the next.

In this lesson, you will apply transitions to an existing slide show. Choose transitions wisely. Effects that are too jarring end up distracting from a presentation instead of enhancing it.

New Skills

Applying Slide Transitions • Applying Effect Options to Transitions

Instructions

1. Open the **INDIVIDUAL** presentation you previously created in Lesson 8.9.
2. Save the file as **INDIVIDUAL2**.
3. Make the following changes to the slides in the presentation.

SLIDE 1:

4. Apply a Wipe transition and select the From Top effect option (if available).

SLIDES 2–7:

5. Apply a Split transition and select the Horizontal Out effect option (if available).

ALL SLIDES:

6. Format the size, style, and placement of the text and elements (if applicable) so that this presentation projects a professional appearance.
7. Carefully proofread your work for accuracy.
8. Be sure that all changes have been saved.
9. View your presentation as a slide show.
10. Print a copy of the presentation if required by your instructor.
11. If required, present this presentation to your instructor and/or your class.

Team Sports 2

Applying Special Effects to Transitions

Overview

You have learned how to add transitions to slides in a presentation. There are times when applying a sound effect can add an extra punch to gain the attention of the audience. Adding sound and transitions with each new slide can be a fun way of keeping the audience's interest. However, overusing these features can distract from the main message of your presentation.

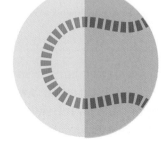

In this lesson, you will use a previously created slide show to apply sound to a transition. You will also set timings to the transitions.

New Skills

Using Sound • Timing Transitions • Previewing Transitions

Instructions

1. Open the **TEAM** presentation you previously created in Lesson 8.10.

2. Save the file as **TEAM2**.

3. Make the following changes to the slides in the presentation.

SLIDE 1:

4. Apply the Reveal transition and insert the Applause sound option (if available).

5. Change the Duration to 3.00 seconds, and apply these settings to all slides.

6. Preview the transitions you created for each slide.

ALL SLIDES:

7. Format the size, style, and placement of the text and elements (if applicable) so that this presentation projects a professional appearance.

8. Carefully proofread your work for accuracy.

9. Be sure that all changes have been saved.

10. View your presentation as a slide show.

11. Print a copy of the presentation if required by your instructor.

12. If required, present this presentation to your instructor and/or your class.

Business Meeting Agenda

Working with Animation Tools

Overview

You are the chairperson of the planning committee for a Band Booster fundraising event. Your first task is to call a committee meeting to brainstorm event ideas that will attract more people and generate greater interest than last year's event.

New Skills

Applying Animation • Applying Effect Options to Animations • Previewing Animations • Reordering Animation

In this lesson, you will use presentation software to create an agenda for a meeting. You will explore the animation features and apply special effects to text and images.

Instructions

1. Create a new blank presentation.

2. Save the presentation as **AGENDA**.

3. Insert five new slides using a slide layout that is appropriate to the instructions and content provided for each slide in **Figure 8.13-A**.

4. Change the background of all slides to a solid fill color of your choice.

SLIDE 1:

5. In separate text boxes, type the text as shown.

6. Change the font size of text box 1 to 80 point and center align.

7. Change the font size of text box 2 to 40 point, italics, and center align.

8. Change the font color in both text boxes to a color that contrasts well with the background color.

9. Insert an image related to a marching band and position it below text box 1.

   NOTE: Resize and reposition text box 2 if necessary.

10. Copy and paste the image in the bottom right-hand corner of **each** slide (except for Slide 1).

11. Apply the Wave animation option to text box 1 (if available).

12. Apply the Fly In animation option to text box 2 (if available).

13. Apply the From Right effect option to text box 2 (if available).

14. Reorder the animation sequence as you see fit.

SLIDES 2-6:

15. In separate text boxes, type the text as shown.

16. Change the font size of text box 1 to 60 point and center align.

17. Use a numbered list to format the items in text box 2, and change the font size to 40 point.

    NOTE: If necessary, resize the text box and image to ensure that the text is properly displayed and presents a professional appearance.

18. Apply the Float In animation option to text box 2 (if available).

19. Animate the numbered lists one number at a time.

20. Change the font color of all text boxes to a color that contrasts well with the background.

21. Preview the sequence of animations.

ALL SLIDES:

22. Format the size, style, and placement of the text and elements (if applicable) so that this presentation projects a professional appearance.

23. Carefully proofread your work for accuracy.

24. Be sure that all changes have been saved.

25. View your presentation as a slide show.

26. Print a copy of the presentation as a handout using 3 or 6 slides per page if required by your instructor.

27. If required, present this presentation to your instructor and/or your class.

Figure 8.13-A

Slide 1

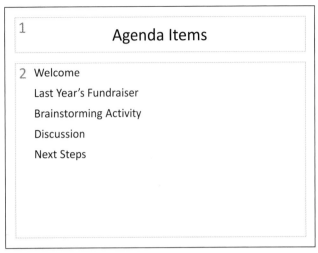

Slide 2

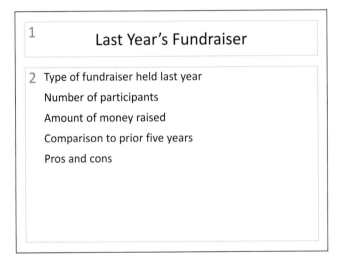

Slide 3

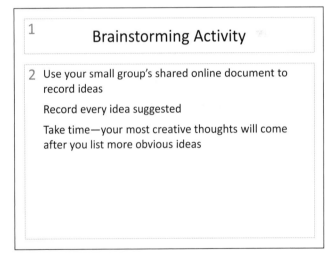

Slide 4

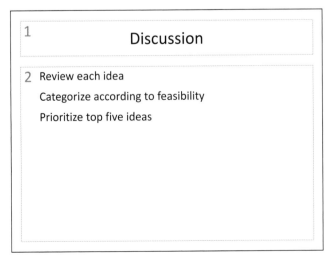

Slide 5

Slide 6

Presentation Tips

Using Tools to Help You Present

Overview

This lesson is intended to provide you with several tips for creating and making effective presentations. There are four broad areas to consider: fonts, graphics and design, color, and making the presentation. You will create a presentation offering advice in these categories. These tips will help you present well-designed presentations every time.

In this lesson, you will prepare a presentation using different views, as well as add notes to the presentation for easy reference.

New Skills / TEKS

Working with Presentation Views • Using Slide Sorter View • Adding Notes to Slides • Using Notes Page View • Printing Slides with Notes

TEKS: 12.A.i, 12.A.ii, 12.A.iii, 12.E.i

Instructions

1. Create a new blank presentation.
2. Save the presentation as **TIPS**.
3. Read through the instructions prior to inserting your slides.
4. Insert seven new slides using a slide layout that is appropriate to the instructions and content provided for each slide in **Figure 8.14-A**.
5. Change the background of all slides to a solid fill color of your choice.

SLIDE 1:

6. In separate text boxes, type the text as shown.
7. Change the font size in text box 1 to 80 point and center align.
8. Change the font size in text box 2 to 48 point and center align.
9. Insert an image of your choice. Select an image that best illustrates the contents of the slide.

   NOTE: Resize and reposition the text boxes if necessary.

10. Resize and position the image below text box 2.

SLIDES 2–8:

11. In separate text boxes, type the text as shown.
12. Change the font size in text box 1 to 60 point and center align.
13. Use standard bullets for the list in text box 2. Remove the bullet on the first line in Slides 3, 4, 7, and 8 if necessary.

14. Change the font size in text box 2 to 40 point.

15. Use Slide Sorter View to move Slide 6 so that it is positioned after Slide 2.

16. Move Slide 8 so that it is positioned after Slide 4.

17. Move Slide 6 so that it is positioned after Slide 7.

18. Use Notes Page View to add the notes for Slides 1 – 8 as shown in **Figure 8.14-B**.

ALL SLIDES:

19. Format the size, style, and placement of the text and elements (if applicable) so that this presentation projects a professional appearance.

20. Carefully proofread your work for accuracy.

21. Be sure that all changes have been saved.

22. View your presentation as a slide show.

23. Print a copy of the presentation **including the notes** if required by your instructor.

24. If required, present this presentation to your instructor and/or your class.

Figure 8.14-A

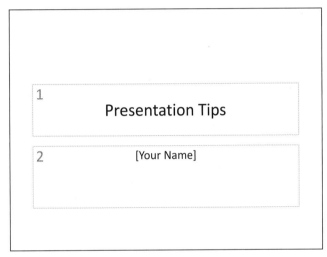

Slide 1

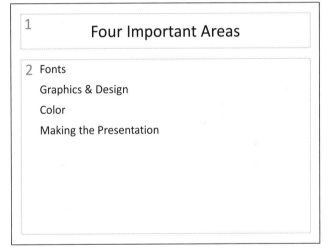

Slide 2

Figure 8.14-A (Continued)

Graphics & Design

2 Graphics Tips:
Keep the style of graphics consistent
Ensure they are related to the topic
Use them to enhance the topic

Slide 3

Making the Presentation

2 Before giving the presentation:
Ask a friend for feedback
Practice giving the presentation
Prepare speaking notes
Prepare handouts, if needed

Slide 4

Color

2 Choose a color scheme that is easy to see
Light backgrounds with dark text are easiest to read
Use no more than two or three colors per slide

Slide 5

Fonts

2 Two or three fonts per presentation
Sans-serif fonts are easier to read
Italicized fonts are hard to read
It's okay to make titles all capital letters

Slide 6

Making the Presentation

2 During the presentation:
Speak slowly and clearly
Have bulleted or numbered points appear one at a time
Do not read slides aloud—they are not a script

Slide 7

Graphics & Design

2 Design Tips:
Use subtle backgrounds
Avoid cluttered slides; include white space
Limit use of sound effects and animation
Choose transitions carefully
Five points per slide, six to eight words per line

Slide 8

Figure 8.14-B

Slide 1	This brief presentation will help you review important presentation tips.
Slide 2	Explain that this presentation will cover the four points shown on this slide, in this order.
Slide 3	Examples of sans-serif fonts are Arial or Helvetica. Examples of serif fonts are Times New Roman or Book Antiqua.
Slide 4	Whenever possible, use graphics instead of text. If you have not created the graphics yourself, make sure the graphics you use are in the public domain.
Slide 5	Slide design is extremely important. Simple is better.
Slide 6	Once you've selected the colors you plan to use, project the slides and view them from a distance to see if they are easy to see and read.
Slide 7	This slide identifies several things you need to do to prepare for a presentation. When asking for feedback, ask the person helping you to proofread slides for errors in spelling and grammar. Ask for his or her opinion about the graphics and design, too.
Slide 8	Keep these tips in mind as you make your presentation.

Kiosk Presentation

Applying the Finishing Touches

Overview

You've seen presentations in public places that are on a continuous loop and are designed to show information relevant to passers-by. Typically, these slide shows are displayed on mounted monitors or freestanding structures called kiosks located in public areas, including shopping malls, airports, banks, and school lobbies.

Flat-screen monitors have recently been installed throughout your school. Your principal wants to use these monitors to share information about current and upcoming events, and has asked you to create a brief slide show that can be easily updated and displayed each day.

In this lesson, you will use your creativity and software skills to create a presentation that will loop continuously. You will choose your own design elements and add special effects as needed.

New Skills

Setting Up a Slide Show • Rehearsing Timings for a Slide Show • Making Your Own Design Decisions

Instructions

NOTE: Unless otherwise noted, the layout and design, font size(s), and style(s) for this lesson are left for you to decide.

1. Save the presentation as **KIOSK**.

2. Read through the instructions prior to inserting your slides.

3. Insert two new slides using a slide layout that is appropriate to the instructions and content provided for each slide in **Figure 8.15-A**.

SLIDES 1–3:

4. In separate text boxes, type the text as shown.

5. Change the background of all slides to a fill color of your choice.

6. Change the font, font size, font color, and alignment of the text so that it is readable and projects a professional appearance.

7. Apply a transition to each slide.

8. Add an image to each slide to enhance the contents of the presentation.

9. Apply animations and effects to each image.

10. When your presentation design is complete, set up your slide show to loop continuously.

11. Set the timing for each slide to display for 6–8 seconds.

ALL SLIDES:

12. Format the size, style, and placement of the text and elements (if applicable) so that this presentation projects a professional appearance.

13. Carefully proofread your work for accuracy.

14. Be sure that all changes have been saved.

15. View your presentation as a slide show.

16. Print a copy of the presentation if required by your instructor.

17. If required, present this presentation to your instructor and/or your class.

Figure 8.15-A

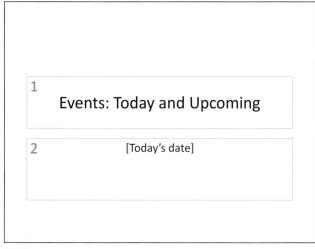

Slide 1

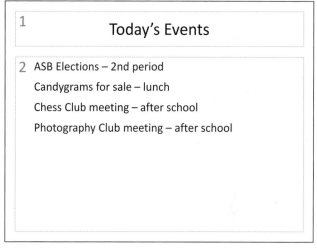

Slide 2

Slide 3

My Kind of Town!

Creating, Editing, Collaborating, and Sharing

Overview

The ability to collaborate and share using online presentation software, such as Google Slides, offers a variety of advantages for users. Several people can contribute to the slide content by editing slides, adding special effects, etc., all at the same time. This is ideal for group presentations as the workload can then be distributed evenly. In addition, comments can be shared on the document to allow for fast and convenient communication.

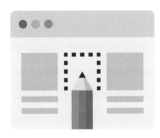

In this lesson, you will collaborate to create a slide show about Austin, Texas to be displayed in the Chamber of Commerce.

The Chamber of Commerce in Austin, Texas has decided they need a new presentation that will highlight some of the attractions Austin has to offer to its visitors. This presentation will be set up on a monitor in their lobby. They have provided a list of points of interest they would like to showcase, and have asked you and a partner to create the presentation.

New Skills / TEKS

Creating, Editing, and Sharing an Online Presentation • Collaborating Using Online Presentation Software

TEKS: 12.F.i, 12.F.ii, 12.F.iv

Instructions

IMPORTANT NOTE BEFORE YOU BEGIN: To complete this lesson, you must be assigned a partner with whom you will collaborate. Once partners have been assigned, determine who will take on the role of Student A and who will take on the role of Student B. As you complete this lesson, refer to **Figure 8.16-A** for visual guidance.

STUDENT A

1. Using Google Slides, or a similar online presentation application, create a new blank presentation.

2. Save the file as **AUSTIN**.

3. Read through the instructions prior to inserting your slides.

4. Insert five new slides using a slide layout that is appropriate to the instructions and content provided for each slide in **Figure 8.16-A**.

5. Share the presentation with Student B and assign the "Can Edit" permission.

SLIDE 1:

6. In separate text boxes, type the text as shown.

7. Change the font in text box 1 to Cambria, the font size to 60 point, and center align.

8. Change the font size in text box 2 to 24 point, italic, and center align.

9. Apply an animation of your choice to text box 2.

    NOTE: Apply the After Previous option for all animations (if available).

10. Insert an image that best illustrates the contents of the slide.

11. Insert a shape (or shapes) with a fill color of your choice to enhance the appearance of the slide.

12. Apply animations of your choice to the image and shape(s).

13. Apply a transition to this slide.

SLIDE 3

14. In separate text boxes, type the text as shown.

15. Change the font in text box 1 to Cambria, the font size to 40 point, bold, and center align.

16. Change the font size in text box 2 to 20 point and format the list of **attractions** using custom bullets.

    HINT: Remove the bullet on the first line if necessary.

17. Insert an image that best illustrates the contents of the slide, then add a picture border.

18. Apply an animation of your choice to the image.

19. Apply a transition to this slide.

SLIDE 5:

20. In separate text boxes, type the text as shown.

21. Change the font in text box 1 to Cambria, font size to 40 point, bold, and center align.

22. Change the font size in text box 2 to 20 point and format the list of **restaurants** using a numbered list.

23. Apply an animation of your choice to text box 2.

24. Hyperlink the restaurant "Chi'lantro" to the restaurant's website.

25. Insert an image that best illustrates the contents of the slide, then add a picture border.

26. Apply an animation of your choice to the image.

27. Apply a transition to this slide.

STUDENT B

28. Retrieve and open the **AUSTIN** presentation from your "Shared with me" folder on your Google Drive. (if applicable).

SLIDE 2:

29. In separate text boxes, type the text as shown.

30. Change the font in text box 1 to Cambria, the font size to 40 point, bold, and center align.

31. Change the font size in text box 2 to 20 point and format the list of **historic sites** using custom bullets.

    HINT: Remove the bullet on the headings if necessary.

32. Apply an animation of your choice to text box 2.

    NOTE: Apply the After Previous option for all Animations (if available).

33. Change the font size in text box 3 to 20 point and format the list of **historic sites** using custom bullets.

    HINT: Remove the bullet on the first line if necessary.

34. Apply an animation of your choice to text box 3.

35. Insert an image that best illustrates the contents of the slide.

36. Apply an animation of your choice to the image.

37. Apply a transition to this slide.

SLIDE 4:

38. In separate text boxes, type the text as shown.

39. Change the font in text box 1 to Cambria, the font size to 40 point, bold, and center align.

40. Change the font size in text box 2 to 24 point and format the list of **places** using a numbered list.

41. Insert an image that best depicts the contents of the slide, then add a picture border.

42. Apply an animation of your choice to the image.

43. Apply a transition to this slide.

SLIDE 6:

44. In separate text boxes, type the text as shown.

45. Change the font in text box 1 to Cambria, the font size to 40 point, bold, and center align.

46. Change the font size in text box 2 to 24 point and center align.

47. Hyperlink the text "www.austintexas.org/visit" to the Austin Tourism website.

48. Insert an image that best illustrates the contents of the slide.

49. Insert a shape (or shapes) with a fill color of your choice to enhance the appearance of the slide.

50. Apply animations of your choice to the image and shape(s).

51. Apply a transition to this slide.

STUDENTS A AND B

52. Use the Comment feature to collaborate and inform each other that you have completed your portion of the lesson.

53. Use the Comment feature to decide who will change the background of the slides.

54. When your presentation design is complete, use the Comment feature to decide who will set up the slide show to loop continuously (if available).

55. Format the size, style, and placement of the text and elements (if applicable) so that this presentation projects a professional appearance.

56. Carefully proofread your work for accuracy.

57. Be sure that all changes have been saved.

58. View your presentation as a slide show.

59. Use the Comment feature to decide which of you will share the presentation with your instructor.

60. Print or share a copy of the presentation if required by your instructor.

61. If required, present this presentation to your instructor and/or your class.

Figure 8.16-A

Slide 1

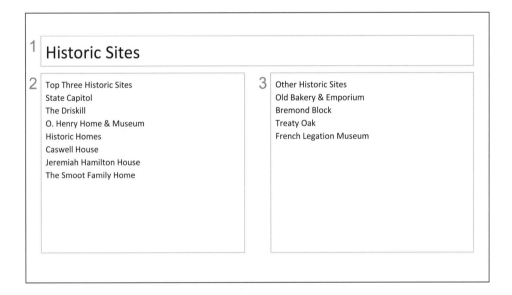

Slide 2

Figure 8.16-A (Continued)

1 **Main Attractions**

2 There are so many ways to learn more about Austin. The city's main attractions all help visitors see the city from different points of view. Some of these attractions include:

McKinney Falls State Park
South Congress Avenue
HOPE Outdoor Gallery
The Hideout Theatre
Austin Zoo

Slide 3

1 **Free Things to Do**

2 Other fun places to visit in Austin include:

Zilker Park
Barton Springs Pool
Mount Bonnell
The Veloway
Austin Nature & Science Center

Slide 4

Figure 8.16-A (Continued)

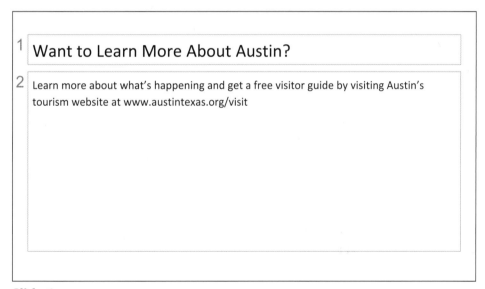

1 Dining Out

2 Austin's restaurants are world famous. Here are several inexpensive places you will want to try with the family:

Lulu B's
Chi'lantro
Mighty Dogs Café
Shake Shack
Guantanamera

Slide 5

1 Want to Learn More About Austin?

2 Learn more about what's happening and get a free visitor guide by visiting Austin's tourism website at www.austintexas.org/visit

Slide 6

Unit 9
Desktop Publishing

Part 1   Introduction to Desktop Publishing

Hands-on Lessons:

Part 2   Publication Basics   Lessons 9.1 – 9.5

Part 3   Designing Professional Publications   Lessons 9.6 – 9.11

TEKS

13.A.i, 13.B.i, 13.B.ii

What is Desktop Publishing?

Desktop publishing software enables users to create professional-looking print and digital documents such as flyers, brochures, posters, magazines, and books. Desktop publishing tools provide many ways to enhance the look of a document. A user can incorporate multiple font styles, create illustrations, insert and manipulate images, and much more. While some of these features are available with word processing software, desktop publishing applications provide more precise control of layout design, typography, and graphics.

Why Learn Desktop Publishing?

Large and small businesses, non-profit organizations, individuals, and students can all find a need for well-designed desktop publishing documents in either digital form or as hard copy prints. A business can create informational or advertising publications such as flyers, product catalogs, and direct mailers, while users at home can design everyday documents like personal calendars, invitations, and family newsletters. Even with simple desktop publishing tools and skills, students can enhance their school projects, including posters and reports.

Desktop publishing software is flexible and generally easy to use. It allows publications to be sent electronically, published online, or printed for distribution. With some basic familiarity of graphic design principles, such as page layout, typography, and graphic styles, users can easily create eye-catching publications regardless of their level of expertise.

Because so many businesses use some form of desktop publishing in their daily operations, possessing desktop publishing skills gives individuals a competitive edge as they enter the job market.

Types of Desktop Publishing Software

Individuals and businesses must take many factors into consideration when deciding which type of desktop publishing software to use, including cost and task. Adobe InDesign is an industry standard for graphic designers, but a web-based application such as Google Drawings is effective for personal projects, especially those that require collaboration with others in the creation of a publication. Whether desktop publishing software is used as a creative outlet or as a tool for producing documents necessary for a business, it is vital to choose the right software for the task at hand.

The Most Popular Desktop Publishing Software

Microsoft Publisher is a widely used desktop publishing software designed by Microsoft. Publisher is a component of the Microsoft Office Suite, but can be used as a stand-alone product. Publisher was initially launched in 1991, and is an easy-to-use software with a focus on the small business market. Publisher is available on Windows and Macintosh operating systems.

Adobe InDesign is a desktop publishing software that was developed by Adobe Systems. InDesign is used primarily by graphic designers and production artists, but has set the standard for other desktop publishing software. The first version of InDesign was released in 1999, and was Apple's first native desktop publishing software. Today, InDesign is available on Windows and Macintosh operating systems.

Google Drawings is a free web-based application in which users can collaborate and work together in real time to create and edit documents such as flowcharts, website wireframes, concept maps, and diagrams. These documents can be stored online, and files can be accessed from any computer with an Internet connection and a full-featured web browser. Google Drawings was released to the public in 2010, and is integrated with Google Drive.

Identifying Desktop Publishing Technologies

It is important for individuals and businesses to be able to identify the many technologies used with desktop publishing software. Desktop publishing encompasses all aspects of design, layout, and formatting before the publication goes to "press." There are many tools and resources used in the production of desktop publishing publications. Some of these tools and resources are listed below.

Computers and Tablets

Today, most devices, including some smart phones, are more than adequate for creating desktop publishing publications. However, projects that require the use of large, high resolution images, large amounts of text, complex graphics, and multiple pages often require a computer or tablet with enough processing power to handle these tasks.

Displays

Having a high resolution computer monitor (or display) is extremely useful when creating desktop publishing publications because of the need to edit and preview designs in progress. In addition, desktop publishing publications are often created to be displayed on a screen such as a kiosk at the mall, a menu at a restaurant, or a digital billboard. It is important that users are aware of the type of display the presentation will be viewed on to ensure it appears professional and engaging.

Scanners and Cameras

Scanners are used to digitize and import flat art, pictures, and even text into a desktop publishing publication. With scanners, resolution and color depth are vital so that high quality images may be captured and reproduced with minimal changes. Professional grade "drum scanners" tend to deliver the best quality; however, high resolution flatbed scanners are typically the most popular choice. Additionally, photographs from digital cameras are easily incorporated into desktop publishing software. Photographs and scans can be edited, manipulated, and enhanced in desktop publishing applications or other software tools such as photo management software and online image editors.

Digital Drawing Tablets

Digital drawing tablets are a unique resource that have capabilities including freehand drawing with a stylus that acts as a "pen" or "brush" for different effects, giving users a great range of creativity. Many digital artists favor the pressure-sensitive abilities of a drawing tablet over a mouse because it gives them more control, simulating the real-life flow of a pencil, paint brush, or another traditional drawing tool. Additionally, drawing tablets offer many timesaving editing functions, such as the ability to select and control objects.

Image/Asset Libraries

High quality stock images are available from online resources and can enhance the professionalism of desktop publishing documents. There are many benefits to using stock image/asset libraries in desktop publishing. Users are able to find the exact image they need and use it with multiple designs. Additionally, stock images can be relatively inexpensive and are readily available from multiple image galleries including Getty Images, iStock, and Adobe Stock.

Printers

Printers are an important tool when using desktop publishing software. Most desktop publishing publications are intended to be distributed in a printed format, so businesses often require printers that can print good quality black and white and color documents. Desktop publishing printers specified for an office, home, or school environment often do the trick for projects on a smaller scale. For more professional-grade uses or large distribution quantities, such as magazine advertisements, brochures, and posters, high end printers (i.e. four-color, offset, or digital) are needed.

Media

In addition to printed documents, desktop publishing software can create digital publications that are meant to be viewed electronically. These electronic documents are typically intended to be seen on a screen, either via the Internet on a device such as a computer, tablet, or smart phone, or directly from CDs, flash cards, thumb drives, or other portable computer media. With the evolution of the Internet, digital media is becoming increasingly more common to audiences, and many businesses are taking advantage of digital advertising and technology.

Desktop Publishing Design Tips and Guidelines

The following desktop publishing design tips and guidelines will help you in the preparation of each document you will be designing and creating. By carefully planning and following the proposed guidelines, you will be inspired to create professional, attractive, and eye-catching documents.

The following is a checklist of items that will make a well-designed document stand out with professionalism and creativity:

- ☐ The document is attractive and pleasing to look at and read.
- ☐ The document is well-organized.
- ☐ The document is self-explanatory.
- ☐ The text and imagery are carefully linked to each other.
- ☐ The design and content are appropriate for the targeted audience.

Below are some fundamental desktop publishing design tips to follow as you produce each document. Following these tips and guidelines will help you create first-rate professional documents.

Know Your Audience

Determine the single most important message of your document by asking yourself: If my viewer carries away one idea, what do I want it to be? The answer will be the central theme that determines your entire document design.

White Space

White space is the area of a document not covered by text or images. The general rule of thumb when considering white space is to not have too much or the viewer's eye will wander, and to not have too little or you'll confuse and overwhelm your viewer. A guideline to follow is that if your page looks cluttered, eliminate the least important text and/or images from the page.

Working with Fonts and Styles

Take a look at your favorite magazine, shopping website, or social media website. It is likely that they contain no more than a total of two or three fonts. Too many fonts will make your document cluttered, unprofessional, and difficult to read. As a general rule, use no more than a total of two to three fonts per document.

Select one font that will serve as the primary font (used for areas that contain more than two or three sentences in one area) and one font to serve as your secondary font (used for headlines, headings, or subheadings).

Here are some general guidelines to follow when working with fonts:

- Fonts and font sizes for headlines, subheadings, and body text should be kept consistent within each document.

- When considering type styles, with the exception of titles, avoid using all capital letters.

- Avoid excessive use of underlines, italics, and bold text.

- Select a font that is appropriate to the document's subject.

- Be consistent with your font choices throughout each document. This will help to establish a consistent look, which will add to the professionalism of the document.

Keep the Document Design Symmetrical and Proportional

Creating balance and symmetry throughout a document is crucial to its final appearance. For example, if you are creating a document that contains three separate headings, keep the font size of the headings relatively similar. Otherwise, your document will look out of proportion, giving it an amateur look and feel.

These guidelines will help keep your documents looking balanced and in proportion:

- Use the same fonts throughout each document to give the document a crisp, clean, consistent look.

- When using columns, keep the width and distance between each column the same.

- Use the same style and size of images.

- Use the same font size for different headings and the same font size for the body of your document.

Margins and Spacing

All margins of a document should be straight and even. Don't overcrowd the space, and make sure to balance content from top-to-bottom and side-margin to side-margin.

Consider organizing your text into columns rather than stretching it across the page. This will make the document easier to read and more balanced in appearance.

Working with Images

You've heard it a million times: "a picture is worth a thousand words." This is especially true when it comes to document design. Select images that have the same look and style. This helps establish consistency throughout the document and gives it a polished, professional look.

Establish a Professional Identity

When businesses communicate through print, they rely heavily on the look and design of their documents to convey their intended image and identity to consumers.

To help establish a professional image, you should:

- Use the same fonts throughout your publications.
- Use the same color scheme (if using a color printer).
- Use the same style of objects and design elements.
- Use the same style of images.

Proofread for Spelling, Grammar, and Design

Nothing spoils a well-designed document more than a typo. When you are nearing the completion of a document, take time to proofread it for spelling, grammar, and design. Before submitting any document, ask yourself the following questions: Are there any misspelled words? Do the sentences make sense? Did you leave out any required text or design elements?

A great way to check your work is to give your document to one or two people and let them proofread the document. They may find an error or omission that you didn't see.

Revise, Revise, Revise

Desktop publishing design rarely comes out right the first time around. Look at your starting point as just that—a starting point. Print your document early on in the design phase and plan on making several revisions, additions, and deletions to attain a professional, well-designed final product.

When in Doubt, "KIS"

If you are spending precious time pondering over the use of one image over another or haggling over selecting a particular font, then "KIS."

"KIS" is an acronym commonly used by designers. It stands for "Keep It Simple." When faced with making a decision, always go with the one that is simplest.

Have a Paper Plan

One of the worst habits a desktop publisher or graphic designer can establish is to start designing on a computer without first having a plan on paper. Good design starts on paper first! A sheet of paper, a pencil, and a ruler are the only tools you'll need to get your imagination and creativity going. It is much easier and faster to experiment with shapes, images, font styles, and borders on a piece of paper than on a computer.

Hardware Requirements for Desktop Publishing Applications

In this unit, you will create a series of publications that require the use of desktop publishing software. As with all software applications, there are certain hardware requirements necessary to complete this task.

Hardware refers to the physical elements of a computer, so in this case, in order for you to use desktop publishing software, you will need some type of computer to run the software, such as a desktop computer, tablet, or mobile phone. Some input devices that you would need include a mouse and a keyboard, or a scanner if you plan on importing flat art or print images into your publications. Of course, if you are going to print any of your documents, you will need a printer. If the desktop publishing software requires access to the Internet, such as Google Drawings, then a router and Internet connection are required.

A LOOK AHEAD TO YOUR FINAL ASSESSMENT

Pitch It!™

As a final assessment (Unit 10), you will be divided into teams and "pitch" a new product idea to your instructor. This assessment will give you exciting, first-hand knowledge of how desktop publishing software can be used as a tool for creating and organizing information. Pay close attention to the skills you will be learning in this unit, as you will draw on them again in the "Pitch It!" final assessment.

Unit 9 Review

1. Visit **www.MyCompanionSite.com**.
2. Download and complete the **Unit 9 Review** worksheet.
3. Submit your completed worksheet to your instructor.

SOFTWARE NOTES

If you encounter a skill or feature that is not available in the software you are using, use an equivalent feature or adjust your document accordingly.

Unless otherwise stated, use the default font of the desktop publishing software being used. For example, the default font in Microsoft Publisher is Calibri, and Adobe InDesign is Minion Pro.

It is important to note that all of the lessons in this unit are written in a generic format and, in most cases, the skills required can be achieved using any type of desktop publishing software.

Due to the creative nature of desktop publishing software, your publications may vary in design from other students in your class.

Toy Drive

Working with Text

Overview

The Student Council at Hamilton High School has volunteered to help market an upcoming Toy Drive at the local children's hospital. In order to solicit donations, you have been asked to create an informational handout listing the types of toys needed.

New Skills

Creating a Blank Publication　•　Saving a Publication　•　Inserting and Moving Text Boxes

In this lesson, you will create a new publication and practice typing in different text boxes.

Instructions

1. Create a new 8.5" by 11" desktop publishing document.

2. Save the publication as **TOY DRIVE**.

3. Create a text box that measures approximately 7.5" wide and 1" high and position as shown in text box 1 in **Figure 9.1-A**.

4. Type the text in text box 1 as shown in **Figure 9.1-A**.

5. Create seven additional text boxes and type the remaining text as shown in **Figure 9.1-A**.

6. Position each text box as shown in **Figure 9.1-A**.

7. Carefully proofread your work for accuracy.

8. Be sure any changes have been saved.

Figure 9.1-A

1
Toy Drive for Kids

2
March 1 through March 31

Sponsored by the Student Council at Hamilton High School

3
Here is a categorized list of some of our most popular items:

4
Arts and Crafts

Crayons, water-soluble markers, watercolor paints, coloring books and posters, drawing paper, arts and crafts kits, crochet hooks, yarn, and simple needlepoint kits

5
Music and Books

Portable DVD and CD players, age-appropriate DVDs for children and teens, music CDs, new picture and chapter books for young readers, and new young adult books

6
Games and Toys

Playing cards, dominoes, checkers and chess, board games for young children and teens, LEGOs, wooden blocks, snap-together model kits

7
Infants and Toddlers

Board books, rattles, squeeze toys, busy boxes, stuffed animals, sound books, sorting and stacking toys

8
Donations are greatly appreciated!

Toy Drive 2

Formatting Text

Overview

Now that you have the basic text (also called copy) that needs to be included on the Toy Drive handout, it's time to make it more visually appealing. You decide to change the color, size, and alignment of the text so that the handout is more likely to grab the readers' attention and encourage them to donate to the cause.

In this lesson, you will open an existing publication and format the text to increase its visual appeal.

New Skills

Opening an Existing Publication • Using Save As • Changing Font • Changing Font Size • Changing Font Color • Applying Bold, Italic, and Underline • Changing Alignment • Changing Case and Character Spacing • Resizing Text Boxes • Printing a Publication

Instructions

1. Open the **TOY DRIVE** publication you previously created in Lesson 9.1.

2. Rename and save the publication as **TOY DRIVE 2**.

3. Make the following changes to the text in text box 1:
   a. Change the font to Arial Black.
   b. Change the font size to 36 point.
   c. Change the font color to green.
   d. Apply bold to the text.
   e. Change the case to all caps.
   f. Change the character spacing to loose.
   g. Change the alignment to center align.

4. Change the font of the text in each remaining text box to Arial Black.

5. Change the font size of the text in text boxes 2 and 3 to 16 point.

6. Underline the text in text box 3.

7. Change the font size of the first line of text boxes 4, 5, 6, and 7 to 18 point and apply italic.

8. Resize the text boxes so that all text is visible.

9. Change the font size of the remaining text in text boxes 4, 5, 6, and 7 to 11 point.

10. Make the following font color changes:

    a. In text box 4, change "Arts and Crafts" to blue, and italicize.

    b. In text box 5, change "Music and Books" to red, and italicize.

    c. In text box 6, change "Games and Toys" to orange, and italicize.

    d. In text box 7, change "Infants and Toddlers" to light blue, and italicize.

11. Change the font size of the text in text box 8 to 24 point and center align.

12. Move each text box to the appropriate position as shown in **Figure 9.2-A**.

13. Type your name and project name in the bottom corner of your publication.

14. Carefully proofread your work for accuracy.

15. Be sure any changes have been saved. When complete, your publication should look similar to **Figure 9.2-A**.

16. Print the publication if required by your instructor.

Figure 9.2-A

1 — # TOY DRIVE FOR KIDS

2 — **March 1 through March 31**

Sponsored by the Student Council at Hamilton High School

3 — <u>**Here is a categorized list of some of our most popular items:**</u>

Arts and Crafts

4 — **Crayons, water-soluble markers, watercolor paints, coloring books and posters, drawing paper, arts and crafts kits, crochet hooks, yarn, and simple needlepoint kits**

Music and Books

5 — **Portable DVD and CD players, age-appropriate DVDs for children and teens, music CDs, new picture and chapter books for young readers, and new young adult books**

Games and Toys

6 — **Playing cards, dominoes, checkers and chess, board games for young children and teens, LEGOs, wooden blocks, snap-together model kits**

Infants and Toddlers

7 — **Board books, rattles, squeeze toys, busy boxes, stuffed animals, sound books, sorting and stacking toys**

8 — # Donations are greatly appreciated!

Science Fair Tips

Aligning Text

Overview

With the science fair only a few months away, your science teacher needs a poster that offers helpful hints on how to prepare for the event. She would like the poster to remind students of the scientific method and suggest pointers on how to create an exceptional project. Your teacher has offered extra credit to any student who can design the required poster.

In this lesson, you will create a poster that offers reminders and advice for the upcoming science fair.

New Skills

Creating Numbered and Bulleted Lists • Changing Line Spacing • Using Find and Replace • Using Print Preview

Instructions

1. Create a new 8.5 x 11" desktop publishing document.
2. Save the publication as **SCIENCE FAIR**.
3. Using separate text boxes, type the text as shown in **Figure 9.3-A**.
4. Resize and arrange each text box as shown in **Figure 9.3-A**.
5. Center align the text in text box 1, and change the font to Arial Black, the font size to 36 point, and the font color to dark red.
6. Change the font of text boxes 2 and 4 to Arial Black, the font size to 16 point, and the font color to dark red.
7. Using the bullet style of your choice, format the text in text box 3 as a bulleted list.
8. Format the text in text box 5 as a numbered list.
9. Change the line spacing of text boxes 3 and 5 to 1.5.
10. Change the font of the text in text boxes 3 and 5 to Arial, and the font size to 14 point.
11. As needed, resize the text boxes so that all text is visible.
12. Using Find and Replace, replace the word "information" with the word "data."
    HINT: When complete, you should have made three replacements.
13. Type your name and project name in the bottom corner of your publication.
14. Use Print Preview to preview your publication.
15. Carefully proofread your publication for accuracy.
16. Be sure any changes have been saved.
17. Print the publication if required by your instructor.

Figure 9.3-A

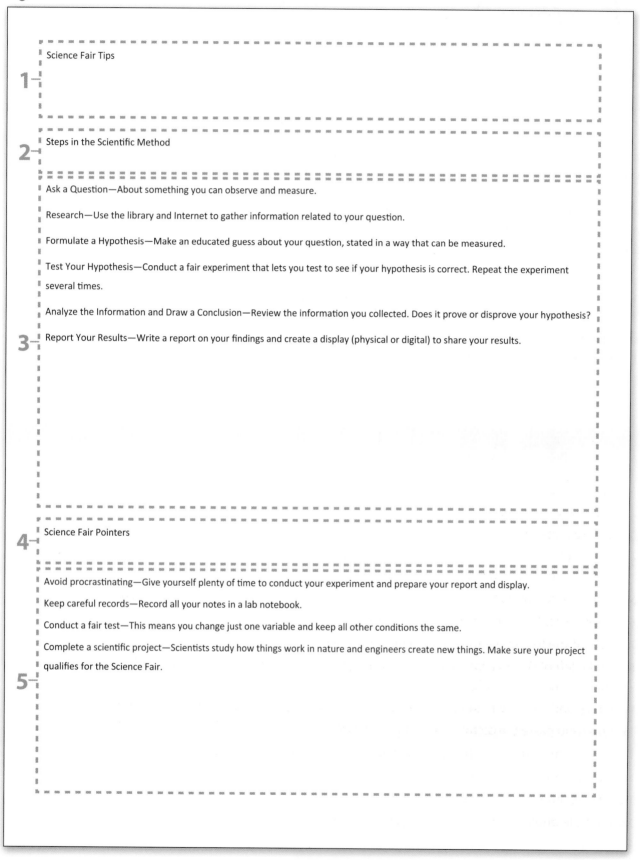

1→ Science Fair Tips

2→ Steps in the Scientific Method

Ask a Question—About something you can observe and measure.

Research—Use the library and Internet to gather information related to your question.

Formulate a Hypothesis—Make an educated guess about your question, stated in a way that can be measured.

Test Your Hypothesis—Conduct a fair experiment that lets you test to see if your hypothesis is correct. Repeat the experiment several times.

Analyze the Information and Draw a Conclusion—Review the information you collected. Does it prove or disprove your hypothesis?

3→ Report Your Results—Write a report on your findings and create a display (physical or digital) to share your results.

4→ Science Fair Pointers

Avoid procrastinating—Give yourself plenty of time to conduct your experiment and prepare your report and display.

Keep careful records—Record all your notes in a lab notebook.

Conduct a fair test—This means you change just one variable and keep all other conditions the same.

Complete a scientific project—Scientists study how things work in nature and engineers create new things. Make sure your project qualifies for the Science Fair.

5→

Coffee Mug Design

Working with Shapes and Pictures

Overview

Your annual family reunion is only a few weeks away. Your mom has decided to commemorate the occasion by giving everyone a specially designed coffee mug, which will include a celebratory photo or image. She has purchased clear plastic mugs and has asked you to design an insert that will make the gift attractive and memorable.

In this lesson, you will use text, shapes, and images to design an insert for a commemorative coffee mug.

New Skills / TEKS

Changing Page Orientation • Inserting Shapes • Inserting, Resizing, and Cropping Pictures • Using Copy and Paste • Horizontally Flipping a Picture

TEKS: 13.C.ii

Instructions

1. Create a new 11 x 8.5" desktop publishing document.
2. Save the publication as **COFFEE MUG**.
3. Draw a rectangle that measures 10" wide by 3.75" high.
4. Position the rectangle in the center of the page as shown in **Figure 9.4-A**. You will place the contents of your coffee mug design within this rectangle.
5. Draw a text box that measures 4" wide and 1.5" high and position as shown in **Figure 9.4-A**.
6. Type the text "<Your Last Name> Family Reunion."
7. Format the text to the font, size, color, and alignment of your choice.
8. To the left of the text, insert a picture that best illustrates the message of your coffee mug design and position as shown in **Figure 9.4-A**.
9. Resize and crop the picture (if necessary) so that it fits appropriately on your coffee mug design.
10. Copy and paste the picture on the right side of the text box.
11. Flip this second picture horizontally and position as shown in **Figure 9.4-A**.
12. Carefully proofread your work for accuracy.
13. Be sure any changes have been saved.
14. Print the publication if required by your instructor.

Figure 9.4-A

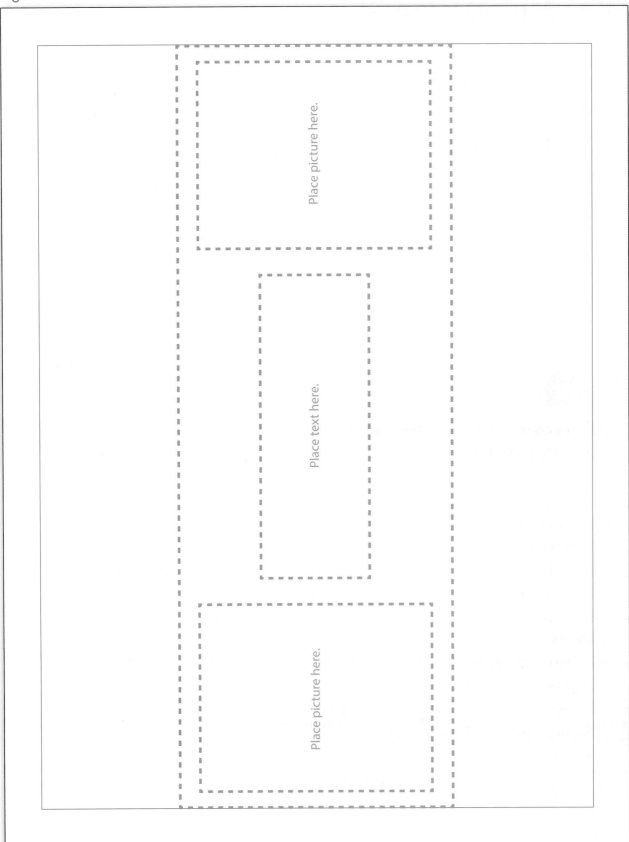

Coffee Mug Design 2

Enhancing Shapes

Overview

A week before the family reunion, you show your parents the coffee mug insert you created in Lesson 9.4. While your parents approve of the basic design, they offer a few suggestions on how to make the mug more festive.

New Skills

Changing Shape Fill and Outline • Changing Shape Size • Rotating a Shape • Using Horizontal Guides • Grouping Objects

In this lesson, you will use shapes to enhance visual interest, use horizontal and vertical guides to help you align objects in your publication, and group the objects.

Instructions

1. Open the **COFFEE MUG** publication you previously created in Lesson 9.4.

2. Save the file as **COFFEE MUG 2**.

3. Place three horizontal guides at 2.5", 3.25", and 6" as shown in **Figure 9.5-A**.

4. Insert a 4-point star (or similar shape), then change the height and width of the star to .5", apply a horizontal gradient fill style of your choice, and change the outline color to dark red.

5. Rotate the star 45 degrees.

6. Place the star in the top left corner so that the **top** of the star aligns with the horizontal guide at 2.5".

7. Copy and paste the star 21 times and align them with the horizontal guide at 2.5".

8. Group all of the stars, and copy and paste them so that the **bottom** of the stars align with the horizontal guide at 6".

9. Align the top of both pictures with the horizontal guide at 3.25" as shown in **Figure 9.5-A**.

10. Change the fill color and the outline color of the rectangle and the text box to a color of your choice.

11. Type your name and project name in the bottom corner of your publication.

12. Carefully proofread your work for accuracy.

13. Be sure any changes have been saved.

14. Print the publication if required by your instructor.

Figure 9.5-A

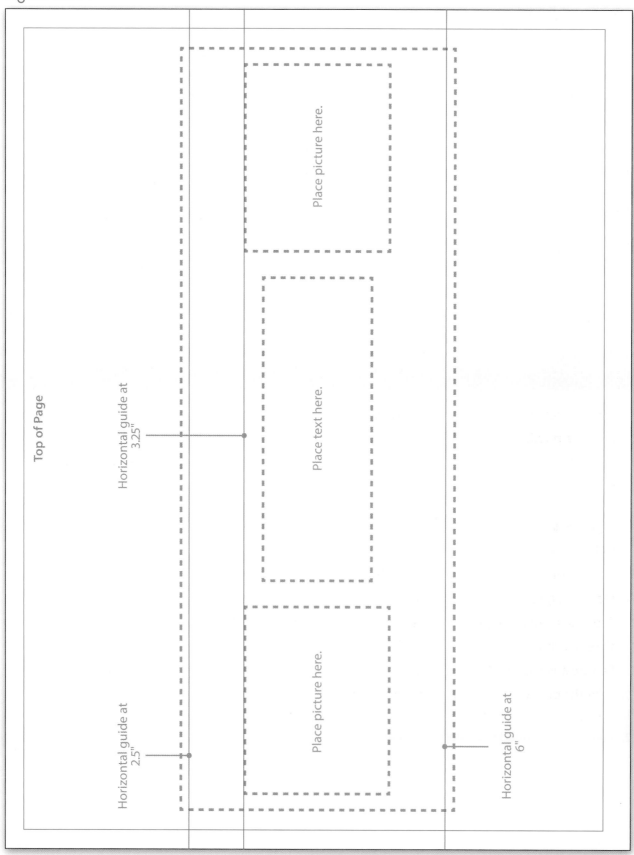

Top of Page

Horizontal guide at 2.5"

Horizontal guide at 3.25"

Horizontal guide at 6"

Place picture here.

Place text here.

Place picture here.

Lunch Menu

Importing Text

Overview

One of the many benefits of desktop publishing software is the ability to import text from a file. The file easily converts into the correct format, giving you the ability to enhance the appearance of the original text and create a professional design.

In this lesson, you will import text from a previously created word processing document to create and design a visually appealing lunch menu.

New Skills / TEKS

Importing Text

TEKS: 13.C.i, 13.C.ii

Instructions

1. Create a new 8.5" by 11" desktop publishing document.

2. Save the publication as **MENU**.

3. Create a text box that measures 7.5" wide by 10" high and align with the margin guides as shown in **Figure 9.6-A**.

4. Import the text from the **LUNCH** file previously created in Lesson 5.16 in Unit 5 as shown in **Figure 9.6-A**.

    NOTE: Delete your name and project name from the imported text as shown.

5. Change the font and size of the text so that the lunch menu projects a professional design.

6. Insert images, shapes, and/or additional text to enhance the look and design of the lunch menu.

7. Type your name and project name in the bottom corner of your publication.

8. Carefully proofread your work for accuracy.

9. Be sure any changes have been saved.

10. Print the publication if required by your instructor.

Figure 9.6-A

LUNCH MENU FOR TUESDAY

Starter

Clam Chowder

Option 1

Prime Rib

Option 2

Vegetable Lasagna

Sweet

Strawberry Shortcake

Note Card

More Formatting with Text and Borders

Overview

In the world of social media posts, text messages, and email, people seldom take the time to write and mail a personal note. But there are still occasions when a personal message is the best form of communication. Thank-you notes, thinking-of-you cards, and birthday wishes are an especially meaningful way to connect with a loved one.

In this lesson, you will insert and format images and text in order to design a personalized note card.

New Skills

Changing Text Direction • Inserting and Formatting a Picture Border • Setting Margins

Instructions

1. Create a new 8.5 x 11" desktop publishing document.
2. Save the publication as **NOTE CARD**.
3. Set the margins to 0.25" on all sides.
4. Place vertical guides at 4", 4.25", and 4.5" as shown in **Figure 9.7-A**.
5. Place horizontal guides at 5.25", 5.5", and 5.75" as shown in **Figure 9.7-A**.
6. Include the following on the **front cover** of your note card:

    HINT: Be sure to place the contents of the front cover panel in the **lower right** quadrant of the document.

    a. A graphic image or photograph of people, places, or things that are important to you.

    b. A border. Select a picture style border for the image that complements the front of the note card. Format the border color and weight so that it best enhances the image.

    c. A short caption for the image you have selected.

7. Change the direction of the text and rotate the image so that both are 90 degrees to the left.
8. Include the following on the **interior panel** of your note card:

    HINT: Be sure to place the contents of the interior panel in the **upper left** quadrant of the document.

    a. An image that is related to the image you selected on the front cover.

    b. The text of your note. This may be a one-line personal motto or famous quote that represents you. Select the font and color of your choice.

    c.   A border. Place a border around the text and change the border color and weight so that it enhances the design of the note card.

9.   Change the direction of the text and rotate the image so that both are 90 degrees to the right.

10.   Include the following on the **back cover** panel of your note card:

    HINT: Place the contents of the back cover panel in the **lower left** quadrant of the document.

    a.   The text "Designed by" and insert your name.

11.   Change the direction of the text by rotating it 90 degrees to the right.

12.   Add additional text and/or graphic elements to enhance the appearance of the note card.

13.   Format the size, style, and placement of the text and other elements on the document so that it projects a professional design.

14.   Carefully proofread your work for accuracy.

15.   Be sure any changes have been saved.

16.   Print the publication if required by your instructor. If so, fold the paper in half horizontally then vertically, making sure the front cover panel of the note card is facing outward.

Figure 9.7-A

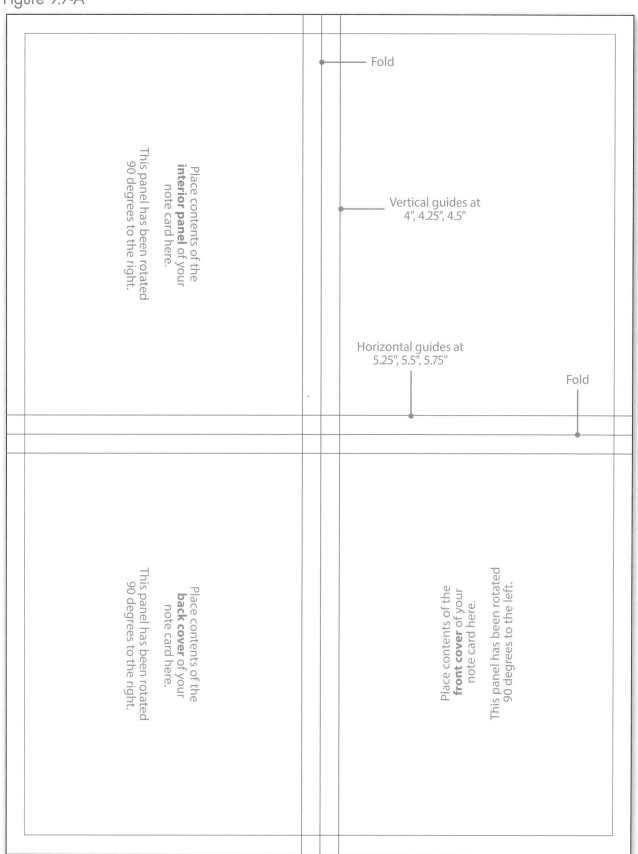

Fold

Vertical guides at
4", 4.25", 4.5"

Horizontal guides at
5.25", 5.5", 5.75"

Fold

Place contents of the
interior panel of your
note card here.

This panel has been rotated
90 degrees to the right.

Place contents of the
back cover of your
note card here.

This panel has been rotated
90 degrees to the right.

Place contents of the
front cover of your
note card here.

This panel has been rotated
90 degrees to the left.

Beginners Design Tips

Using Customary Standards and Styles

Overview

You are a student assistant for your school's desktop publishing class. The teacher has asked you to create a poster that displays a list of publication design tips for beginners. The text for the tips has been provided for you; however, the design has been left for you to decide.

In this lesson, you will create and design a poster that expresses the importance of using basic design strategies.

New Skills / TEKS

There are no new skills being introduced in this reinforcement lesson.

TEKS: 13.B.i, 13.B.ii, 13.C.ii

Instructions

1. Create a new 8.5 x 11" desktop publishing document.

2. Save the publication as **DESIGN TIPS**.

3. Using separate text boxes, type the text as shown in **Figure 9.8-A**.

4. Resize and arrange the text boxes as needed.

5. Change the size and font of the title in text box 1 so that it is the largest element on the page.

6. Insert one or two graphic images to enhance the poster topic.

7. Add additional text and/or elements to enhance the appearance of the poster.

8. Format the size, style, and placement of the text and other elements so the poster follows customary standards and styles of design.

9. Type your name and project name in the bottom corner of your publication.

10. Carefully proofread your work for accuracy.

11. Be sure any changes have been saved.

12. Print the publication if required by your instructor.

Figure 9.8-A

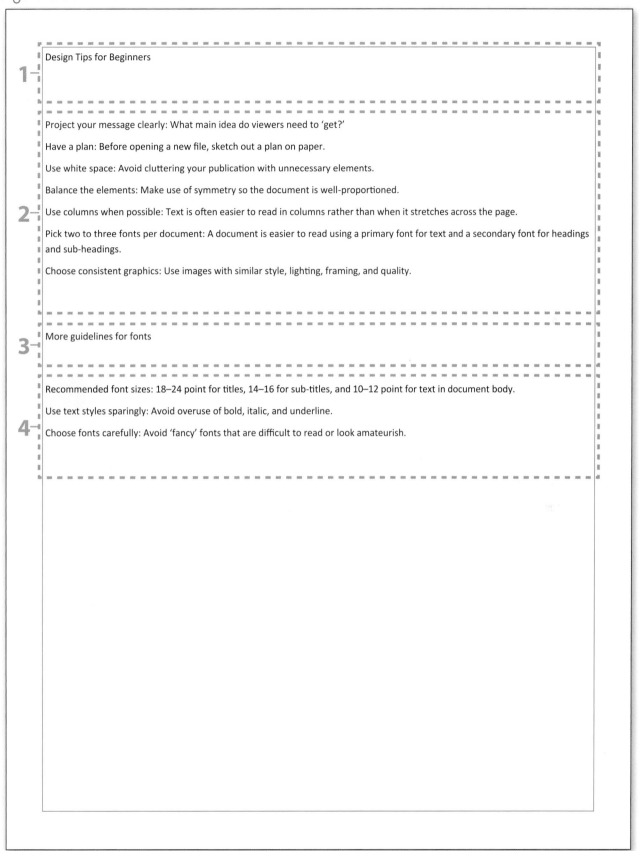

1 →

Design Tips for Beginners

Project your message clearly: What main idea do viewers need to 'get?'

Have a plan: Before opening a new file, sketch out a plan on paper.

Use white space: Avoid cluttering your publication with unnecessary elements.

Balance the elements: Make use of symmetry so the document is well-proportioned.

2 → Use columns when possible: Text is often easier to read in columns rather than when it stretches across the page.

Pick two to three fonts per document: A document is easier to read using a primary font for text and a secondary font for headings and sub-headings.

Choose consistent graphics: Use images with similar style, lighting, framing, and quality.

3 → More guidelines for fonts

Recommended font sizes: 18–24 point for titles, 14–16 for sub-titles, and 10–12 point for text in document body.

Use text styles sparingly: Avoid overuse of bold, italic, and underline.

4 → Choose fonts carefully: Avoid 'fancy' fonts that are difficult to read or look amateurish.

Doorknob Hanger

Formatting a Doorknob Hanger

Overview

The type of doorknob hanger you may be most familiar with is the "Do Not Disturb" sign found on hotel room doors. However, doorknob hangers can actually have a variety of uses, from spreading information about a political campaign to informing an occupant of a missed delivery. Many businesses even use doorknob hangers as a clever marketing strategy in order to communicate with current and potential customers. For this doorknob hanger, the message, layout, and design decisions will be entirely up to you.

In this lesson, you will create a two-sided doorknob hanger that effectively conveys a message to a specific target audience.

New Skills

There are no new skills being introduced in this reinforcement lesson.

Instructions

1. Create a new 8.5 x 11" desktop publishing document.

2. Save the publication as **DOORKNOB HANGER**.

3. Set the margins to 0.5" on all sides.

4. Place a horizontal guide at 1" as shown in **Figure 9.9-A**.

5. Insert a rectangle measuring 3.5" wide by 10" high. Align the rectangle with the top and left margin as shown in **Figure 9.9-A**.

6. Insert a 2.25" circle. Align the top of the circle with the horizontal guide and center it horizontally within the rectangle as shown in **Figure 9.9-A**.

7. Group the circle and rectangle. This grouped object will be used for the front side of the doorknob hanger.

8. Copy and paste the front side of the doorknob hanger onto the right side of the page as shown. Align this object with the top and right margin as shown in **Figure 9.9-A**. This new object will be used for the back side of the doorknob hanger.

9. As you begin to plan and design the doorknob hanger, think of a purpose or cause for creating the doorknob hanger. For example, you may want to create a doorknob hanger for your office or bedroom door.

10. Include the following on your doorknob hanger:

    a. Two different messages, one for the front side and one for the back side.

    b. A maximum of two graphic images per side that correlate with the messages used.

11. Add additional text and/or graphic elements to enhance the appearance of the doorknob hanger.

12. Format the size, style, and placement of the text and other elements so the doorknob hanger projects a professional design.

13. Type your name and project name in the bottom corner of your publication.

14. Carefully proofread your work for accuracy.

15. Be sure any changes have been saved.

16. Print the publication if required by your instructor.

Figure 9.9-A

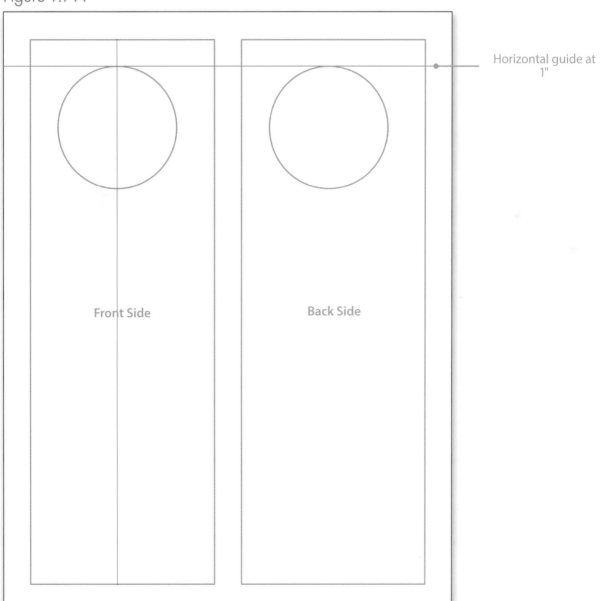

Horizontal guide at 1"

Front Side

Back Side

Join the Club!

Formatting a Brochure

Overview

Three-panel brochures are used to promote organizations, programs, businesses, and more. Brochures are designed to grab the readers' interest and encourage them to take some sort of action, such as volunteering, taking a trip, or joining an organization. Brochures allow a substantial amount of information to be organized into a relatively limited amount of space.

In this lesson, you will see how to organize and create a three-panel brochure promoting a school club or special activity of your choice.

New Skills / TEKS

There are no new skills being introduced in this reinforcement lesson.

TEKS: 13.C.ii

Instructions

1. Choose a school club, organization, special event, or athletic team you would like to promote to other students in your school. This will be the topic of your brochure.

2. Create a new 2-page, 11 x 8.5" desktop publishing document.

3. Save the publication as **BROCHURE**.

4. Set the margins to 0.25" on all sides.

5. Use page or column guides to divide both sides of the brochure into three equal panels as shown in **Figure 9.10-A**.

   NOTE: Leave a 0.5" gutter space between each column to allow for folding. When folded in thirds, the pages will form a brochure.

6. Include the following on the outside right panel (front cover) of your brochure:

   a. Headline. This is the title of the brochure and should include the name of the club, organization, or athletic team. For example: Welcome to Future Business Leaders of America; Drama Club—Channel Your Inner Performer; or Ballin' with the North Kingstown Girls' Basketball Team.

   b. Tagline. This phrase or short sentence should briefly describe your topic. For example: Changing Lives; Learning by Doing; or, It's Above the Rim!

   c. Images and/or additional text to enhance the look and design of the front cover.

7. Include the following on the outside middle panel (back cover) of your brochure:

   a. The club's, organization's, or athletic team's contact information: advisor's name, classroom number, email address, website address, etc.

   b. Images and/or additional text to enhance the look and design of the back cover.

8. Include the following on the outside left panel of your brochure:

   a. Information on how to join the club, organization, or athletic team along with two or three short testimonial statements from members or participants saying why they enjoy being part of the group or team.

   b. Images and/or additional text to enhance the look and design of the outside left panel.

9. Include the following on the inside left, middle, and right panels of your brochure:

   a. The inside content and design of the brochure is entirely up to you to decide. Include information that prospective club or team members need to know. For example: academic eligibility requirements for members; where and when the group meets, sample activities, events, meeting schedules, competitions, and so on.

   b. Images and/or additional text to enhance the look and design of the inside of the brochure.

10. Format the size, style, and placement of the text and other elements on the document so it projects a professional design.

11. Type your name and project name in the bottom corner of your publication.

12. Carefully proofread your work for accuracy.

13. Be sure any changes have been saved.

14. Print the publication if required by your instructor.

Figure 9.10-A

Page 1

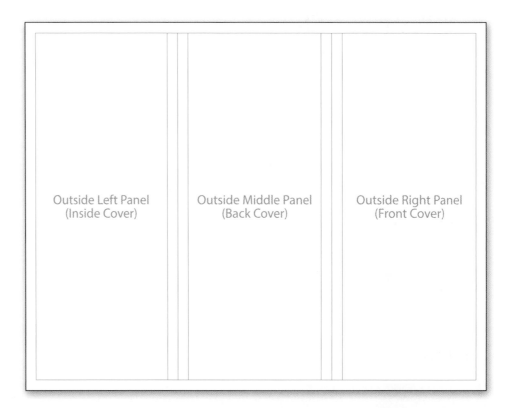

Outside Left Panel
(Inside Cover)

Outside Middle Panel
(Back Cover)

Outside Right Panel
(Front Cover)

Page 2

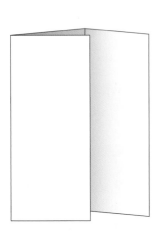

Inside Left Panel

Inside Middle Panel

Inside Right Panel

Fall Festival Flyer

Redesigning a Promotional Flyer

Overview

Throughout this unit, you have developed a variety of desktop publishing skills, from working with text and images to learning page layout and design rules. Now it's time for you to apply these customary standards and styles of desktop publishing and demonstrate what you've learned.

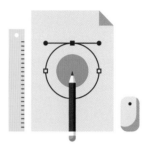

In this lesson, you will redesign an existing document—one that is poorly designed and in need of an intensive makeover.

New Skills / TEKS

There are no new skills being introduced in this reinforcement lesson.

TEKS: 13.B.i, 13.B.ii

Instructions

1. Carefully review the flyer shown in **Figure 9.11-A**. Make a list of things that are wrong with the publication and what you will do to improve it. Below are some questions to consider as you analyze the flyer:

    a. Are the fonts easy or difficult to read?

    b. Is the font size too small, too large, or just right?

    c. Do the graphics support the theme of the flyer?

    d. Are the graphics of high quality?

    e. Does the use of a border enhance the appearance of the flyer?

    f. Is the message clear and easy to understand?

    g. Does the existing text provide all necessary information or are some things missing?

    h. Does the flyer look professional? Why or why not?

2. Create a new 8.5 x 11" desktop publishing document.

3. Save the publication as **FALL FESTIVAL**.

4. Set the margins to 0.5" on all sides.

5. Using your notes and the desktop publishing skills you've learned thus far, redesign the flyer. You may edit the text, replace images, add missing information, or delete unnecessary information; however, be careful not to change the overall message of the flyer.

6. Add additional text and/or graphic elements to enhance the appearance of the flyer.

7. Format the size, style, and placement of the text and other elements on the document so it projects a professional design.

8. Type your name and project name in the bottom corner of your publication.

9. Carefully proofread your work for accuracy.

10. Be sure any changes have been saved.

11. Print the publication if required by your instructor.

Figure 9.11-A

Fall Festival

Saturday, October 27

4 p.m. to 10 p.m.

Food

Music

Raffle

Games

Admission: $5

Tickets available in the school office

If you plan to come, you need to buy your ticket by Wednesday 24 so we can order food and beverages.

Unit 10
Pitch It!
Final Assessment

Pitch It!

I N C O R P O R A T E D

"Making Your Idea The Next Big Thing"

What is the Pitch It! Project?

TEKS

1.A.i, 1.Di, 1.Fi, 1.F.iii, 1.F.iv, 1.F.v, 14.A.i

The Pitch It! unit is an exciting mini-simulation where you will use and apply a variety of technology skills you have learned in this book to complete a final assessment. From word processing to desktop publishing, you will integrate computer applications in a real-world simulation. There are many benefits to integrating computer applications, including convenience, efficiency, and producing professional business documents. Software integration allows you to use many different features to create a variety of documents that match your exact needs. For example, you can use spreadsheet software to analyze and calculate data, and then import the spreadsheet into word processing or presentation applications. You can also create a presentation from a word processing outline, use publications or presentations to design a visual aid for business documents, and more. Integration is used in this project to produce marketing materials, to estimate annual sales and create a vendor database, and to collaborate with your partner to create your final slide show presentation. For this entire unit, you will be working with a fellow classmate with whom you will collaborate to complete each project. The essence of this unit is provided in the "Pitch It!" scenario below.

The "Pitch It!" Scenario

Throughout the Pitch It! unit, you will assume the role of a young entrepreneur. Your task will be to invent a new product. You will be required to conduct research and develop a variety of documents that you will use to support and "pitch" your idea to the CEO of Pitch It!, Inc. (your instructor).

The unit culminates with a final presentation, similar in format to the popular reality TV show, "Shark Tank." In Shark Tank, budding entrepreneurs get the chance to bring their dreams to reality as they present their product ideas to industry-leading entrepreneurs and investors.

Although you will be working in a classroom environment, you will experience exactly what happens in the real world, where aspiring entrepreneurs create "elevator pitches" to potential investors.

The goal of this unit is simple: To have Pitch It!, Inc. hear and love your idea so that they give you the necessary financial backing to make your product idea a reality.

Who is Pitch It!, Inc.?

An entrepreneur is a person who organizes, operates, and assumes the risk for a business venture. Most commonly, the term "entrepreneur" applies to someone who establishes an entity (or business) in order to offer an original or existing product or service into a new or established market. Most entrepreneurs who invent a new product seek out investors who will provide the financial backing, allowing the entrepreneurs to manufacture, market, and sell their products. Pitch It!, Inc. is a privately held company that specializes in developing and creating new products to market.

To bring new products to the market, Pitch It!, Inc. regularly receives proposals from aspiring entrepreneurs (like yourself) who "pitch" their ideas in hopes of getting an investment backing. If an idea is accepted by Pitch It!, Inc., the ball begins to roll forward. By successfully obtaining a contract with Pitch It!, Inc., prospective entrepreneurs get the financial backing they often require to get their ideas to market.

Meet the CEO of Pitch It!, Inc.

Your instructor will serve as the Chief Executive Officer (CEO). The CEO has the right to change or modify any of the project requirements, criteria, and instructions.

Review the company profile provided below in **Figure 10.0** to become familiar with Pitch It!, Inc.

Figure 10.0

Company Name	Pitch It!, Inc.
Chief Executive Officer (CEO)	Your Instructor
Tagline	"Making Your Idea the Next Big Thing"
Logo	Pitch It! INCORPORATED
Mission Statement	To act as an active partner for aspiring entrepreneurs who want to bring their new product to market. Once partnered with a client, our sole purpose is to provide ongoing assistance, commitment, and support in all aspects of not only bringing an idea to market, but to also sustain its product life.
Address	23 Elevator-pitch Avenue • Fort Worth, TX 76179
Contact Information	Phone: 817.123.1875 • Fax: 888.123.1857 • Email: contact@pitchitinc.com • Web: www.pitchitinc.com
Average Number of Proposals Accepted Annually	20% (2 in every 10)
Average Annual Gross Earnings for Pitch It! Clients	$625,000
Highest Earning Client	$11,575,000

Working in Teams

As previously mentioned, you will be working in groups of two throughout the Pitch It! unit. For the purposes of this project, look at your team as "your business." Each member of your team will need to work together closely and efficiently to achieve the final goal of convincing the CEO of Pitch It!, Inc. (your instructor) that your team's new product idea is a winner. As is the case with all businesses, remember that professionalism, respect, and sound communication skills within your group will be the key to success.

You will have the benefit of brainstorming together and sharing the workload as a team. You may even be able to meet deadlines faster. However, collaborating can have its downsides, as well. If a team member does not pull his or her weight, the whole group can suffer. Not only will this bring the team's morale down, but you may have to rush to finish your assignment last-minute. You may even miss deadlines, which can hurt your grade. Make sure that you communicate with your team often to ensure that everything is on track for a great final project.

Time Management

Throughout this final assessment, your instructor will determine and set due dates that you must meet. As a result, it is important for you to consider how you can effectively manage your time to meet the required deadlines. Use a calendar to stay on track, or make a list of priorities to help you decide which task should be completed next. You can also utilize any downtime throughout the day by dedicating a few minutes to working on your project. By figuring out what time management strategies work best for you, you will be able to reduce stress, learn self-discipline, improve your decision-making skills, and finish this project well within the deadline.

Software Note

Software Note

The projects in this unit are intended to be completed collaboratively. The work required to complete each project should be shared equally by each team member. It is recommended that you use a software application that supports collaboration and sharing, such as Google Drive or Microsoft Office 365. If your class does not use an application that supports collaboration and sharing, then the projects in this unit can still be completed by each member of your team. However, some modifications may be required.

Grading

Pitch It! consists of a total of nine projects and is designed to serve as a final assessment for this textbook. The last seven projects in this unit require your team to complete a variety of steps to produce different documents, which are then used in **Project 10.9**. In this project, you will incorporate all of the previous projects into an oral presentation. Your instructor may grade each project individually, or issue one grade based on the outcome of this project.

Although you will be working in teams throughout this unit, your instructor may issue different grades based on the level of participation, effort, and quality of work put forth by each team member.

Grading for this unit will be based on the following categories:

- Collaboration
- Participation
- Effort
- Demonstration of skills

Required Setup Instructions

Before you begin the projects in this unit, read and follow the steps below.

Step 1: Set Up Your "Pitch It!" Team

All of the projects in this unit are intended to be completed collaboratively by a team of two students. Your instructor will determine how students are paired.

Before moving on to Step 2, establish who your teammate will be for this unit.

NOTE: If a team consists of more than two members, some modifications will be required for some or all of the projects in this unit.

Step 2: Name Your Business (Your Team)

Once your team is established, it's time to name your "business." Since you will be presenting your team's idea to Pitch It!, Inc., you need to look at your team as a business. All businesses have names to help consumers identify and recognize who they are. Before proceeding, spend some time brainstorming with your team to create a business name.

TIP: So it's easy to remember, most business names are short and usually only contain one to three words. Think about business names we all know very well: Walmart, McDonald's, Microsoft, Apple, Best Buy, and Nike. They are all short and easy to pronounce—hence, they are easy to remember.

Step 3: Submit Your Business Name

1. Download and complete the **Project 10.1 Planning Form** on the Business Information Management Companion Website: **www.MyCompanionSite.com**.

2. Submit the completed planning form to your instructor for approval.

Project 10.2: What's the Big Idea?

Inventing Your New Product

Overview

With your team established, it's time to get to work. The goal in this project is to create the "big idea" that your team will be proposing to Pitch It!, Inc. While there are millions of possibilities for creating a new product, your challenge is to create just one. The key to this project is to create a new product that consumers either *need* or *want*. The product must bring some type of benefit to the consumer. For example, it might make a task easier, faster, or more convenient, it might add pleasure to something, or it might solve a problem. Keep in mind that Pitch It!, Inc. has strict guidelines as to what type of products they will consider. The "Pitch It!, Inc. New Product Guidelines" are introduced in the **Project 10.2 Planning Form**, which you will download shortly.

In this project, you will collaborate with your team to brainstorm new product ideas, research the competition, and survey your target market to ultimately decide on a final product idea that you will present to Pitch It!, Inc. Finally, you will write a memo to your instructor seeking approval of your product idea.

New Skills / TEKS

There are no new skills being introduced in this final assessment.

TEKS: 1.A.i, 1.Di, 1.Fi, 1.F.iii, 1.F.iv, 1.F.v, 6.D.iii, 14.A.i

Instructions

1. Download and complete the **Project 10.2 Planning Form** on the BIM Companion Website: **www.MyCompanionSite.com**.

2. Using word processing software, create a new document.

3. Set up your document using the memo format provided in **Lesson 5.26**.

4. Save the file as **PITCH IT! MEMO**.

5. Using the information from the completed **Project 10.2 Planning Form**, create a memo addressed to your instructor seeking approval of your new product idea.

   Your memo must include:
   - ☐ Proper memo format (see **Lesson 5.26** as a reference)
   - ☐ Title of the memo
   - ☐ Three body paragraphs
   - ☐ Two approval checkboxes

6. Carefully proofread your work for format and grammatical accuracy.

7. Submit a copy of your document and completed Planning Form packet to your instructor.

Project 10.3: Creating Your Product's Identity

Turning Your Product Into a Brand

Overview

Congratulations! Your team has made it to the next step in the Pitch It! final assessment. As part of the new product presentation for potential clients, Pitch It!, Inc. requires a "product identity" component. **Product identity** is what makes a product unique. Similar to your own identity, which includes your name, what you look like, your social security number, and so on, products need an identity, as well.

Product identity can include a variety of different things depending on the product type. However, every product needs a name, a logo, and a slogan (or a tagline). The product's name and logo is what makes the product unique compared to its competitors.

Think about some of the products we've come to know and trust through their identities. When we think of Kellogg's Frosted Flakes, for instance, we instantly recognize the name, how it's designed and, of course Tony the Tiger saying "They're Gr-r-reat!" As you work on this project, remember that how you brand your product is almost as, if not just as, important as the product itself.

In this project, your team will develop an identity by creating a name, logo, and slogan for your new product. Once the identity has been established, you will create a product business card for your team.

New Skills / TEKS

There are no new skills being introduced in this final assessment.

TEKS: 1.A.i, 1.Di, 1.Fi, 1.F.iii, 1.F.iv, 1.F.v, 12.D.i, 13.A.i, 14.A.i

Instructions

1. Download and complete the **Project 10.3 Planning Form** on the BIM Companion Website: **www.MyCompanionSite.com**.

PART 1: LOGO

2. Using desktop publishing or illustration software, create a new 8.5" x 11" desktop publishing document.

3. Save the file as **PITCH IT! LOGO**.

4. Using the information from the completed **Project 10.3 Planning Form**, design your product logo.

Your logo must include:

- ☐ Product name
- ☐ Product slogan
- ☐ Additional design elements at your discretion (optional)

5. Depending on the software you are using, save or export the file in JPEG format. Save the file as **PRODUCT LOGO IMAGE**. This will allow you to insert your logo as an image into other documents.

6. Submit a copy of your logo for instructor approval.

PART 2: PRODUCT BUSINESS CARD

7. Using desktop publishing or illustration software, create a new 8.5" x 11" document.

8. Set up your document using the instructions provided in **Lesson 5.29**.

9. Save the file as **PITCH IT! BIZ CARD**.

Your business card must include:

- ☐ Product name
- ☐ Product slogan
- ☐ Product logo
- ☐ Team member names
- ☐ Team's business name
- ☐ A fictitious address, city, state, zip code, phone and fax numbers, email address, and website address
- ☐ Optional: Additional elements that enhance the appearance and professionalism of the business card

10. Depending on the software you are using, save or export the file in JPEG format. Save the file as **BIZ CARD IMAGE**. This will allow you to insert your business card as an image in a later project.

11. Carefully proofread your work for format and grammatical accuracy.

12. Submit a copy of your logo, business card, and completed Planning Form packet to your instructor.

Project 10.4: Bringing Your Product to Life

Creating a Prototype of Your Product

Overview

Now that you have your product, product name, logo, and slogan, it's time to bring the product to life. What started as an idea is about to become a reality. Pitch It!, Inc. is not only interested in hearing about your new product, they want to see it in prototype form.

Before product inventors mass produce a product, they work with prototypes. A **prototype** is a preliminary model of something, or in this case, your product. Depending on the physical dimensions and material of a product, prototypes can take on many forms—from sketches to full working models.

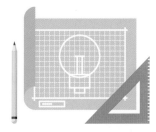

In this project, your team will collaborate to construct a prototype of your product.

New Skills / TEKS

There are no new skills being introduced in this final assessment.

TEKS: 1.A.i, 1.Di, 1.Fi, 1.F.iii, 1.F.iv, 1.F.v, 14.A.i

Instructions

1. Download and complete the **Project 10.4 Planning Form** on the BIM Companion Website: **www.MyCompanionSite.com**.

2. Using the information from the completed **Project 10.4 Planning Form**, create a prototype of your product.

   NOTE: You may utilize any materials and software applications that you feel will help you achieve your goal.

Your prototype must include:

☐ Product logo

☐ Product name

☐ Product slogan

☐ Product specifications, such as ingredients, instructions, etc.

☐ Product package design (if required)

☐ Company contact information

☐ Additional elements and/or materials that will enhance the professionalism and reality of the prototype (optional)

3. Submit your prototype and completed planning form packet to your instructor.

Project 10.5: Estimating Annual Gross Sales

Forecasting the Potential Sales of Your Product

Overview

No matter how great your product looks up to this point, you not only have to convince Pitch It!, Inc. that it will sell, but you must also prove it with numbers. All businesses, both small and large, are in business to make a profit. Due to time constraints, you will be doing a modified version of how a business would estimate annual gross sales. Pitch It!, Inc. has provided you with some preset numbers that you will enter into a spreadsheet to roughly calculate the annual gross sales for your product. **Gross sales** is defined as the total sales value based on a selling price before deducting any returns, discounts, or expenses.

In this project, your team will collaborate and use spreadsheet software to calculate the estimated annual gross sales for your product.

New Skills / TEKS

There are no new skills being introduced in this final assessment.

TEKS: 1.A.i, 1.Di, 1.Fi, 1.F.iii, 1.F.iv, 1.F.v, 12.D.i, 14.A.i

Instructions

1. Download and complete the **Project 10.5 Planning Form** on the BIM Companion Website: **www.MyCompanionSite.com**.

2. Using spreadsheet software, create a new spreadsheet.

3. Save the file as **PITCH IT! GROSS SALES**.

4. Type the data as shown in **Figure 10.5-A**.

   NOTE: The Average Units Sold per month data has been provided and preset for you by Pitch It!, Inc. This data represents the Average Number of Units sold across all clients of Pitch It!, Inc. While this column may not represent what your product's Average Units Sold might be, it gives the evaluation team at Pitch It!, Inc. a starting point.

5. Using the information from the completed **Project 10.5 Planning Form**, input the selling price for your product in the Selling Price/Unit column.

6. Using the appropriate formula, compute the **Gross Sales** column for each month.

7. Using the appropriate formula, compute the **Estimated Annual Gross Sales**.

8. Format columns C and D as Currency displaying 2 decimals.

9. Create a pie chart that compares gross sales by month.

10. Place the pie chart below the data in row 16.

11. Resize the pie chart so that it is in proportion to the data in the worksheet.

12. Apply additional formatting to the spreadsheet so that it projects a professional image and appearance.

13. Depending on the software you are using, save or export the file in JPEG format. Save the file as **GROSS SALES IMAGE**. This will allow you to insert the spreadsheet as an image in a later project.

14. Carefully proofread your work for accuracy.

15. Submit a copy of the spreadsheet and completed Planning Form packet to your instructor.

Figure 10.5-A

	A	B	C	D
1	Estimated Annual Gross Sales for <Your Product's Name>			
2	Prepared by <Team Member Names>			
3	Month	Average Units Sold	Selling Price/Unit	Gross Sales
4	January	1,716		
5	February	2,009		
6	March	952		
7	April	3,030		
8	May	2,300		
9	June	3,200		
10	July	1,740		
11	August	2,900		
12	September	450		
13	October	1,375		
14	November	4,029		
15	December	6,840		
16	Estimated Annual Gross Sales:			

Project 10.6: Marketing Your Product

Designing a Magazine Print Ad

Overview

There's an old adage used in the business world: "People don't know what they want, they only want what they know." Think about it for a moment. You can have the greatest product since the beginning of mankind, but if people don't know about it, they'll never buy it. It's a simple yet very true fact. In order to sell something, you have to get the word out. This is done by marketing. **Marketing** is the action or business of promoting and selling products or services, including market research and advertising.

In this project, your team will create and design a magazine print advertisement.

New Skills / TEKS

There are no new skills being introduced in this final assessment.

TEKS: 1.A.i, 1.Di, 1.Fi, 1.F.iii, 1.F.iv, 1.F.v, 12.D.i, 13.C.ii, 14.A.i

Instructions

1. Download and complete the **Project 10.6 Planning Form** on the BIM Companion Website: **www.MyCompanionSite.com**.

2. Using desktop publishing software, create a new 8.5" x 11" document.

3. Set the margins to 0.25" on all sides.

4. Save the file as **PITCH IT! PRODUCT AD**.

5. Using the rectangle tool, place a 1 pt. border along the margin guides.

6. Using the information from the completed **Project 10.6 Planning Form**, create a print advertisement for your product.

Your advertisement must include:

- ☐ Headline
- ☐ Product logo
- ☐ Product name (if it is not contained within the product logo)
- ☐ Product slogan
- ☐ A call-to-action
- ☐ One or more images (optional—will depend on the message of your ad)

☐ Additional elements and/or text that will enhance the message, appearance, and professionalism of the ad

☐ Your company contact information

7. Depending on the software you are using, save or export the file in JPEG format. Save the file as **PRODUCT AD IMAGE**. This will allow you to insert the advertisement as an image in a later project.

8. Carefully proofread your work for accuracy.

9. Submit a copy of the advertisement and completed Planning Form packet to your instructor.

Project 10.7: Advertising Vendor Database

Expanding the Advertising Potential

Overview

There are many other types of media formats that businesses can utilize for advertising. Exploring new advertising opportunities is an ongoing and necessary process for businesses. From social media to mobile apps, the list of potential advertising opportunities is plentiful. As part of their proposal requirements, Pitch It!, Inc. requires potential clients to create a database consisting of prospective advertising vendors.

In this project, you will use Microsoft Access to create a database of advertising vendors that cater to your new product's target audience.

New Skills / TEKS

There are no new skills being introduced in this final assessment.

TEKS: 1.A.i, 1.Di, 1.Fi, 1.F.iii, 1.F.iv, 1.F.v, 14.A.i

Instructions

1. Download and complete the **Project 10.7 Planning Form** on the BIM Companion Website: **www.MyCompanionSite.com**.

2. Using Microsoft Access, create a new database file.

3. Name and save the database file as **PITCH IT! ADVERTISERS**.

4. Set up the database table using the field names and data types provided below.

Database Structure	
Field Name	**Data Type**
Vendor Name	Text or Short Text
Media Format	Text or Short Text
City	Text or Short Text
State	Text or Short Text
Zip	Text or Short Text
Primary Contact	Text or Short Text
Phone	Text or Short Text
Email	Text or Short Text
Website	Hyperlink

5. Name and save the table as **ADVERTISING VENDORS**.

6. Using the information from the completed **Project 10.7 Planning Form**, enter the data into the **ADVERTISING VENDORS** table.

7. Adjust the column widths so that all data displays properly.

8. Create and run a query that displays only the Vendor Name and Website fields.

9. Save the query as **VENDOR LINKS**.

10. Carefully proofread your work for accuracy.

11. Submit a copy of the table, query, and completed Planning Form packet to your instructor.

Project 10.8: Putting It All Together

Creating the "Big Pitch" Presentation

Overview

The big moment is almost here! Your team has completed all but three tasks that remain in this unit (a visual presentation, the actual oral presentation, and a project summary report). Presenting your team's new product in a professional format is critical to the overall success of your presentation.

You will not only be judged on your product, but also on how it is presented. Ultimately, your goal is to "sell" your new product concept to Pitch It!, Inc., using the most professional appearance possible. To sell it, you have to market and package your presentation properly.

Creating a visually appealing, well organized, and professional computer presentation will be a critical piece in the outcome of your final grade in this unit.

In this project, your team will work collaboratively to create a persuasive slide show presentation that encompasses and summarizes all of the requirements defined by Pitch It!, Inc.

New Skills / TEKS

There are no new skills being introduced in this final assessment.

TEKS: 1.A.i, 1.Di, 1.Fi, 1.F.iii, 1.F.iv, 1.F.v, 12.F.i, 12.F.ii, 12.F.iii, 12.F.iv, 14.A.i

Important Notes for This Project:

1. This project is written and intended for your team to create a presentation using Google Slides. The intent is for each team member to share and work on their team's presentation collaboratively. However, if your class does not use Google Slides, your team can use an alternative program such as Microsoft PowerPoint to create this presentation. If you are using an application that does not support sharing capabilities, simply divide the tasks in the instructions equally for each team member.

2. Unless otherwise indicated in the instructions, the layout, design, and format of your presentation is entirely up to your team to decide.

Instructions

1. Go to the BIM Companion Website: **www.MyCompanionSite.com**.

    a. Download and review the **Project 10.8 Computer Presentation Tips** document.

    b. Download and print the **Project 10.8 Planning Layout Form**.

    c. Download the Pitch It! logo.

2. Read through all of the instructions in this project, including **Figure 10.8-A** before starting any work on the computer. Using the **Project 10.8 Planning Layout Form**, collaborate with your team to plan the contents and layout of your slide show presentation.

3. Designate one team member (this is **STUDENT A**) to log into Google Drive, create a new Google Slides presentation, and do the following:

    a. Name the presentation as **PITCH IT! SLIDE SHOW**.

    b. Insert eight slides. Remember, you can always change the number of slides, layout, and theme as you continue through the instructions.

    c. Share the presentation with **STUDENT B** (your partner) and assign the "Can edit" permission.

STUDENT B:

4. Retrieve and open the **PITCH IT! SLIDE SHOW** file from the "Shared with me" folder on your Google Drive.

STUDENTS A AND B:

5. Refer to **Figure 10.8-A** to complete the slide show. The figure indicates the content that must be included, and which slides are assigned to be completed by each student (A and B), respectively.

> Remember that the text, layout, design, and format of your presentation is entirely up to your team to decide. However, your presentation must include the following:
>
> ☐ At least one occurrence of the animation feature
>
> ☐ A least one use of sound
>
> ☐ 8 to 10 slides

6. Carefully proofread your work for accuracy.

7. Use the Comment feature to communicate and determine which of you will share the file with your instructor.

8. Share the file with your instructor so you can receive feedback on your presentation. Be sure to select the "Can comment" permission when sharing with your instructor.

    NOTE: If you are using a program other than Google Slides, print a copy of the slide show for your instructor to review.

Figure 10.8-A

STUDENT A	STUDENT B

Slide 1

- The text "Pitch It! Final Project"
- The Pitch It! logo (available at **www.MyCompanionSite.com**)
- A photo of your team members (optional). If a team photo is not available, insert your team's product business card
- Presented by <Team member names>
- Add additional images, elements, and/or text to enhance the professional appearance of the slide (optional)

Slide 2

- A heading that introduces your new product
- The product name, logo, and slogan
- A brief overview and description of your product
- A photo of your product prototype (if a prototype photo is not available, your physical prototype will suffice)
- A brief description of why there is a need or want for your new product by consumers
- Describe the target audience of your product
- Add additional images, elements, and/or text to enhance the professional appearance of the slide

Slide 3

- A heading titled "Who Are the Competitors?"
- List several competitors of your product
- A brief description of how your product is different from its competitors
- Add additional images, elements, and/or text to enhance the professional appearance of the slide

Slide 4

- A heading titled "Estimated Annual Gross Sales"
- Information about the cost and selling price of your product. Describe and explain how you calculated each.
- Insert the **GROSS SALES** spreadsheet completed in **Project 10.5**. If a different file format is required, insert the file named **GROSS SALES IMAGE**.
- Include a shape or object to highlight the "Estimated Annual Gross Sales" amount
- Add additional images, elements, and/or text to enhance the professional appearance of the slide

Figure 10.8-A (Continued)

STUDENT A	STUDENT B

Slide 5

- A heading titled "Print Advertisement"
- List the magazines you selected for your print advertisement from **Project 10.6**
- A brief description of why you selected each magazine
- Insert the **PRODUCT AD IMAGE** you created in **Project 10.6**
- Describe the advertisement and explain why it would appeal to the readers of the magazine you selected
- Add additional images, elements, and/or text to enhance the professional appearance of the slide

Slide 6

- A heading titled "Other Potential Advertising Opportunities"
- List several other advertising vendors and their media formats from **Project 10.7**
- Describe how these vendors and media formats can be utilized to advertise your product to reach potential customers
- Add additional images, elements, and/or text to enhance the professional appearance of the slide

Slide 7

- A very brief summary of all of the slides
- A closing statement that persuades and convinces Pitch It!, Inc. that you have created a product that they should approve as worthy of being developed
- Add additional images, elements, and/or text to enhance the professional appearance of the slide

Slide 8

- A closing statement thanking Pitch It!, Inc. for meeting with your team and taking the time to review your presentation
- Add additional images, elements, and/or text to enhance the professional appearance of the slide

Slide 9 (Optional)

- The contents and design of this slide are entirely up to you. You can also move this slide to a different location if necessary.

Slide 10 (Optional)

- The contents and design of this slide are entirely up to you. You can also move this slide to a different location if necessary.

Project 10.9: The Big Pitch!

Delivering Your Presentation to Pitch It!, Inc.

Overview

It's time to deliver your oral presentation to your class and the CEO of Pitch It!, Inc. (your instructor).

It's no secret that speaking in front of an audience can cause shivers to run down your spine. It's okay to be nervous. After all, the three things people fear most are death, taxes, and public speaking. So, you are not alone. The secret to success is planning and preparation.

Carefully crafting what your team will say, when they will say it, and how it will be said during your oral presentation will lessen the nervousness you might be experiencing. Like any fear, the more you do it, the less fearful it becomes. Giving presentations is no exception. Get ready to put your best foot forward, because the real-world practice you are gaining now will undoubtedly help you tremendously in your future career. This is your moment to shine and showcase your new product to Pitch It!, Inc.

In this project, your team will work collaboratively to prepare and deliver a persuasive presentation to convince Pitch It!, Inc. to accept your new product proposal.

You will export your slide show as a PDF and save it on a thumb drive. By doing so, it can be opened and viewed by a user who may not have access to the software application.

New Skills / TEKS

There are no new skills being introduced in this final assessment.

TEKS: 1.A.i, 1.Di, 1.Fi, 1.F.iii, 1.F.iv, 1.F.v, 12.D.i, 12.E.i, 12.F.iii, 14.A.i

Instructions

1. Before you begin, read through all of the instructions included in this project. This will get you familiar with all of the project requirements.

2. The CEO of Pitch It!, Inc. (your instructor) will inform your team of the date and time of your presentation. Take note of this "due date" so that you can plan and manage your time accordingly.

3. Carefully review the Pitch It! Final Presentation Grading Criteria provided in **Figure 10.9-A** on the following page. In addition to the project documents your team has created, your oral presentation will be graded on the criteria categories shown.

4. Go to the BIM Companion Website: **www.MyCompanionSite.com**.

    a. Download and print the **Project 10.9 Oral Presentation Tips** document.

    b. Download and complete the **Project 10.9 Planning Form**.

5. Execute your backup plan:

   a. Print out copies of your slide show and other required documents well in advance of your presentation date.

   b. Export your slide show as a PDF and save it on a thumb drive.

6. Deliver your Pitch It! Oral Presentation.

7. At the conclusion of your presentation, submit copies of the following documents (in the order provided below) to your instructor. Check with your instructor regarding what format (print, email, or share) is required for submitting the documents.

   Closing comments: You should be receiving feedback and your grade from Pitch It!, Inc. shortly. Give yourself a round of applause on completing the projects in the Pitch It! unit.

Project #	Document	File Name(s)
10.2	Instructor Approval Memo	PITCH IT! MEMO
10.3	Logo, Slogan, and Business Card	PITCH IT! LOGO and PITCH IT! BIZ CARD
10.4	Product Prototype	NOT APPLICABLE
10.5	Estimated Annual Gross Sales	PITCH IT! GROSS SALES
10.6	Print Advertisement	PITCH IT! PRODUCT AD
10.7	Advertiser Database	PITCH IT! ADVERTISERS
10.8	Slide Show (Share or print)	PITCH IT! SLIDE SHOW
10.9	Oral Presentation Planning Form	PITCH IT! PRESENTATION

Figure 10.9-A

Pitch It! Final Presentation Grading Criteria*	
Time	The presentation must be 5-10 minutes in length
Attire	This is a business presentation; you are expected to dress professionally
Participation	Each team member is expected to participate equally
Visuals	The following visuals are required during the presentation: ☐ Computer slide show presentation (Project 10.8) ☐ Business cards to distribute (Project 10.3) ☐ Product prototype (Project 10.4) ☐ Print advertisement (Project 10.6)

* **NOTE:** Your instructor may choose to modify this criteria.

Project 10.10: Project Summary Report

Summarizing Your Pitch It! Project Experience

Overview

Congratulations, you've reached the final project! You've come this far working with a partner; now it's time to reflect on this unit independently. Teamwork is an important skill both at school and in the workplace, so it helps to think about what went well in your collaboration process and what could have gone better. What did you like about working in a team? What challenges did you face? You will address these topics and more as you create your project summary report.

In this project, you will write a 2-3 page double spaced project summary report (MLA style) to reflect on your experiences in this final assessment. You will also cite the sources you and your teammate used at the end of your document.

New Skills / TEKS

There are no new skills being introduced in this final assessment.

TEKS: 1.A.i, 1.Di, 1.Fi, 1.F.iii, 1.F.iv, 1.F.v, 6.D.iii, 6.D.iv, 6.E.iii, 14.A.i

Instructions

1. Using word processing, create a new document.
2. Save the document as **PITCH IT! SUMMARY REPORT**.
3. Before you begin, read through all of the instructions in this project. This will get you familiar with all of the project requirements.
4. Using MLA style, write a 2-3 page summary report about the Pitch It! final assessment.

Your project summary report must include:
- ☐ Proper MLA style report (see **Lesson 5.32** as a reference)
- ☐ Properly cited sources used throughout the assessment
- ☐ What you enjoyed about the project
- ☐ How the collaborative process went
- ☐ What you learned from the collaborative process
- ☐ The challenges or obstacles you faced
- ☐ The benefits of working in teams
- ☐ The downsides of working in teams
- ☐ How you managed your time
- ☐ The challenges of meeting deadlines

□ The most challenging project you tackled and why (be specific—for example, the prototype, the magazine print ad, etc.)

□ What you would do differently if you completed "Pitch It!" a second time

□ Any additional information that you consider important in the process of completing the final assessment

5. Carefully proofread your work for grammatical accuracy.

6. Submit a copy of the Project Summary Report to your instructor if required.